THE ORDEAL OF
IVOR GURNEY

THE ORDEAL OF
IVOR GURNEY

MICHAEL HURD

OXFORD UNIVERSITY PRESS
OXFORD   NEW YORK   MELBOURNE

Oxford University Press, Walton Street, Oxford OX2 6DP

OXFORD LONDON GLASGOW
NEW YORK TORONTO MELBOURNE WELLINGTON
IBADAN NAIROBI DAR ES SALAAM CAPE TOWN
KUALA LUMPUR SINGAPORE JAKARTA HONG KONG TOKYO
DELHI BOMBAY CALCUTTA MADRAS KARACHI

British Library Cataloguing in Publication Data

Hurd, Michael
The ordeal of Ivor Gurney.
1. Gurney, Ivor   2. Composers – England – Biography
1. Title
780'.92'4   ML410.G9/   78-40194
ISBN 0-19-211752-1

Printed in Great Britain by
Lowe & Brydone Printers Limited, Thetford, Norfolk

Contents

Contents

England: 1917–1922

Asylum: 1922–1937

Aftermath: 1937–1959

Conclusion: 1977

Plates

Illustrations

Acknowledgements

Being by nature a predator, the biographer must inevitably involve himself in a debt of gratitude to a great many people. In the present instance the debt is widespread (for I began tentative researches in 1963), and I fear that time may have erased the exact memory of how and when certain small but vital clues were run to earth. If any there be whose help I now overlook, may I beg their forgiveness — the slight being unintentional.

Of the greater debts I am well aware, and so acknowledge my grateful thanks to the following people. To the surviving members of Ivor Gurney's immediate family: Miss Winifred Gurney, Mrs. Dorothy Hayward, his sisters; and Mrs. Ethel Gurney, the widow of his brother Ronald, who also, years ago, was most generous with his help. To Mrs. Joy Finzi and Dr. Howard Ferguson, who helped Gurney and enormously helped and encouraged me. To Dr. Herbert Howells, and Professor William H. Trethowan; and to Mr. Peter Bayley, with whom at one time it seemed as if I would collaborate. To the Head Librarian and staff of the Gloucester City Public Library, for their kindness and forbearance during the many years when I have pestered them.

I am most grateful also to Mr. George Bowles, Mr. William Bubb, Mrs. E. M. Ford, Mrs. Winifred Miles and her sister Mrs. Freeman, Mr. Brian Frith, Mr. R. A. Lusty, Mr. Geoffrey Marwood, Mrs. Margaret Rouse, Mrs. Edith Sterry, and Mrs. Lavinia Taylor, all of whom supplied the kind of detail a biographer craves.

Two poets, Geoffrey Grigson and P. J. Kavanagh, talked, listened, and were most helpful; and two books, *Eye Deep in Hell* by John Ellis (Croom Helm, 1976), and *The Great War and Modern Memory* by Paul Fussell (Oxford, 1975), proved invaluable.

I am most grateful to Messrs. Sidgwick & Jackson, Chatto & Windus, and Hutchinson & Co. for permission to reprint poems originally published by them; and to the Gurney family and Mr. Robert Haines (Sole Trustee of the Gurney estate) and to Mrs. Joy Finzi (to whom Marion Scott bequeathed her extensive Gurney archive) for permission to make use of the manuscript poems, letters, and other documents.

The heirs, executors, and representatives of Mr. Robert Bridges, Mr. Walter de la Mare, Mr. C. Scott-Moncrieff, Miss Marion M. Scott, and Mrs. Adeline Vaughan Williams have allowed me to make use of certain letters, and I am most grateful. So also am I to the editors and management of *Music and Letters*, and the *R.C.M. Magazine*, and the executors of Mrs. Helen Thomas for permission to quote articles about Gurney. It would have been nice to thank the Crypt House Press, Gloucester, for permission to quote from A. F. Barnes's *The Story of the 2nd/5th Gloucestershire Regiment*, but they have left the publishing world.

In the matter of photographs to illustrate this book, I am most indebted to the Gurney family (Mrs. Dorothy Hayward in particular), Mr. John L. Moulsdale, the City of Gloucester Public Library, the Royal College of Music, and the Imperial War Museum.

And, last of all, I am most grateful to the editorial staff of the Oxford University Press, first Jon Stallworthy, and then his successor, Jeremy Lewis, for their guidance and encouragement.

West Liss, Hampshire   Michael Hurd
December 1977

The songs I had are withered
    Or vanished clean,
Yet there are bright tracks
    Where I have been,

And there grow flowers
    For other's delight.
Think well, O singer,
    Soon comes night.[1]

I

There is no date. No day, no month, no year. Only an address where time did not matter. Then page after yellowing page of cheap, thin paper, with line upon line of pencilled words, upright and clear:

Stone House
Dartford
Kent

To the London Metropolitan Police Force

Sirs,
      After leaving my studies at the Royal College of Music in London, July 1921, I returned to Gloucester; again returning to London where I worked for a fortnight at Cold Storage. Being dismissed, and having hurt myself, I went partly by train, partly by cycle back to Gloucester, sleeping out one night. After which I lived mostly with my Aunt at 1 Westfield Terrace, and partly on her kindness; working hard, staying up long hours and being active, digging, walking, cycling. Advertisments for Cinema Posts were inserted and answered. I had a post at Plumstead for two weeks or so; and lost that. Returned again; gained a post at Bude, which I lost after a week, but for no reason that I agreed with.

      After which I went back to Gloucester and worked there, staying up night after night, striving not to eat, living with my Aunt, partly on her kindness, partly on an Army Pension. Digging, walking, riding, doing gymnastics.

      But working harder than most people, and answering advertisments — having advertised for a farm post with 5/– a week and keep. One job I refused — of picking up stones one morning.

      My pension and some royalties and earnings helped to keep me, with my Aunt's kindness; but I eat little, though drinking much tea, and working late with too much light. But I slept by my work often, washing my body every morning and trying not to go to bed. Seeing many dawns; writing much, walking much; almost any active employment I would have taken, at 5/– a week and keep. An enema was used, but I eat little, drinking much; working much; sometimes walking 17 miles at a time.

I took a dog out for walks (for kindness), saved it from eating; kept its health, and sometimes beat it, but was kind to it.

Not much I spent — tobacco, music paper, a few books for myself — on a pension, and gifts (small) and small royalties.

Much I walked (about May), worked harder than almost anybody, dug, and did gymnastics. Waiting for almost any active work; digging, washing my body every morning, and doing gymnastics. Hoping for work — seeing Cinema playing as probability, but ready for any manual work. However hoeing wheat proved beyond me and unprofitable for so slow a worker. After which I went for a week's walk; earned a little at playing the piano.

Much I drank, eat little, smoked much, working at music and verse until 5, 6, or 7 in the morning. Electrical tricks began to be played on me. I used a wood axe more, on hard wood.

At last obtaining an office post (Income Tax) in Gloucester, I held this for twelve weeks. The reasons for losing it were partly that the work (it was said) might have been better done at cheaper rate, and that I held an Army Pension. This I dared not give up until Unemployment Benefit was obtained.

Again I was left to wait till work was obtainable in farm or Cinema. Electrical Tricks were played on me of bad kind. My attempts at work were often spoiled. I went out time after time for death. Would have gone on tramp, but was too much in pain save once.

During the Electrical Control of Gloucestershire many risks were taken, much endured. I worked still, but such wickedness at night was terrible. I worked and walked still.

Removed to my brother's house in Gloucester, where still they were continued. I applied many times for permission to carry a revolver or poison at the local Police Station (Gloucester). My pain was made nothing of. The danger I faced made nothing of.

Certain people (whom I knew except one) arranged for my removal for protection to Barnwood House. Six weeks was the period given. The electrical torture suffered there was bad also — many times one would pray for death daily.

This after a life for a year of longer days than are usual now. Often I worked or walked from 11pm – 7pm or thereabouts. It was the best life I knew of. Much work and activity. For 28 days I touched meat or bread only once, and little at that. Many people knew the truth and should have admired so good a life; made possible by the kindness of my Aunt. I drank much, not really too much, smoked much, eat as

2

little as possible. Did gymnastics, digging, used an enema, washed my body every morning.

Beat a dog, but was kindest in the best way to it of anyone. Thanked my Aunt for her kindness sincerely every night — worked as hard as possible under the circumstances. It was a life to admire. Before God a good one. I needed money to support me in taking a post. Why betrayed is not known.

I had made application for full pension of 25/– instead of 12/– because I wished to write with it — believing my work in music and verse to be good. It had been promised for this reason; but I gave in application the reason of 'after shell shock', which was false, but it seemed best to believe that the pension was to be given, and the reason not then important. But considering my courage and hard work, it was dreadful to be so broken.

The torments were bad; the courage deserving reward. I have appealed to the Carnegie Trustees and to the Royal College to appeal for my death.

My life was in many ways so good — the best I ever led considering all things — when so many times I stayed up all night to work or walk.

Sometimes an hour or two of sleep sufficed. The work produced seemed good enough — I believed in myself, read Carlyle and others, and usually went on in work or activity or certain courtesies as long as my ordinary strength would allow — and further. Once staying up for thirty-six hours; often skipping, digging, doing gymnastics.

The harm of such a life was small. Employment for but approximately sixteen weeks only — because (roughly) there was none to be had. I read the papers, occasionally sought work, and strove as few can have striven perhaps to work, or stay up.

An appeal is made for Justice, or Trial, or to be allowed the die, or to receive Chance of Death. Many times daily has the writer prayed for Death, and asks that his pain may be ended, either by Death or Release. Having so much use left in him, if he were free and allowed to get well.

I should have been released after three weeks (by instinct) or six weeks by assurance.

For six months and a half now my confinement and pain has endured.

My music, my verse — my War service should have saved me from so much pain.

So many times I had gone to honour, and really injured none.

Asking for Death, Release, or Imprisonment. An end to pain.

I. B. Gurney

many letters have not been
forwarded through
accident

3

Having twice escaped, and once broken parole and escaped. Ready for Death.

Also (under influence) I wrote a letter to the London Metropolitan Police Force, and to (Mr) D Lloyd George asking for money to continue my work. I would ask that unfriendly feelings to one who often walked at night should be forgotten.[2]

GLOUCESTER: 1890-1911

The ploughed field and the fallow field
They sang a prudent song to me:
We bide all year and take our yield
Or barrenness as case may be.

What time or tide may bring to pass
Is nothing of our reckoning,
Power was before our making was
That had in brooding thought its spring.

We bide our fate as best betides
What ends the tale may prove the first.
Stars know as truly of their guides
As we the truth of best or worst.[1]

II

It would have pleased Ivor Gurney to know that deep in the earth beneath the house in which he was born lay the still massive remains of the Roman wall that once guarded the eastern approaches to Gloucester. That house, 3 Queen Street, vanished long before the Second World War — the row of cramped buildings giving way to the needs of larger, more imposing shops on parallel Brunswick Road. More recently the street itself has disappeared, to be reborn as Queen's Way — a link in the Via Sacra that threads the changing city in a line above the old, buried walls. Yet there is still much in Gloucester that he would recognize: the pattern of its ancient streets, the great cathedral and intimate churches, the docks, canal, and Severn river, the glorious countryside. Above all, the spirit of place remains — a tangible presence to shape the receptive mind, as once it did his.

Ivor Bertie Gurney was born on 28 August 1890. He was the second of a family of four children: a sister, Winifred, had been born in 1886; a brother, Ronald, was to follow in 1894, and a sister, Dorothy, in 1900. Between the birth of Winifred and Ivor, briefly mourned and then all but forgotten, there was a still-born child, a boy.

In all essentials the Gurney family was typical of its class and period. David Gurney, the father, was a tailor and ran his own business. The small house in Queen Street was home and shop in one. Florence, his wife, had also trained in tailoring and, when domestic duties were done, worked alongside her husband with needle and thread. They differed from other couples only in one small detail: she was five years his senior. By the standards of the time they could be considered to have gained a tenuous foothold on the ladder of middle-class comfort and respectability. They were certainly not rich, but neither were they poor. The horizons that opened up before them were clearly defined, and

7

circumscribed. There would be no hardship as such, but little to encourage the creative imagination.

As in so many Gloucester families, the Gurney parents united two quite different geographical types. David Gurney was a Severn Valley man, from the low-lying fields around Maisemore. Florence Lugg came from Bisley, high in the hills above Stroud. He was gentle, placid, ruminative. Her temperament was much chillier, and given to anxious storms. In an age which married for better or for worse, the mixture worked — after a fashion. It passed on to the children, however, an uneasy background for which none, in later years, were able to feel much gratitude.

The Gurneys of Maisemore were builders: bricklayers, carpenters, stonemasons, almost to a man. David was the youngest of seven brothers, the sons of William Gurney and Mary Hawkins. Only two of them wandered from their father's trade — William, who ended as a waiter in Cheltenham, and David, who at his mother's insistence was apprenticed to a tailoring firm in Wimborne. The other boys — Thomas, Joseph, John, Walter, and Guy — banded together and settled in Gloucester as 'Gurney Bros. Builders and Contractors'. They grew mildly successful.

Though music played no very outstanding part in Gurney family life, both parents enjoyed and respected it, and with the purchase of a pianoforte in 1896 (a sign of increasing respectability) the children were offered music lessons as a matter of course. Various cousins figured as organists and singers in Gloucester musical circles, and Florence Gurney, in one of her many rambling, unpunctuated, but vivid letters, laid claim to a strong vein of ancestral musicality:

Mother could sing very nicely she was always singing Scotch songs and English Irish and Welsh Father was alto in the Bisley Choir but he didnt sing at home like Mother did my dear old Grandfather and his brother uncle Robert he was a Batchelor and Mother said he nursed his Mother till she died and wouldnt let anybody else do a thing for her her arm chair was covered with white dimity and he used to wash everything himself and after he had dug the garden the spade and the fork and all the diggers were shone like silver and put down in the cellar and the white stones which showed up through the dirt was scrubbed white and he would give us some flowers if we wouldnt put them on the graves that was popery well I wish I knew where they

8

came from they were not the regular sort of Bisley people they had too much in them . . .

Grandfather was a good man the Luggs round Stroud are the most respected of anybody and you can say what you like a good ancestor is something to be proud of but Ivor hasnt seen a lot of the Luggs he knew the Gurneys better and they hadnt a note of music in them . . .[2]

Exactly what brought Florence Gurney to Gloucester is not known. Her three brothers and four sisters seem to have remained resolutely in the Bisley area, where her father, William Lugg, worked as a house decorator. Possibly it was to train as a seamstress. What matters is that she became a regular member of the congregation of All Saints' Church, and there met the young David Gurney.

The choice of All Saints' as a place of worship not only shaped the lives of David and Florence Gurney, but was also to have a profound effect on the way their eldest son was to develop — cutting clean across what might have been anticipated for him. It was a stroke of the greatest good fortune that brought them there.

The church itself — one of Sir Gilbert Scott's less ambitious flights — is not remarkable. A solid, purposeful structure, it had been built in 1875 to serve the rapid proliferation of artisans' dwellings that had spread in mean rows across the fields on either side of Lower Barton Street, burying the gentle River Twyver in melancholy culverts. Indeed, All Saints' abutted the Midland Railway's London line and lay cheek by jowl with the level-crossing that separated Lower Barton Street from Barton Street proper, and thus, even in its heyday, must have been considered outside the range of Gloucester's politer society. On the edge of poverty and shaken by every passing train, it nevertheless enjoyed the services of an enlightened vicar and an unusual curate. And this was just as well, for when, on 24 September 1890, David and Florence Gurney presented their son for baptism, they were alone. The vicar, the Reverend Herbert Foster, stood as one of the necessary godparents; his curate, Alfred Hunter Cheesman, became the other.

Mr. Cheesman was twenty-five. After studying at Worcester College, Oxford, he had been ordained in 1888, and the curacy of All Saints' was his first appointment. He was one of a prosperous Sussex family, yeomen-farmers well-known in the Bosham area, where his father also had interests in the 'Brick, Tile and Fancy Pottery Works'. He delighted in literature and history, and though he had no ambition to write, he was the kind of man to nourish enthusiasm in others. Indeed, devotion and enthusiasm characterized his whole career. He was content to remain where fortune had placed him. Twenty-four years passed before he left All Saints', and the remaining twenty-nine slipped as quietly by as vicar of the tiny country parish of Twigworth, a few miles out of Gloucester. In 1925 he became an honorary Canon of Gloucester Cathedral, and at this modest level his career rested. He was a good man, kind and gentle; and he remained a bachelor.

In the 1890s, Gloucester observed and cheerfully accepted the fact that the Reverend Cheesman 'had a liking for lads of all ages'.³ Our own cruder age would, no doubt, have noted his romantic attachments with less charity. But Gloucester merely smiled when Cheesman, remote and chaste in gown and biretta, walked arm in arm with the favourite of the moment. No breath of scandal ever clung to his name. If indeed he loved, he kept his love to himself, content to be guide, philosopher, and friend to such boys as had ears for his counsel.

It was inevitable that Ivor Gurney would become 'one of Mr. Cheesman's boys'⁴ — the one he influenced the most. But it was to be some years before his interest would ripen into something over and above a concern for a member of his congregation. In the meantime, the infant had to grow up.

Shortly after his birth, Ivor Gurney's family moved from the cramped conditions of Queen Street into marginally more spacious premises at 19 Barton Street. The building was mid-Victorian and undistinguished. Double-fronted shop windows faced the street, the entrance set back somewhat and not especially inviting. Display screens at the back of the windows added to the gloom of the interior, and only on exceptional days was it possible to do without the pale gleam of gaslight. Customers made their choice from bolts of cloth held close to the glass-panelled door. Behind the shop lay the family's living room. It too was poorly lit, the windows hugging one end and overlooking a small backyard flanked by kitchen, scullery, and outside privy.

Upstairs and over the shop there was a broad, spacious room. It should have been the living room, and did in fact contain a piano, hauled up through the outside window. But as the family grew, it was pressed into service as a bedroom. In later years it became a workroom where suits were stitched and buttonholes worked by hand. Three small bedrooms, one little more than an attic, completed the very cramped, oppressive living space. Winifred Gurney, reminiscing in later years, wondered 'how any of us managed to keep well, and how mother managed to keep sane'.[5]

Life certainly cannot have been easy for Florence Gurney, and her own temperament did nothing to lighten the load. She fretted about trifles, and saw in her husband's understandable desire to escape to the nearby Conservative Club after the long day's work was done, a slippery slope to ruin. She complained when he attended the Saturday afternoon football match at Kingsholm, for it was then that local farmers might be expected to place their orders. Nor did she approve when he abandoned football and went instead to the Conservative Club's bowling green on early closing day. She took to nagging and, when that failed, to outbursts of temper. Winifred Gurney's recollections of life at 19 Barton Street are quite specific on this point:

Happiness revolved around Father. As very small children Mother certainly did her best to bring us up well, but when we grew to be more independent it seemed too much for her. She possessed us as babies, but couldn't do so later and her iron rule led to nagging. Life for us was something akin to a bed of stinging nettles, and to keep the peace Father's efforts had to be applied when and where possible, but taking care to walk warily . . . The pity of it was that Mother did not seem to enjoy her children, and so far as I could see she did not win their love. Worse still, Father was not allowed to give us as much love as he had for us . . .[6]

Sunk in her own anxieties, Florence Gurney left few pleasant memories behind.

David Gurney was different. Quiet and gentle, he did his best to sidestep conflict. Though capable enough as a craftsman, he was not naturally suited to running his own business, and would almost certainly have preferred a more peaceable existence working under someone else's direction. Ivor Gurney remembered him as a countryman, and as the thwarted, uncomplaining shadow of what might have been:

My father looked on ploughland and willed me.
His was the friendliness of every hill and tree
In all West Gloucestershire, in all West Gloucestershire.
Born of that earth, of like love brought to birth;
Knowing the flight of birds, and the song of the smallest
Bird — the names of flowers and the likeliest place
Where first Spring might bring Her lovely trifles in.
So on a night when Orion ruled with majestic light,
He remembered his past dreams, all broken, and hoped for grace
Whereby a son should say what he had never never
Been able to say or sing of such well beloved Earth.[7]

The poetry, it would seem, came from the father; the tension, and hence the will to create, from the mother.

In this somewhat uneasy atmosphere the young Ivor Gurney began to feel his way towards independence. We have only his mother's jumbled recollections of his early days, but they, as always, are vivid and delightful:

Now to tell you some of his little sayings he was learning his Collect for Sunday School he was conning it over about twice he always knew a thing directly and I thought how reverent he sounded and thought I believe Ivor is going to be a good boy and he clapped the book together and said all men no women good gracious what a come down and there was a scrubbing brush with made in England on it and he wrote what a wonder till it was worn out the others were curly Ronald was Bubbles but Ivor's was straight and silver theirs was gold and he used to look up at people so affectionate but they wouldnt take any notice of him and he was a lovely boy and the others people offered so much money for them he cut every tooth with Bronchitis and his teeth grew projecting out and that was very painful pulling them in besides the teeth cant bite as well because they are not opposite and then they took out his teeth to try to make him better and made it worse . . .[8]

More solid facts, and dates, begin to emerge only gradually. He appears to have started Sunday school at All Saints' in October 1896, attracting, almost immediately, the sympathetic interest of Alfred Cheesman. He must also, at roughly this time, have begun to attend the National School in London Road. Though not far from Barton Street (the short cut taking you past the delights of Gloucester's busy Cattle Market), it was still a tidy step for a small boy. When he was eight he joined the choir at All Saints' as a probationer, graduating to full membership on 3 December 1899.

Though the fact that his cousin Joseph was now organist of All Saints' may have helped his promotion, it seems clear that Ivor Gurney not only possessed a good voice but showed signs of a musicality that went far beyond that of the ordinary choirboy. Encouraged by the watchful Cheesman, he competed for a place in the Cathedral Choir. It was secured without difficulty, and in the autumn term of 1900 he duly took his place.

It meant, of course, that he must now become a pupil at the King's School, which had served the needs of the Cathedral since the time of Henry VIII. Inevitably the process of general education at such an establishment took second place to the musical routines of the Cathedral's daily life. Moreover, the fortunes of the school were at a particularly low ebb in 1900 and numbers were down. 'Discipline,' it was said, 'was very lax at this time, and the Headmaster was often drunk!'[9] And Gurney's own recollections of his school-days are memorials to cricket and football rather than to high learning.

Nor were the musical standards particularly high. According to one of Gurney's fellow choristers 'all you needed was a voice and to be able to read music. [It] was not a thorough training.'[10] School began at 8.45 a.m., but was interrupted by morning service from 10.15 to 11.30. Music practice took place between 12 noon and 1 p.m., and lessons were resumed after lunch at 2 p.m. Evensong, from 4 p.m. to 4.45, brought the day's work to an end. Compensations for such a straitened regimen might have been found in an enlightened musical diet. But the service music at Gloucester was typical of its time, and Gadsby in C took precedence over Wesley, while the great masters of English polyphony were ignored altogether.[11]

The organist of the day was Dr. Herbert Brewer. He had been a Gloucester chorister himself, receiving his appointment to the Cathedral in December 1896, in succession to an ailing Charles Lee Williams. His autobiography suggests that he was by no means as dull as his rather pedantic appearance might imply. He was an excellent organist and inspired the kind of general respect that was eventually rewarded with a knighthood. The *Musical Times*, recording his death in 1928 and evidently unable to light upon any one outstanding quality, described him as an 'Admirable

Crichton', adding that his choice of works for the Three Choirs Festival was unusually adventurous and enlightened.

As Brewer firmly believed that each choir boy should learn to play a musical instrument, Gurney was duly farmed out to Charles H. Deavin, the organist of St. Michael's Church. Deavin was a talented man, a member of a Gloucester family of some musical renown. Lessons in piano, basic theory, and simple harmony and counterpoint seem to have gone smoothly and profitably.

Altogether, life at the King's School presented Ivor Gurney with few problems. He did all the usual things, recording with pride that he achieved a second best batting average and, in his last term, a third best bowling record. He also, it seems, played centre-forward to some effect — though a fellow pupil recalled that 'he was most selfish and seemed to think that he could beat the other side on his own'.[12] And if some thought that he was 'not boyish' and 'never took part in any pranks' and seemed more often than not to 'live in a world of his own', it did him no special harm in the eyes of his fellow students. He gave his name and initials to cheerful, loutish puns in double-Gloucester accents — 'Oi be Gurney' echoing down the corridors and over the fields surrounding Paddock House. He wrote doggerel verse to amuse his friends, and 'plastered his school books with drawings of little men, and what they said — with instructions to turn to page so-and-so for the rest of the conversation'.[13] He was, in all essentials, a very ordinary, unsurprising schoolboy:

When I was small and packed with tales of desert islands far
My mother took me walking in the grey ugly street,
But there the sea-wind met us with a jolly smell of tar,
A sailorman went past to town with slow rolling gait.

The trees and shining sky of June were good enough to see,
Better than books or any tales the sailormen might tell —
But tops'le spars against the blue made fairyland for me;
The snorting tug made surges like the huge Atlantic swell.

Then thought I, how much better to sail the open seas
Than sit in school at spelling-books or sums of grocers' wares.
And I'd have knelt for pity at any captain's knees
To go see the banyan tree or white Arctic bears.[14]

Only one incident stands out in Ivor Gurney's early years, and it is best told in his mother's words, for, among other things, it reveals that by this date (1904) he had begun to write music. The Festival is, of course, the Gloucester meeting of the Three Choirs, and 'Madam Albani' was making the last of her many appearances:

. . . as soon as we got into a shop my husband did not care anything about his home life when Ivor said he was minding the shop he first tried to write some music he was gone to the football of a Saturday afternoon when we always had horse-dealers coming in for clothes and I was lying on the couch with acute indigestion and was quite helpless well this photo was taken by Stanley Son & Jackson an Irish linen merchant at Belfast came to the festival and Ivor was top dog he sang with Madam Albani 3 Madams had to sing the trio lift thine eyes and the one when she was fetched down from the Bell Hotel said she didnt know it was time and so it had to be done and Dr Brewer said Ivor was to do it and Madam Albani would have him by her and he looked such a Boy to her but they said he done it beautiful an unrehearsed piece and he was so frightened at his success when he got home he hid in the kitchen everybody saying Ivor Gurney had been singing with Madam Albani . . .[15]

According to Winifred Gurney, however, his subsequent reaction was less modest and retiring. Finding that his gallant gesture was not to be officially recorded — either to save him from the dangers of a swollen head, or to spare the feelings of the missing Madam who, it seems, had enjoyed the Bell Hotel's hospitality to an extent that was good neither for her nor for Mendelssohn — he promptly set about ruining his voice by shouting and bawling on the football field.

It is not until the onset of puberty that signs of individuality begin to crop up in accounts of Ivor Gurney's life. He loved nature and was particularly sensitive to its beauties. 'I remember once,' wrote his sister, 'when we were at Huntley, he pointed out a beautifully shaped hedge which seemed like a huge wave rising up and across the landscape.'[16] He was beginning also to turn more and more to literature for companionship, to read deeply and widely and far beyond the range of the few books he was able to find at home; he was beginning to write music seriously now, imitating the anthems and services of his daily work, short organ pieces and, most significantly of all, songs; and he was beginning to turn away from home, finding companionship and understanding among older people outside his class.

In all this he was helped by Alfred Cheesman. His library was at the boy's disposal, as was his conversation. He offered himself gladly as someone far removed from the nagging, restrictive atmosphere of the shop in Barton Street, someone who knew about books and painting and architecture, who revelled in the details of local history and smiled encouragement at youthful ambition. His influence can scarcely be exaggerated, for he treated the young Ivor Gurney as an adult.

According to Cheesman, the years of their intimacy began in 1905 when he prepared him for confirmation so that he could take his first Communion on Easter Day:

From 1905 I saw him constantly till 1911 when he took up the RCM scholarship — and you will be amused to know that during those years he came to see me 2,000 times! almost every day. He used to write down his visits in my diary. I think I was guilty of introducing him to Kipling, Tennyson and other poets — which I used to make him read aloud, but I think from his very early years he had a love of reading. I remember that when he was only ten, during the Sermon in Church he used to read the Preface of the Prayer Book — lovely English, but a bit stiff for a boy of ten.

Of course in my Journal for those years, 1905–1911, I have a good deal about his doings and sayings. He was not always easy, as you will imagine — but he always showed me much affection, and I remember a charming remark of his. He had promised to bring me Crockett's *Lad's Love* and came one day and had forgotten the book, and said 'I haven't brought you "Lad's Love" — at least, not the book.'

Naturally I frequently got him books he wanted and also music . . .

Once I spent a day with Rudyard Kipling — and Ivor sent most warmly respectful messages and the gift of Housman's *Shropshire Lad* — and I had to write a minute description of my visit and everything Kipling did and said . . .[17]

Cheesman was also probably responsible for introducing Ivor Gurney to the two maiden ladies who were to become extremely influential in his artistic development.

The Misses Emily and Margaret Hunt were sisters. They lived in Wellington Street, close to the park and a short walk from the Gurney shop. They enjoyed a modest income from private sources. Emmy played the piano, and Margaret the violin — both well enough to teach others, as they had done professionally in South Africa in the years before the Boer War. Like Cheesman they were exactly the type of person to whom a young and sensitive nature would be drawn.

It was the younger sister, Margaret, delicate of health and always fragile, who became Gurney's particular confidante. Old enough almost to be his mother (she was born in 1875), she breathed encouragement as he poured out his dreams. He wrote music for her violin, and together they played it. Her quiet, spinster home, so different from the cramped anxieties of Barton Street, became a place of refuge and an inspiration. Echoes of what her sympathetic interest meant sound in his poetry, even in the darkness of his later years:

She had such love and after my music sent
Me out to woodlands, and to wander by meadow or bent
Lanes of Severn — I got them all into my music —
I would wander my soul full of air, and return to her quick . . .
Gloucestershire's air made clear loveliest wrappings of heart:
She blessed it, and took with one touch the foldings apart,
Who was love and music and companion's help and most dear
Work — thought in the dear room with the Bechstein and Holbein
    there.[18]

All this was observed at home with a mixture of pride and jealousy. Pride that the boy had been accepted as an equal by people who were not 'in trade'; jealousy that these new friends were taking him away from the home circle, encouraging his high-flown ideas and making him discontented and ambitious for things they knew nothing about. His schoolfriends observed a change, too. He was no longer one of them. He was a solitary. 'We used to laugh at him,' said one, 'and call him "Batty Gurney"!'[19]

III

Gloucester was, and is, a special city. The four great central streets, charted by the Romans, have not only established its basic shape for all time, but underline also its geographical, economic, social, and cultural importance: its very reason for existence. Northgate Street reaches out to Cheltenham and the busy industrial Midlands; Southgate Street to Bristol and the open sea. Eastgate Street boldly faces the high ridge of the Cotswolds; Westgate Street runs downhill to the Severn River and on, through the Forest of Dean, into Wales. It is in every sense a crossroads: a place of arrival and departure, of mingling and sifting, blending and separating.

It is not one city; it is several. And at the turn of the century its different faces would have been more obvious than they are perhaps today. Down from the hills and up from the Severn plain came sheep and cattle, wheat and vegetables, all heading for Gloucester the market town. Along the roads, along the Gloucester–Berkeley Canal, along the Midland Railway and the Great Western (for here the narrow gauge and the broad gauge had met in bitter rivalry) went goods from Gloucester the industrial centre. Up and down that canal floated barges and sailing ships to the Port of Gloucester — the furthest inland in the whole country. Magnificent and serene above the bustle stood the great Cathedral Church of St. Peter. In Gloucester, town met country and country met the sea.

To a composer and poet in the making, Gloucester at the turn of the century offered riches for the imagination. As the young Ivor Gurney roamed the narrow streets of a still largely medieval city, he fell deeper and deeper under its spell. The history of the place entranced him: the Roman legionaries marching out to face the marauding Welsh; King William and the Domesday Book; the murdered Edward and the martyred Bishop Hooper; the

18

Royalists outside the city walls and unyielding Colonel Massey within — they were as real to him as the Railway Carriage and Wagon Works, the timber yards along the canal, or Moreland's 'England's Glory' matches. There were signs and symbols everywhere: in the giant anchor, guarding the docks at Llanthony Bridge; in Queen Anne's mouldering statue, target and challenge of every Spa cricketer; in the Raven Tavern, home of Mayflower men. About the cathedral reminders lay on every hand: in the great Crécy window that formed the eastern wall, a miracle of light thrown up in defiance of structural probability; in the massive Norman pillars of the nave, and the lacy exuberance of delicate stonework with which the fourteenth-century masons had transformed their solemn heritage; in the great tower itself.

There were pleasures, too, in the sights and sounds of Gloucester's daily life. Each September the street outside his father's shop would hum with Barton Fair — an army of cheapjacks, showmen, quacks, and fortune-tellers haunting the side streets, ready to dash in wild rivalry to favoured sites along Barton Street and Eastgate at the stroke of midnight. Farm labourers for hire, sheep and horses for sale, amusements and swindles on every side. Here too, in spring, he would start to the cry 'Live elvers!' and see the white and wriggling mass, scooped from the Severn and their frantic race upstream. There on the streets the horses pulled the trams, till progress, in 1904, brought the snap and crackle of electricity. There in Westgate Street the Theatre Royal had beckoned since 1791 — though soon it would change its name to Palace Theatre of Varieties, so that 'Jimmie Shields the one-legged dancer and comedian' (August 1906)[1] might triumph where Henry Irving had trod. There in lower Northgate Street Goddard's Assembly Rooms would introduce a rival 'Electric Theatre', grandly called the 'De Luxe' (and ever afterwards mispronounced), where a new race of flickering heroes would supplant all memories of Miss Violet Perry's Operatic Class and its 1907 production of *H.M.S. Pinafore*, which had boasted, with sublime irrelevance, 'a revolving lighthouse light'.[2]

More important than his beloved city, though only in degree, was the countryside that surrounded it. In those days it lay close at hand, an easy stroll along sweet lanes, by leafy hedgerows. The Gurney family made it part and parcel of their leisure:

It was the rule for Father to walk to Maisemore on Sunday evenings, summer and winter when the weather permitted, taking Grandma Gurney her weekly tea and butter. Those of us who were old and well enough were pleased to accompany him — this being, there and back, eight miles, or longer if he took us off the beaten track, through the woods in bluebell time. When Ivor was in the Cathedral Choir he was allowed to invite another choirboy, or more, to have tea with us before setting off. In these things, combined with trips down the Canal or the River, as well as country walks, Mother generally accompanied us, and they were the pleasant days of our lives . . .[3]

With Ivor, the simple family habit — something they shared with most Gloucester families — grew into a way of life, loved with obsessive passion. As his school-days melted away, his ramblings increased; along the river, up into the hills — the litany of places he visited chiming in his poetry and letters over and over again:

> God, that I might see
> Framilode once again!
> Redmarley, all renewed,
> Clear shining after rain.
>
> And Cranham, Cranham trees,
> And blaze of Autumn hues.
> Portway under the moon,
> Silvered with freezing dews.
>
> May Hill that Gloster dwellers
> 'Gainst every sunset see;
> And the wide Severn river
> Homing again to the sea.
>
> The star of afterglow,
> Venus, on western hills;
> Dymock in spring: O spring
> Of home! O daffodils!
>
> And Malvern's matchless huge
> Bastions of ancient fires —
> These will not let me rest,
> So hot my heart desires . . .

Here we go sore of shoulder,
Sore of foot, by quiet streams;
But these are not my rivers . . .
And these are useless dreams.[4]

Such was the need, even in student days, that once, as Herbert
Howells recalls, when playing for morning service in the Cathedral and the great east window was aflame with light, he cried
'God, I must go to Framilode!',[5] walked out, a Scholar Gypsy,
and stayed away for three whole days.

To a young composer Gloucester had one final gift to offer: it
was a Three Choirs city and for nearly two hundred years, along
with Hereford and Worcester, had shared in a music festival
that had become world-famous. In an age without wireless, tele-
vision, or gramophone records, it meant that fine music, decently
performed, was to be heard with some regularity. True, the
festivals themselves were not adventurous, for they were largely
choral and thus, almost by definition, conservative. They relied
heavily on *Elijah*, *Messiah*, and *The Creation*, and spawned a deplor-
able number of debilitated cantatas and oratorios from minor
English musicians. But there were occasional ventures into the
unknown and worthwhile. Coleridge Taylor's orchestral *Ballade*
enlivened the 1897 Gloucester meeting, Elgar's 'Cockaigne'
Overture that of 1901. *The Apostles* made its appearance in 1904,
and *The Kingdom* in 1907. By 1910 the Protestant clergy of
Gloucester at last felt able to follow Worcester and Hereford in
permitting a complete and unexpurgated performance of *The
Dream of Gerontius*. Emboldened (for the Cathedral did not collapse), and possibly misled by biblical precedent, they lost their
heads completely in 1913 and made room for the final scene of
Strauss's *Salome*![6]

Music-making in the city itself profited by the triennial feast of
professionalism. In 1901 an Orchestral Society was founded and
soon became available to accompany the Choral Society (nursery
for the Festival Chorus itself) in a more ambitious range of concerts. A male-voice Orpheus Society had flourished since 1898,
and free Sunday organ recitals had been a feature of the Cathedral
organist's contribution since 1886. At one level or another there
was in Gloucester a great deal of music-making; even Rosalind,
Bishop Ellicott's daughter, wrote charming cantatas and, together

with her mother (who 'possessed a rich contralto voice')[7] sang madrigals in the Palace library.

Though much of this was meat and drink to the young Ivor Gurney, he could not swallow everything that musical Gloucester had to offer. In 1907, readers of the *Citizen*, though long accustomed to the kind of heroic understatement that only a truly provincial newspaper can give voice to (4 September 1907: 'Kitchenmaid in Flames. Exciting Scenes in Gloucester Hotel'), and by now thoroughly bored by the annual sanctimonious objections to 'turning the Cathedral into a concert hall', were stirred by a series of letters that seemed, in part, to snipe at the essentially trivial nature of local musical life.

It began on 8 November, when 'A Lover of Music' wrote, in all innocence, to enquire why there were not more concerts of good music in Gloucester. On 12 November Mr. J. Embling replied by agreeing with the need, but pointing out that there was 'a good class concert held at the Sherborne Street Mission Hall every Saturday evening, free, where they avoid the mere trashy, always endeavouring to give a good class concert to lovers of music.'

At this, 'A Lover of Music' fell silent, but 'Another Lover of Music' joined the fray and went so far as to say 'I don't know whether Mr. Embling quite understands what we true lovers of "good" music mean. We don't want sentimental, semi-operatic, comic songs, and violin and piano solos, such as are generally given in "Mission" and other rooms, but rather want to hear something of the Masters, through the medium of an orchestra.'

On 14 November Mr. Embling replied, with some feeling, that it was his 'firm opinion [that] if you want to hear anything from the Masters you will have to pay dearly for it'. He, he declared, was 'quite content to listen to the singing of those who are trying to uplift mankind'.

The argument raged back and forth until 23 November, when Mr. Embling issued a challenge to 'Another Lover of Music', saying 'I wish he would furnish me with his name and address, then I would give him an invitation to my home, and let him hear a bar or two on the banjo, when he would have an idea what high-class music really is'. Silence, not surprisingly, then fell.

It seems highly likely that 'Another Lover of Music', who so earnestly wanted to hear 'something more solid than such things as

the "Little Snowdrops" waltz, or the "March to Timbuctoo" ',
was the seventeen-year-old Ivor Gurney, even though in one
letter he described himself as 'a very modest amateur player and
musician'. Certainly the legend of his engagement in some kind
of anonymous newspaper correspondence became current in
Gloucester circles, and nothing else printed in those years seems
quite to fit the bill.[8]

At seventeen, however, Ivor Gurney was now wholly committed to the task of becoming a professional musician. On leaving the Cathedral Choir in 1906, he had enrolled as an articled
pupil to Dr. Brewer. And it says much for his parents that they
were prepared to underwrite the venture, even though there was
precious little money to spare for each term's fees, and they can
scarcely be expected to have had any real appreciation of his
talent and where it might lead. Doubtless the Revd. Cheesman
helped to smooth his path, and perhaps the Misses Hunt. Dr.
Brewer does not appear to have been enthusiastic, but duly
instructed his wayward and unpredictable pupil in the mysteries
of harmony and counterpoint, piano and organ. As for composition, well, Gurney composed and nobody could curb or direct
him, least of all Brewer, whose own turgid efforts added leaden
echoes to many a Three Choirs meeting.

Partly for the experience, and partly to help out financially,
Gurney now contrived, on Cheesman's recommendation, to hold
several minor organist posts in and around Gloucester. Two, at
Whitminster and Hempsted, did not last long. 'I am afraid,' wrote
Alfred Cheesman, 'that he was rather wanting in tact, and gave
offence by being rather too outspoken — sometimes even to the
Vicars' wives!'[9] The third post suited him better; it was at the
tiny Mariners' Church in the centre of Gloucester's dockland
area where, doubtless, susceptibilities were less easily ruffled. As
an articled pupil he would also have had opportunities to play the
cathedral organ and even deputize for Dr. Brewer — though he
was in no sense, as has sometimes been claimed, the Cathedral's
Assistant Organist; such a post did not exist in those days.

More powerful than any of these experiences, however, were
his friendships. Two were now supremely important.

The first he had formed in his King's School days. It was with
F. W. Harvey — Will Harvey — whose family lived at Minsterworth, on the banks of the Severn a few miles out of Gloucester:

A creeper-covered house, an orchard near;
A farmyard with tall ricks upstanding clear
In golden sunlight of a late September. —
How little of a whole world to remember!
How slight a thing to keep a spirit free!
Within the house were books,
A piano, dear to me,
And round the house the rooks
Haunted each tall elm tree;
Each sunset crying, calling, clamouring aloud.[10]

Though Gurney adopted the entire Harvey family, Will was his special friend. Not only were they of an age, but both were in love with the countryside, intoxicated with the very fact of being Gloucester bred. And, most important of all, Will Harvey had begun to express these feelings in verse. There can be no doubt that it was his example that first set Gurney on the poet's path.

The other important friend was an articled pupil of Dr. Brewer's — not Ivor Novello, who, improbably enough, was also studying with them at this time, but a boy from Lydney, Gurney's junior by two years. His name was Herbert Howells.

The little town where Howells was born lies a few miles downstream from Gloucester, close to the Forest of Dean. His father, like Gurney's, was 'in trade', as a builder and decorator, but ran his affairs so badly that he was eventually declared bankrupt. The young Howells was only able to exploit his obvious musical talents through the generosity and understanding of the Bathurst family, the local squires. He became a private pupil of Dr. Brewer in 1907, and then, a little later on, an articled pupil alongside Ivor Gurney.

The two boys got along famously. Not only were they from a similar background, and thus aware that only native talent and good luck could rescue them from the petty indignities of a class-conscious society, but both worshipped Gloucestershire and fine poetry. It is not hard to imagine them, walking the Gloucester streets, staking out the musical territories they meant to conquer, and talking, always talking. And on at least one occasion, after the first performance of Vaughan Williams's *Tallis Fantasia* (described by Brewer as a 'queer, mad work by an odd fellow from Chelsea'[11]) there was much to talk about, for both were aware that something of great importance had happened in English music.

They were, however, very different in temperament and appearance. Howells, small and dapper and strikingly handsome, stood in complete contrast to the awkward, bespectacled and rather shambling Ivor Gurney, whose indifference to clothes and personal appearance was breath-taking. Different, too, were their ultimate solutions to the problems that faced them in society. Howells's innate good sense and practicality enabled him to build a solid career and, despite ill-health, climb steadily to a respected position in the musical establishment. Gurney, for all his charm, possessed no such instinct. He remained his own blundering self, and to all intents and purposes opted out of the race. The impression they made on Dr. Brewer is significant. In 1931 when, three years after his death, his autobiography was published, it was found that he mentioned Herbert Howells with pride. He mentioned even the ubiquitous Ivor Novello. But he did not mention Gurney.

His indifference was scarcely surprising. Gurney was intractable and opinionated, carried along by a rush of enthusiasm for all the things his bright mind was discovering. He had no time for academic caution, or the kind of gentlemanly reticence that stultified his master's compositions. This was not the path that he, Ivor Gurney, would tread; and though he may never have said as much, Brewer must have sensed the contempt he felt. As master and pupil, they did not get on.

And by this time Gurney's personal behaviour had begun to settle into patterns that were to become typical. Some were frankly disconcerting. His family saw little of him, and understood even less. He would go for long walks, sometimes stopping out all night — sleeping, perhaps, under the stars or in some friendly barn. 'It was useless to interfere. The truth was, he did not seem to belong to us . . . he simply called on us briefly, and left again without a word.'[12]

His eating habits were also far from reassuring. He seemed unable and unwilling to sit down to a proper meal, but preferred to go without, often for long periods, and then suddenly purchase great quantities of apples or buns and consume them voraciously. Howells records how once they went to Botherway's restaurant in Eastgate Street, and Gurney, having earlier rejected an ordinary meal, wolfed down a dozen fancy cakes, one after the other.[13] At home, and even in other people's homes, he would creep into the pantry and stuff himself with all manner of unsuitable foods — half a pound of butter, or some ill-considered jumble of left-overs. It is scarcely surprising to find that he began to suffer cruelly from digestive troubles.

But if his family saw little of him, his friends saw a great deal. Their homes became his home, and he would drop in unannounced at any time of day, and sometimes at any time of night. The Harveys learned to accept that a noise at two in the morning was likely to be no more than Ivor entering by a downstairs window. The Hunts kept open house for him, and so did Alfred Cheesman. Another friend was the solicitor John Haines, passionately devoted to literature, a man who actually knew a whole clutch of rising young poets, and who himself wrote tolerable verse when torts and conveyances became unbearable. They were all pleased to see him. For however unorthodox his behaviour may have been, his talent and enthusiasm were infectious, and he possessed above all a kind of guileless charm and good humour that was not to be resisted. Finding no comfort in his own family, he simply adopted the families of other people.

He was, by now, writing music to some purpose. The earliest pieces to survive belong to 1904 and are clearly first efforts of no real significance. There is nothing in them to suggest anything more than a desire to compose — certainly nothing to indicate genuine talent, great or small. The first songs of any consequence are dated November 1907: settings of 'There is a Lady sweet and kind', wrongly ascribed in the manuscript to Herrick, and Housman's 'On your midnight pallet lying'.

The following year saw other Housman settings, two of which survived in a revised form as part of the song cycle *The Western Playland*, published by the Carnegie Collection of British Music in 1926. A letter from Housman to his publisher, Grant Richards, dated 16 May 1908, suggests that Gurney gave, or at least planned, a public performance of some of these songs — though where and when is not known:

Mr. I. B. Gurney (who resides in Gloucester Cathedral along with St. Peter and Almighty God) must not print the words of my poems in full on concert programmes (a course which I am sure his fellow lodgers would disapprove of); but he is quite welcome to set them to music, and to have them sung, and to print their titles on programmes when they are sung.[14]

As these Housman settings were revised in the early 1920s, it is not really possible to judge their value as first-fruits of a budding talent. Probably they were no better than the other surviving songs of 1908–9. These include a setting of W. E. Henley's 'Dearest, when I am dead' and of a translation from Heine, 'I would my songs were roses'. There is also a rather tumultuous setting of Robert Bridges' 'The Hill Pines'. They are all of them competent and show a sensitive response to words. But they are all derivative, reflecting, on the one hand, sentimental drawing-room ballads ('I would my songs were roses'), and Grieg's chromatic side-slipping ('The Hill Pines') on the other. The real point of interest is not so much the musical quality as the choice of words. Henley, as a Gloucester poet, may perhaps be discounted; but Stevenson, Housman, and Bridges all hint at the way Gurney's mind was reaching out to the work of contemporary poets, almost as if he felt himself to be one of them.

To this period belong also a number of pieces for piano solo, and violin and piano, many of them dedicated to Margaret and Emily Hunt, and all probably written for them to play. Three movements of a piano sonata have survived, and there are a great many single-movement works, many of which have poetic titles —'Song of the Summer Winds', 'Ocean Legend', 'Autumn', and so forth. There are similar pieces for violin and piano, and, from 1910, three complete violin sonatas, in C minor, G major, and E minor.

In all these works it is as it was with the songs: they are derivative. The single movement pieces are particularly indebted to Grieg, though echoes of Brahms, Dvořák, and Schumann can also be felt. They reflect, in fact, just the kind of music that cultured maiden ladies might be expected to approve. The sonatas present a much tougher proposition, and here the influence of Brahms is paramount. Almost without exception each movement begins in fine heroic style, but then starts to waver — partly through melodic short-windedness (evident also in the one-movement pieces), and partly through lack of structural drive; the themes simply do not develop in a convincing way. In the duo-sonatas the

writing for both piano and violin is inclined to be desperate —
cluttered and ill-disciplined, an enthusiastic welter of notes sadly
in need of a pruning. Nevertheless, despite the shortcomings of
inexperience, it is manifestly the work of a musical talent moving
towards genuine originality.

By now it was clear to everyone that music would be Ivor
Gurney's career and that he stood in need of more advanced training than Gloucester could offer. His first step was to take the
matriculation examination at Durham University, where he hoped
eventually to read for a degree. He was coached for this by the
Revd. Cheesman, who accompanied him to Durham in September
1907 when he went to sit the exam. Little doubting that his pupil
would be successful (and he was), Cheesman turned the journey
into a memorable expedition. They visited York, Lincoln, Nor-
wich, Ely, and Cambridge, marvelling at the great cathedral
architecture and the changing beauties of the English countryside.
At Durham itself, Cheesman even arranged matters so that his
pupil could play the cathedral organ.[15]

The next step was to sit for an open scholarship to the Royal
College of Music. Dr. Brewer did not approve. 'Why does he
bother?' he grumbled. 'He can get all he wants here.'[16] But
Gurney knew better and duly presented himself, together with a
portfolio of his music. His examiners were Sir Hubert Parry, Sir
Charles Stanford, Dr. Walford Davies, and Dr. Charles Wood —
as formidable an inquisitorial team as London music could have
mustered. Legend has it that Parry and Stanford were intrigued
by the number and quality of the songs submitted and commented
on a certain Schubertian touch in them and even a similarity of
handwriting. When Gurney appeared before them it is said that
one or the other — it varies with the telling — burst out,
amazed, 'By God! It *is* Schubert!'

Thus, auspiciously, in the autumn of 1911, Ivor Gurney enrolled as a student of the Royal College of Music. His scholarship
was worth £40 a year. Back home in Gloucestershire the faithful
Cheesman moved heaven and earth and somehow found the means
to double the sum.

Who says 'Gloucester' sees a tall
Fair fashioned shape of stone arise,
That changes with the changing skies
From joy to gloom funereal,
Then quick again to joy; and sees
Those four most ancient ways come in
To mix their folk and dust and din
With the keen scent of the sea-breeze.
Here Rome held sway for centuries;
Here Tom Jones slept,
Here Rufus kept
His court, and here was Domesday born,
Here Hooper, Bishop, burnt in scorn
While Mary watched his agonies.
O Christ, O God, what deeds of shame
Have here been done in thy Love's name,
What Beast lit what dread flames.
Time out of mind these things were dreams,
Mere tales, not touching the quick sense,
Yet walking Gloucester History seems
A living thing and an intense.
For here and now I see the strength
In passing faces, that held bay
Proud Rupert in an arrogant day
Till Essex' train bands came at length,
And King's Power passed like mist away.
Courage and wisdom that made good
Each tiny freedom, and withstood
The cunning or the strength of great
Unscrupulous Lords; and here, elate,
The spirit that sprang to height again
When Philip would conquer the wide Main
And England, and her tigerish queen.
Countenances here of antique grace
And beautiful smiling comedy look
That Shakespeare saw in his own place
And loved and fashioned into a book.
Beauty of sweet-blood generations
The strength of nations
Hear the passion-list of a fervent lover:
The view from Over,
Westgate Street at Night, great light, deep shadows,
The Severn meadows,

The surprising, the enormous Severn Plain
So wide, so fair
From Crickley seen on Coopers, my dear lane
That holds all lane-delightfulnesses there
(O Maisemore's darling way!)
Framilode, Frampton, Dymock, Minsterworth . . .
You are the flower of villages in all earth!
Whatever those may say
That have been cursed with an unlucky birth
Poor blinded multitudes
That far from happy woods,
Like these, in towns and hovels make their stay.
If one must die for England, Fate has given
Generously indeed for we have known
Before our time, the air and skies of Heaven
And Beauty more than common has been shown,
And with our last fight fought, our last strife striven
We shall enter unsurprised into our own.[17]

LONDON: 1911-1915

Of course not all the watchers of the dawn
See Severn mists like forced-march mists withdrawn;
London has darkness changing into light,
With just one quarter hour of any weight.

Casual and common is the wonder grown —
Time's duty to lift light's curtains up and down.
But here Time is caught up clear in Eternity,
And draws as breathless life as you or me.[1]

IV

Far from his beloved Gloucestershire, Ivor Gurney settled into the routines of college life and the melancholy comforts of 'digs' in Fulham. There were new wonders, new delights — walks along the Embankment or in the crowded fascinating City streets, music to hear for the first time, new friends to make and fresh minds to explore — but it was not the same: it was not Gloucester. In all the heady splendour of Imperial London in the year of King George V's coronation, he cut a strange and isolated figure. He simply did not belong.

He cut a strange figure at the Royal College too; standing out even in that place of marked individualities:

For one thing the boy was wearing a thick, dark blue Severn pilot's coat, more suggestive of an out-of-door life than the composition lesson with Sir Charles Stanford for which (by the manuscript tucked under his arm) he was clearly bound. But what struck me more was the look of latent force in him, the fine head with its profusion of light brown hair (not too well brushed!) and the eyes, behind their spectacles, were of the mixed colouring — in Gurney's case hazel, grey, green and agate — which Erasmus once said was regarded by the English as denoting genius. 'This,' I said to myself, 'must be the new composition scholar from Gloucester whom they call Schubert.'[2]

The writer was Marion Scott. She was impressed by what she saw and moved by intuition, but can scarcely have guessed how closely her life would become involved with that of the new 'Schubert', or for how long.

Miss Scott was thirteen years Gurney's senior. She had studied at the Royal College and had remained closely in touch with its affairs, as secretary of the R.C.M. Union and editor of the college magazine. Though trained primarily as a violinist, her interest

33

had turned to musicology, and she was later to make a particularly valuable contribution to an understanding of Haydn's life and work. Though she never completed the book on Haydn for which her many articles and papers were preliminaries, she did write successfully, though not in depth, about Beethoven and Mendelssohn. She was active as a music critic, and took a keen interest in the Society of Women Musicians, of which she was President in 1915–16. Comfortably placed and not wholly dependent on music for her living, she kept house with her parents in Westbourne Terrace.

Exactly how the relationship grew we shall never know, but by 1912 Ivor Gurney was on close terms with 'Miss Scott' and clearly regarded her as a friend and confidante. She thus joins, and indeed heads, that select group of maiden ladies, older by many years, to whom he instinctively turned for comfort and encouragement. It has been suggested that he was in love with them, and they with him. Though possible, it seems more likely that the affection, on his side at least, was more of the kind he might have expected to find at home. Where Florence Gurney failed, Margaret Hunt and Marion Scott succeeded.

There were, of course, other friends. In 1912 Herbert Howells came to London and the Royal College, and the pair formed a particular friendship with a young Australian student, Arthur Benjamin, who was a year younger than Howells and three years younger than Gurney. He was also relatively wealthy, but seems never to have abused the fact. They make a strange trio: very different in character and talent, and marked out for very different destinies. Benjamin, a cheerful bachelor, extrovert and facile, directed his engaging talents with extraordinary skill and made money out of music. Howells, quiet, contemplative, and soon to be happily married, directed his deeper and more mystically inclined talents with an equal sense of purpose. Gurney, muddled, inhibited, enthusiastic, did not enjoy their 'talent', but was caught up instead in the crueller demands of genius, and scarcely knew which way to turn.

But for the time being they were students on an equal footing, enchanted by hope and a lively sense of the world's possibilities. Marion Scott paints a particularly vivid picture of them at the first London performance of Vaughan Williams's 'Sea' Symphony in February 1913:

Coming through the vestibule at Queen's Hall I found Gurney (who had been ill and had dragged himself there from Fulham), Herbert Howells and Arthur Benjamin almost speechless from the shock of joy the music had given them, and all trying to talk at once in their excitement.[3]

The impression it left on Gurney was profound, and letters for many years after the event echo the thrill they all felt.

It is perhaps a pity that Vaughan Williams was not then available as a composition teacher, for Gurney did not get on at all well with Sir Charles Stanford. There can be no doubt that he was a fine teacher — the list of pupils who grew to a genuine individuality under his tuition is staggering. But he was spikey and authoritarian. He preferred order to chaos, a controlled aim to an inspired hit. Gurney, whose manuscripts were models of confusion, quite simply got his goat. Howells recalls a typical scene in which Sir Charles subjected a Gurney manuscript to half an hour's silent contemplation, took out a gold pencil, made a few rapid alterations, smiled and said: 'There, me boy! that puts it right.' Gurney looked, pursed his lips and sighed 'Well, Sir Charles, I see you've jigged the whole show', and was promptly thrown out. But afterwards, when the door was safely closed, Stanford turned to an apprehensive Howells and chuckling said: 'You know, I love him more each time.'[4]

And so in fact did most people. 'Gurney', said Howells, 'had an astonishing creative pride. He was a most lovable egotist.'[5] In later years Sir Charles declared that of all his pupils — Vaughan Williams, Ireland, Bliss, and dozens more — Gurney was potentially 'the biggest man of them all'. 'But', he added, 'he was the least teachable.'[6]

Exactly what Ivor Gurney was writing for Stanford is not easy to decide, for no manuscripts have survived that bear obvious marks of an academic red pencil. Four Chorale Preludes for organ may belong to this period, as may a Theme and Variations for piano. But they are of no great interest and simply suggest a certain dogged student determination to do the right thing. Slightly more interesting is a Coronation March for full orchestra, written between December 1910 and January 1911 and submitted in March to the Musicians' Company as an entry in their Coronation Prize March Competition. It was returned, unplaced, on 29 April. It is not a work of any great importance, nor is it typical of Gurney's style, but it makes a brave attempt to be what an Elgarian march should be. The most individual feature, which may not have escaped the judges' notice, is a quotation from *The Merchant of Venice* inscribed on the cover — testimony to Gurney's powerful sense of irony:

> Then if he loses, he makes a swan-like end,
> Fading in music . . .

Much more ambitious, and much more personal, is the String Quartet in A minor, begun in January 1912 and completed during the summer. It is derivative of many different sources: Dvořák in the first movement's second subject; Elgar in the opening of the slow movement; and so on. But the overall effect is lively and competent, and the whole thing is carried off with a certain impetuosity that raises it considerably above the level of most student work. Gurney's fingerprints are much in evidence: intricate cross rhythms, subtle enharmonic changes (and some that are not so subtle: sudden wrenches into the unexpected), flexible, rather wayward melodic lines. The major flaw is the one which so often creeps into his purely instrumental work, and into some of his weaker songs: the tendency to let the line degenerate into a mere scrabble of buzzing semiquavers that leads nowhere in particular.

More alarming, perhaps, is the sight of the individual parts as copied by Gurney himself in readiness for a performance given by the Society of Women Musicians at one of their informal meetings in the winter of 1912–13. An untidy score is one thing: it may well represent a version intended only for the composer. But instrumental parts are copied as a direct means to performance, and in this respect Gurney's are hopelessly inadequate. The confusion and illegibility is such as to suggest a mind that has not even begun to consider the practicalities of music-making — a mind that is, in some respects, already out of touch with reality.

No such problems exist when we come to consider the eleven songs that have survived from this period. For here, suddenly and for no obvious external reason, Gurney's true originality clicks into place. Eight of the eleven were eventually to find a

Ivor Gurney, September 1905

David Gurney, *c.* 1915

Florence Gurney, *c.* 1915

Ronald Gurney, *c.* 1915

Winifred and Dorothy Gurney, *c.* 1905

Marion Scott, *c.* 1922

Herbert Howells, *c.* 1920

Canon Cheesman, *c.* 1935

F. W. Harvey, 1922

Eastgate Street, Gloucester: Barton Fair

David Gurney's shop, 19 Barton Street, second from the left:
taken in 1970, shortly before demolition

publisher, and at least one more, a setting of Thomas Hardy's 'The Night of Trafalgar', is worthy of publication. Two of the published songs are settings of ancient ballads: 'Edward', written probably in 1913, and 'The Twa Corbies', dated 'Summer, 1914' and dedicated to Parry. Both are bleak, grim, and very powerful and show a dramatic side to his talent that is sometimes overlooked. The third song is a setting of Robert Bridges' 'I praise the tender flower' — subtle and flexible and a clear indication of his mature manner.

Far more impressive, however, are the five settings of Elizabethan lyrics which Gurney came to call, affectionately, 'The Elizas'. He himself was fully aware that in writing them he had reached a level he had never touched before. A letter postmarked 5 July 1912 and addressed to Will Harvey makes his delight quite plain. It is the earliest of his letters to survive and from it the charm of his personality and the vitality of his conversation shine out with wonderful clarity:

Dear Willy,
      It's going, Willy. It's going. Gradually the cloud passes and Beauty is a present thing, not merely an abstraction poets feign to honour.

Willy, Willy, I have done 5 of the most delightful and beautiful songs you ever cast your beaming eyes upon. They are all Elizabethan — the words — and blister my kidneys, bisurate my magnesia if the music is not as English, as joyful, as tender as any lyric of all that noble host. Technique all right, and as to word setting — models. 'Orpheus', 'Tears', 'Under the Greenwood Tree', 'Sleep', and 'Spring'. How did such an undigested clod as I make them? That, Willy, I cannot say. But there they are — Five Songs for Mezzo Soprano — 2 flutes, 2 clarinets, a harp and 2 bassoons, by Ivor Gurney, A.R.C.O. Yes, Willy, I got through that exam, and meningite my cerebralis if I didn't get Second Prize!

Well, Will, a truce to my affairs. How do you get on? Have you written much? Doesn't this sacred hunger for Spring nourish that fire in you? If it does not yet, get, as I have just got, Davies *Farewell to Poesy*, *Foliage* (his latest book) and *Songs of Joy* — the finest lyric poetry in English. God bless the day when Haines recommended that last book to the Gloucester Library. What a Treasury of divine simplicity!

Willy, dear, your photograph is on the piano not far from me as I write in bed. Have your confounded family given it their august approval yet? How does the daily round, the common task go? More slippily than formerly I hope.

Someone has donated me 25 golden yellowboys. Teewentyfive quid! and the bloody indigestion is slowly quitting!! 3 hours writing today!!! Dawn of hope!!!! May be well by Midsummer!!!!! Do Müller's Exercises.[7] Please do.

I have more material for you. A little Irish boy is staying here, and lighting up the whole place for us. He has had a devil of a rough time for two years, and was quiet when he came; but now shows himself to have one of the sweetest souls in human body. Last week he sang a delicious folksong I had never known before. It will go to Sir Charles tomorrow.

O Willy, to be well! To stroll around Redland's deep in the keen joy of comparing experience and the taste of verse.

Little scrap from *Foliage*
> I hear the voice of the soft brass instruments
> Led by the silver Cornets clear and high.

Noble, is it not?

Do Müller's exercises!

How's Miss Harvey, Eric, Roy, Bernard, Gladys and the Aunt?

Spring! Spring!! Spring!!!

Play this on the piano (from *Spring*)

Clarinet
canta.

Key E major

Dont think that your poetic gift will not develop because you have to be at office most of the day. I do not believe it. There are too many examples to the contrary.

Remember — 'Daily Telegraph' on Wed and Fri, and 'Academy' every week, and 'Bookman' every month.

> Yours ever,
>
> I.B.G.

With the 'Elizas', Ivor Gurney jumped in one bound from mere competence to mastery and genuine originality. The vocal line is everywhere a sensitive and memorable response to the words. The accompaniment provides an admirable foil, at once supporting yet independent; underlining the detail of the changing moods, but not slavishly illustrative. Unlike some of his later songs the texture is simple and economical, no doubt because the

songs were originally conceived as chamber music. The score,
however, may never have been completed and they are performed nowadays with piano accompaniment. There are delightful and very typical changes of harmony — the unexpected turn
from E major to C major in 'Tears', for example. The songs, in
short, move easily and inevitably, and though they are modest and
undemonstrative they have the ring of true originality. This is
the music that helped to convince Marion Scott that she had
encountered no ordinary student, and that in Gurney, somewhere, was genius.

Moreover, there are no obvious 'models' for the 'Elizas'.
John Ireland was only just emerging as a song writer, and Peter
Warlock had not begun his chequered career. By comparison,
Parry, Stanford, and even Vaughan Williams are more formal and
more obviously beholden to classical tradition. The inspiration,
in fact, seems not to be a musical one, but a direct response to the
lyrical innocence and freedom of the poetry: the musician, as it
were, drawing out the music that the poet could only find words
for, and the two marching hand in hand to produce something
that is neither words nor music, but a new art form in which
each mirrors the other. Such moments of candid unity are rare in
the history of word setting. In English song we do not find it again
(outside Gurney) until the work of Gerald Finzi, who, as we
shall see, was devoted to Gurney's music. The secret the two
composers share is that of artless spontaneity: and they share it
with their mutual ancestor, John Dowland.

Despite the sudden mastery in the 'Elizas', it cannot be said
that Gurney had, as yet, any very clear understanding of the
nature of his particular gifts. He was, as we have seen, still much
concerned to write ambitious chamber music; and we have it on
Herbert Howells's authority that he longed to make a cycle of
operas out of W. B. Yeats's shorter plays, talked of a *Riders to
the Sea* opera, and even of an elaborate music-drama on the
subject of Simon de Montfort.[8]

Something of his youthful swagger can be seen in a letter he
wrote to Marion Scott on 31 August 1913:

Could you possibly let me have a look at Walford Davies' Violin Sonatas
next term, and early? I have fell designs on a V.S. and the pleasant
consciousness of superiority which Prose Sonatas would probably give

me, might be in the highest degree valuable. Observe — I do not ask it as a personal favour, but in the Service of Art, and to the special Glory of English Music.

Later in the same letter he makes reference to the oratorio which Saint-Saëns had written for the Gloucester Three Choirs meeting: 'Have you seen Saint-Saëns' new work? If not, forbear; there is no fool like an old fool. It should be entitled "Reminiscences of the Old Apprentices — Mendelssohn and Gounod" dedicated by the composer to the memory of the designer of the Albert Memorial.'[9] Though scarcely 'respectful', his assessment of both situations was needle-sharp.

This pattern of striving after more obviously 'impressive' things, though common enough in students, remained with Gurney throughout his composing life. Writing songs came so naturally to him that he does not seem to have recognized the uniqueness of his talents. He fretted after symphonies, concertos, sonatas, and quartets. He saw himself cast in a much more heroic musical mould than that of a lyrical miniaturist. And as time went on he became increasingly aware of the gap between his ambitions and his power to achieve them.

Leaving aside any native inability to see himself 'clear', the temper of the times was no help to Gurney in this. In 1913 'great' music meant 'big' music. Here was Howells, two years his junior, putting the finishing touches to his Piano Concerto in C minor (even the brilliant young Arthur Bliss felt disheartened by its 'beautifully resolute calligraphy' and obvious 'technical mastery').[10] And in the world outside college was the clash and glitter of Stravinsky, Mahler, and Strauss, the pomp of Elgar and the frenzies of the young Schönberg. Perhaps a still small voice could be forgiven for misunderstanding the nature of its own validity!

V

Uncongenial as London must have been to him, Ivor Gurney could scarcely have timed his arrival more advantageously, for 1911 marked the beginning of a revival in English poetry, and for the next few years the London literary scene was alive with poets. Though he was too young and uncertain of himself to play any personal part in the new developments, his choice of verse for subsequent songs proves that he was keenly aware of what was going on and was greatly stimulated by it.

During the first decade of the century, English poetry had been in the doldrums. The exciting developments that had taken place in the novel and the drama — it was, after all, the period of Hardy, Wells, Bennett, Galsworthy, Archer, Pinero, and Shaw — were not matched by poetry of any consequence. As the men of the nineties died off, or drained their febrile talents, poetry came to rest in the hands of such minor figures as Stephen Phillips, William Watson, and Coventry Patmore. Kipling's interest in poetry was on the wane; Hardy's poetic genius was only beginning to manifest itself; Bridges would not become a public figure until appointed Laureate in 1913. That office was, for the moment, enjoyed by Alfred Austin, a versifier of almost limitless ineptitude.

Signs of a poetic revival came in 1911 with the publication of John Masefield's *The Everlasting Mercy*, whose 'realism' caught the public imagination and, for the first time since Kipling's *Barrack Room Ballads*, set people arguing about the nature of poetry. It seemed that a genuine revolt against Romanticism was under way, and that a new mode of poetic expression was coming into existence under the banner of sincerity, objectivity, and truth to life.

Catching the mood, Edward Marsh, urged on by his young friend Rupert Brooke, launched the first of his five volumes of *Georgian Poetry* (Volume 1: 1911–12, published in October 1912).

Its success surprised everyone — most of all the poets themselves.
The second volume (1913–15, published in November 1915) was
eagerly awaited. But by that time the revival of English poetry
was assured, for the world was at war and Rupert Brooke had
captured the public's allegiance by dying, romantically 'before
his time', in the Aegean.

Reasons for thinking yourself a poet were plentiful in the pre-
war air, and Gurney would have been conscious of them. He
must, for example, have made his way to the Poetry Bookshop
which Harold Monro had opened in Devonshire Street in December 1912, and perhaps, on Tuesdays and Thursdays, he attended
the public readings that were held there. To be in the same room
as acknowledged poets, even if you had achieved nothing and
were too shy to speak, would be a satisfaction and a stimulus.

The earliest proof we have of Gurney's interest in writing
poetry on a professional level comes in a letter to F. W. Harvey
which, though undated and minus its envelope, belongs probably
to 1912. It contains a poem which he describes as having been
'refused by "Eyewitness", which should not be, as its author is
a great admirer of Hilaire Belloc, and takes in the "Eyewitness"
every week now.' It is a competent piece of versification — the
outcome of poetic whimsy rather than living observation:

> The afterglow slid out of Heaven,
> Heavily arched the vault above,
> Then round my bows, and in my gleaming
> Wake, dim presences 'gan to move.
>
> My boat sailed softly all the night,
> Through wraiths and shapes of mystery,
> But dawn brought once again to sight
> The friendly and familiar sea.[1]

Another letter to the same recipient, and more securely dated
by its envelope at 17 August 1913, makes it quite clear that he
was now deeply involved in the poetic scene:

Did I tell you that Haines had seen Abercrombie? Who asked Haines
whether he knew one named Harvey who showed great promise. What
do you think of a piece of blank verse I have wrought out?

The rough hewn rocks that Neptune's hosts defy
And stem the tower-tall conquering } seas; that granite mass
The kindly tyrant of tern and sailing gull
Is set in sullen joy to mere inert
Expectancy, blunt valour, 'gainst the boyish
Charges and youthful splendours of ocean old.

Have you read 'The Dynasts'? No! Well, then, quickly must you to't, as Captain Hook might say. The verse is sometimes great, sometimes merely good, sometimes downright grey negation of poetry, but the whole characterisation and some of the scenes are colossally good.

By 1913, it may therefore be safely argued, Gurney was sufficiently gripped by the possibilities of poetry to devote time and energy to making technical experiments on a par with those his studentship obliged him to make in music. He may, perhaps, even have begun to wonder which of the two represented his true talent.

If there were any such doubts, they can only have been compounded by the physical problems which began to assert themselves at this time. Ill at ease in the noisy London streets, and cramped in squalid lodgings, unable in term-time to glimpse the restoring countryside, he began to experience fits of deep depression which left him weak and ill. He was, too, plagued by digestive troubles which, though brought on by his erratic eating habits, may also have been an expression of deeper uncertainties. His letters sound a note that was to become increasingly prominent: 'O, to be well!', 'O that this beastly nervousness would pass!', 'The trail of the dyspeptic serpent is over me still', 'The Young Genius does not feel too well, and his brain won't move as he wishes it to.' At twenty-three Ivor Gurney was beginning to show signs of a marked emotional and physical instability, and his friends noticed it with concern: 'Ivor often appears to waste his time and his health seems always to interfere with steady work. [I] have seen him in so many moods, and the joy of life and creation is so marked. But the reaction goes deeper than with anyone else I have ever seen.'[2]

Only Gloucestershire could supply the healing. Some time in May 1913, on the verge of what can only be described as a type of nervous breakdown brought on by the sustained effort of creative work, he escaped to the Lock House at Framilode. There he wrote to Marion Scott:

Please excuse this pencil. I am (if I may say so) in bed a-writing this.

I am very sorry to hear of the rapacious microbe, and the spoilt holiday, and also of the dreadful indignity and pottiness of it all. Me also behold. A very little work did for me. After four days I went to Dr. Harper, who gave me sealed orders for Homeward Bound (What writing!)

I have been here a week. And oh! what a difference! And oh! Framilode on good behaviour! What you want is sailing, I am sure. And if you came here I would give it to you. Could you manage it? You and your sister in distress? As for cost — Bridgewater is not more than 50 miles I should think, and (but I speak personally) at least one lodger here pays 12/6 a week! But lady friends of mine stay comfortably in a dear little cottage for 18/6 each. Oh, I have a promise to go to Swansea in a coaster, perhaps Cork too! Come to Framilode, Fretherne, Elmore, Arlingham, Saul! Framilode on the map is just where the Severn does this sort of antic:

And again, when for some reason she had not replied:

I hope you got my letter; or, that if it reached you safely, nothing in it offended you? I should be sorry to do that. If recommending you to stay at Framilode was a liberty in your eyes, I am again sorry, but it was a very pardonable one considering what Framilode is: although I am not so great an advertisment as to its health-giving properties . . . I think and hope that Shimmin is coming here soon. He will be surprised to see how accomplished I have become. Yesterday was spent in wheeling coal up a plank — barge loading. Today is eeling and haymaking. To-morrow in boat mending and mullet fishing. But nothing seems to improve my defective works much, although I *can* lift a $\frac{1}{2}$ cwt weight with either hand above my head, which is probably more than any other R.C.M-er can do. It will be good to have someone like the gentle Sidney to look on and admire as I splice the mainbrace or cleat the halliards or in other ways bemuse the bourgeois!

He wrote again after he had returned to London and the caged delights of 15 Barclay Road, Fulham:

Well, I had a pretty bad time of it for the first 6 weeks, and then an increasingly better time of it; and I am still on the mend, thank Goodness. And as for Framilode, who could do justice to it?

I will simply say that from a small hill not a mile away from where I stayed (or 'stopped' as they say here) and this hill, lovely in itself, though tiny and probably not 200 feet high, gives one a view of the Forest of Dean, hills on the West, the whole broad Severn on the SW, Gloucestershire to the Southern Border to the S. And the whole line of Cotswolds on the S.SE and E. Likewise the Malverns on the North! Oh, what a place! Blue river and golden sand, and blue-black hills — in fine weather of course.

London is worse than ever to bear after that. Still, let us hope that the Militants will blow it up soon.[3]

I hope everything has been going well with you, and that I shall soon see you. But please dont expect any immortal imaginings from me yet. I am a pricked bladder still. So that Strauss may lie quiet for a while.

Few letters have survived from this period, so it is not possible to know exactly how Gurney spent the summer of 1914. But it is reasonable to guess that he walked the Gloucestershire countryside, his pockets stuffed with books of poetry and the little music manuscript books, $9\frac{1}{2}$ inches by $3\frac{3}{4}$, which he used to buy for tuppence from Wallace Harris's shop in Westgate Street, and that he spent hours with Margaret and Emily Hunt, playing and talking about his latest composition. Or listened avidly when John Haines talked about the poets he knew — Wilfred Gibson and his family had settled near Dymock on the Gloucester–Herefordshire borders, and the Lascelles Abercrombies were at Ryton; Robert Frost had been persuaded to join them and lived in a cottage at Ledbury, and Edward Thomas was a frequent visitor. Or swam in the Severn, or sailed the little leaky boat that Will Harvey was later to describe in verse:

> The *Dorothy* was very small: a boat
> Scarce bigger than the sort one rows
> With oars! we got her for a five-pound note
> At second-hand. Yet when the river flows
> Strong to the sea, and the wind lightly blows,
> Then see her dancing on the tide, and you'll
> Swear she's the prettiest little craft that goes
> Up-stream from Framilode to Bollopool.[4]

Probably, like Harvey, he was writing poetry; he was certainly writing music. Possibly, like other sensitive people, he felt that all was not well with the world, and shivered at the news that Francis Ferdinand, Archduke of Austria, had been assassinated in the obscure capital of Serbia. But where he was, or what he thought on the fourth day of that sweltering August when the nineteenth century came rudely to an end, we do not know.

The Lock Keeper

Men delight to praise men; and to edge
A little further off from death the memory
Of any noted or bright personality
Is still a luck and poet's privilege.
And so the man who goes in my dark mind
With sand and broad waters and general kind
Of fish and fox and bird lore, and walking lank;
Knowledge of net and rod and rib and shank,
Might well stretch out my mind to be a frame —
A picture of a worthy without name.
You might see him at morning by the lock-gates,
Or busy in the warehouse on a multitude
Of boat fittings, net fittings; copper, iron, wood,
Then later digging, furious, electric
Under the apple boughs, with a short stick,
Burnt black long ages, of pipe between set teeth,
His eyes gone flaming on the work beneath —
He up and down working like a marionette.
Back set, eyes set, wrists; and the work self-set.

His afternoon was action but all nebulous
Trailed over four miles country, tentaculous
Of coalmen, farmers, fishermen his friends,
And duties without beginnings and without ends.
There was talk with equals, there were birds and fish to
    observe,
Stuff for a hundred thoughts on the canal's curves,
A world of sight — and back in time for tea;
Or the tide's change, his care, or a barge to let free.
The lowering of the waters, the quick inflow,
The trouble and the turmoil; characteristic row
Of exits and of river entrances;
With old (how old?) cries of the straining crews,
(Norse, Phoenician, Norse, British? immemorial use.)
Tins would float shining at three quarter tide;
Midstream his line of fire, never far wide —
Dimples of water showed his aim a guide,
And ringed the sunset colours with bright ripples.

47

Later, tide being past violence, the gates known safe,
He would leave his station, lock warehouse and half
Conscious of tiredness now, moving lankly and slow,
Would go in a dark time like some phantom or wraith,
Most like a woodsman in full summer glow.
There he was not known to me, but as hearers know
Outside the blue door facing the canal path;
Two hours or three hours of talk; as the fishers know
Or sailors, or poachers, or wandering men know talk.

Poverty or closing time would bring him again.
On the cinder path outside would be heard his slow walk.
It had a width, that Severn chimney-corner,
A dignity and largeness which should make grave
Each word or cadence uttered or let fall, save
When the damp wind in garden shrubs was mourner.
It would have needed one far less sick than I
To have questioned, to have pried each vein of his wide lore.
One should be stable, and be able for wide views,
Have knowledge, and skilled manage of questions use
When the captain is met, the capable in use,
The pictured mind, the skilled one, the hawk-eyed one;
The deft-handed, quick-moving, the touch-commanded one.
Man and element and animal comprehending
And all-paralleling one. His knowledge transcending
Books, from long vain searches of dull fact.
Conviction needing instant change to act.
The nights of winter netting birds in hedges;
The stalking wild-duck by down-river sedges;
The tricks of sailing; the ways of salmon-netting:
Cunning of practice, the finding, doing, the getting —
Wisdom of every various season or light —
Fish running, tide running, plant learning and bird flight.

Short cuts, and watercress beds, and all snaring touches,
Angling and line laying and wild beast brushes;
Badgers, stoats, foxes, the few snakes, care of ferrets,
Exactly known and judged of on their merits.
Bee-swarming, wasp-exterminating and bird-stuffing.

There was nothing he did not know; there was nothing,
    nothing.

Some men are best seen in the full day shine,
Some in half-light or the dark star-light fine:
But he, close in the deep chimney-corner, seen
Shadow and bright flare, saturnine and lean;
Clouded with smoke, wrapped round with cloak of thought,
He gave more of desert to me — more than I ought —
Who was more used to book-poring than bright life.

One had seen half-height covering the stretched sand
With purpose, insistent, creeping-up with silver band,
But dark determined, making wide on and sure.

So behind talk flowed the true spirit — to endure,
To perceive, to manage, to be skilled to excel, to com-
    prehend;
A net of craft of eye, heart, kenning and hand.
Thousand-threaded tentaculous intellect
Not easy on a new thing to be wrecked —
Since cautious with ableness, and circumspect
In courage, his mind moved to a new stand,
And only with full wisdom used that hand.

Months of firelight and lamplight of night-times; before-bed
Revelations; a time of learning and little said
On my part, since the Master he was so wise —
The lesson easy; while the grave night-winds' sighs
At window or up chimney incessant moaning
For dead daylight or for music or fishermen dead.
Dark river voice below heard and lock's overflow.[5]

FRANCE: 1915-1917

Only the wanderer
Knows England's graces,
Or can anew see clear
Familiar faces.

And who loves joy as he
That dwells in shadows?
Do not forget me quite,
O Severn meadows.[1]

VI

According to Marion Scott, Ivor Gurney volunteered for active service as soon as war was declared, but was turned down because his eyesight was defective.[2] Gurney himself, in one of his asylum writings, went into greater detail, declaring the day to have been 8 August and adding that he had been 'driven by Miss M H appeals and scorn'.[3]

It is impossible now to know what degree of truth lay behind the assertion. It does not fit Miss Hunt's known character, but the temper of the times did strange things to decent people, inducing even the gentlest of ladies to hand out white feathers as if they had been red poppies.

Even so Gurney had reasons enough for wanting to be in uniform. A desire to serve his country was undoubtedly one of them, and a general feeling of impatience with the Royal College may have been another. But he also felt that the physical effort of army life would somehow cure his 'neurasthenia' and that he would come to feel as other men: mind and body at peace with one another. Accordingly, early in 1915, he volunteered again. This time authority was less fussy about the nature of its cannon fodder, and on 9 February he was drafted into the army.

From this point onwards it becomes possible to trace the pattern of his daily life and changing moods through his letters. Several hundred have survived, addressed mostly to Marion Scott and Herbert Howells — the two friends who had the keenest instinct for his originality and therefore recognized that his writings might one day be of importance. But hundreds more must also have perished, for in the boring routines of army life he became a compulsive letter-writer.

The unit he joined was the 2nd/5th Gloucesters.[4] It had been raised in September 1914 as a Home Service Battalion and second line to the 1st/5th, who were already in action. At the beginning of February 1915 the battalion left Gloucester itself and settled in billets in Northampton, the assembly point for the whole Division. Gurney was assigned to B Company. 'It was an experience worth writing about, when we recruits stood at ease in the dusk while the 5th Gloucesters crowded around us with cries of welcome and recognition and peered into our faces to make sure of friends. It gave me a thrill such as I have had not for a long time.'[5]

The 2nd/5th Gloucesters did not remain long in Northampton. In April they moved to Chelmsford and it was here that most of their training was carried out, with occasional excursions to Epping to work on the trench system that formed part of the outer defences of London. Somehow Ivor Gurney found the strength to endure and even enjoy the situation:

Well, here I am, a soldier of the King, and the best thing for me — at present. I feel that nowhere could I be happier than where I am (except perhaps at sea), so the experiment may be called a success. What the future holds has to be kept out of sight, and indeed that is easily to be done here where no-one talked of war until the last few days, and only now because the regiment of which we are the reserve has already been in the trenches and perhaps in action.

They are good sorts, most of these boys; and will surely fight as well as those who have already gone — though there is not a word of war: nothing but a gentle grumbling about the rations or the sergeant major.

It is a better way to die; with these men, in such a cause: than the end which seemed near me and was so desirable only just over two years ago. And if I escape, well, there will be memories for old age; not all pleasant, but none so unpleasant as those which would have come had I refused the call.

Now I am tired; but tired with many others. Hungry, but honestly so. And if I *must* grumble there is always good reason somewhere. The army meat would make Falstaff misanthropic (and reduce his bulk).[6]

On 16 June he wrote to Marion Scott:

My health is still slowly improving; and as my mind clears, and as the need for self-expression grows less weak, the thought of leaving all I have to say unsaid, makes me cold. Could I only hand on my gift! Anyway, I have been rejected for second-reinforcements, and Territorial 3rd reinforcements will be late in going. The war however seems like lasting a year, and there is none of the exhilaration of battle in hot weather training.

Still, I chose this path, and do not regret it; do not see what else I could have done under the circumstances ; and if the Lord God should have the bad taste to delete me 'Deil anither word tae God from a gentleman like me'.

Anyway there's the Elizabethan songs, 'Edward', 'The Twa Corbies', 'The Sea', and 'Kennst du das Land' — two of which seem to be lost and one a sketch . . .

Tomorrow we march to camp, somewhere near Epping . . .

From where he was soon to explain:

At the moment of writing, I am precariously on the edge of a pool, watching for signs of khaki over a hedge half a mile away and cursing the army strongly and long. The aim of training troops is to make them as tired as possible without teaching them anything. Take 'em for a route march, stand 'em on their heads, muck about with 'em in any fashion so long as they get tired and sick of soldiering. It is an unintelligent affair for Infantry, nowadays. If you do as you are told, and have no objection to sudden death, that means a good soldier . . .

They are as mad as hatters here. Reveille at 5, Roll Call and Rifle Inspection at 6. Breakfast at 6.30. Parade at 8.15. March or summat. Dinner 1.30–2.30. Bayonet Practice 3.30. Tea 4.30.

So the meals come at 6.30, 1.30 about, and 4.30. O Generation of Vipers! And I joined to cure my belly!! May the Lord play dirty tricks in great abundance on such malapert cock-knaves![7]

Fortunately it was always possible to escape, for a time at least, into thoughts of music and poetry:

You did not at all bore me by your description of the West; if it had been dull, probably I should have skipped it, but every word was read and enjoyed: behind it all, the continual aching current — 'Shall I ever sing it all'? Indeed England has been poorly off for musicians, or at least (I believe) for musical output. Schubert so full of happy memories of orchards, and Mozart as clear in spirit and expression like a Spring sky, cannot we produce these? The country that produced the man who wrote such a speech as 'Ye elves of hills, brooks, standing lakes and groves' could produce anything. Our young men must write on a diet largely composed of Folk Song and Shakespeare.

The Sonnet of R.B. you sent me, I do not like. It seems to me that Rupert Brooke would not have improved with age, would not have broadened; his manner has become a mannerism, both in rhythm and diction. I do not like it. This is the kind of work which his older lesser inspiration would have produced. Great poets, great creators are not much influenced by immediate events: those must sink in to the very foundations and be absorbed. Rupert Brooke soaked it in quickly and gave it out with as great ease. For all that we have very much to be grateful for; but what of 1920? What of the counterpart to 'The Dynasts' which may still lie within another Hardy's brain a hundred years today?

Thank God we leave camp tomorrow! In it we have suffered all the horrors of slum life. They have driven us to distraction with parades and unexpected unnecessary swoops on our (supposedly) free time. Rainy weather was our only respite, and that on claying soil how appalling! Shackles and over and underdone roast. Execrable tea, margarine crying to Heaven and the Sanitary Inspector for deracination. Bread often fit for museums. Bacon virginal — unspoiled pig. The Canteen was a bright spot, but a bright spot cherished and administered by swindlers and rogues of nameless birth.

From this we go to billets — not to grumble; not to grumble; but to make sacrifices before the altar of the Goddess of Home, that estimable female who, like all her sex, is not allowed in camp.

What we are to do, what destiny confronts us the Gods themselves may well be too confused to know in all the rumours, excursions and alarms which surround those condemned for their sins to dwell in camp.

What do you say, for an ending, to an original

To the Poet before Battle
Sonnet

Now, Youth, the hour of thy dread passion comes;
Thy lovely things must all be laid away,
And thou, as others, must face the riven day
Unstirred by the tattle and rattle of rolling drums
Or bugles strident cry. When mere noise numbs
The sense of being, the fear-sick soul doth sway;
Remember thy great craft's honour, that they may say
Nothing in shame of Poets. Then the crumbs
Of praise the little versemen joyed to take
Shall be forgotten; then they must know we are
For all our skill in words, equal in might
And strong of mettle, as those we honoured. Make
The name of Poet terrible in just War,
And like a crown of honour upon the fight.[8]

Please criticise this very frankly . . .

It may reasonably be supposed that Marion Scott found much to admire in Gurney's poem — despite its Rupert Brookeish sentiments, penned in blissful ignorance of war's realities. At any rate, she took the practical step of putting it safely away, sensing, perhaps, that there was more to come.

There was indeed much more. Starved of the chance of expressing himself in music, Ivor Gurney took to poetry with a kind of delighted ease:

At present I am writing a ballad of the Cotswolds, after Belloc's 'South Country' and there are two sonnets that may come with this.

I find ballad writing very grateful and comforting to the mind; and to praise one's own country makes it not less joyous. Someday maybe I'll write music with no less facility.

I call this hefty good verse. Yet it flows (as R.L.S. said) like buttermilk from a jug.

> When I am old and cannot bide
> The grimy townships more,
> When dreams and images will not
> Assuage my longings sore,
> I'll shake their mire from my quick feet
> And shut an alien door,
>
> And get me home to my dear West
> Where men drive ploughing teams,
> And smell the earth, sing earthy songs,
> Drink careless, dance, swim streams
> Of Crystal, Jest with God; I'll have
> Dreams' Substances, not dreams.
>
> There in the creeper clad old houses
> Of beautiful grey stone,
> I'll have my friends, and make amends
> For bleak years spent alone,
> Deep-snug in a black old chimney seat
> Close to the hearth-stone.

I repeat, Madam, that strikes me as being a damgood piece of verse, and yet when I feel like it, it means the simple trouble of sitting down, opening my poetic pores and exuding as fast as pen will write — almost.[9]

Some relief from army futilities came in August 1915 when it was decided to form a military band and Gurney found himself involved, 'playing the baryton, a bass cornet arrangement. It is a fine instrument, and three days practice — even to me — are inadequate to do it justice.'[10] According to a fellow-bandsman he was even allowed to conduct, when the band sergeant was on the sick list, and 'the ease and the phrasing of our playing was unbelievable'.[11] Gurney was delighted with the change and wrote to Marion Scott about it:

I count myself lucky to be in the band. Fancy getting an interesting job in the noble profession of arms! There's something wrong within the state of Denmark. We made our debut at this (Sunday) morning's Church-Parade with that first of all march tunes 'Marching through Georgia' — bugles and brass. O, but it was hard work! The band is a soft job usually, but not on the march. Our chaps march splendidly, as they can when they choose . . .

In this band I have discovered a delightful creature. A great broad-chested heavy chap who has been a morris dancer and whose fathers and grandfathers, uncles and other relations know all the folksong imaginable. 'High Germanie', 'High Barbary', 'O No John', 'I'm Seventeen come Sunday' — whole piles of 'em. He is a very good player too and a kind of uncle to the band. Chock full of an immense tolerance and good humour and easy to get on with. 'I loved him for his great simplicity', and hope to be like him someday. So strong in himself, set fast on strong foundations. Not likely to be troubled with neurasthenia. He whistled 'Constant Billy' which I had never heard before.[12]

Gurney's letters to his friends range widely over a great many topics and encompass many different moods. It is as if he was talking to them, throwing the weight of his whole personality into every utterance. Sometimes artistic matters claim his attention:

You say that Bach and Milton are first cousins. Maybe, but if heredity were a calculable affair, and supposing their fathers really to have been brothers, I should say that Bach's father must have considerably annoyed Milton's dad and vice versa. Oh the dogmatics — the blank stares at fun and humour — the self-absorption and the wide outlook — the difference in ideas on God and the Universe! The tolerant admiration on the one side, and the slightly contemptuous fatheadedness on the other!

Milton is one of the great men not worth crossing the street to speak to. Bach was worth a hungry pilgrimage to see.[13]

Or again:

Colles's face is that of a critic — Shaw's definition of a critic: one who cannot do, but teaches others to do. Does he read Walter Pater? It is very easy for a man like that to throw sand in the eyes of the public — and nearly as easily into his own.

How is he to know whether 'Heldenleben' is music or not? He gets his opinion (unconsciously) from weight of opinion — which does not, Mr. Colles, necessarily make opinion of weight.[14]

Sometimes his humour is heavily ironic:

Jones has a friend, acquaintance, or companion named Brown. Brown is stirred up by his young lady to enlist. Jones is engaged on War Work, tying up parcels at the Admiralty with odd bits of string, which it is his business to untie and use to purpose (as per instructions on Economy). Brown, who becomes sick of the Army, lacks nevertheless the courage to desert, is shipped over to France in a cattleboat, and contracts a severe fit of sea sickness which is only terminated, in a specially violent paroxysm, by a 29.6 shell. Jones rises in the world, gets a string contract from the Government, acquires fame from his superb Collection of Knots (now in the Bruem, otherwise Mittish Bruseum), obtains through influence a free pass, and goes, after the war, on a tour in Flanders. Is it not possible that he, maybe, 'maybe', may hap to exterminate the solitary dandelion which has sprung out of the former friend and companion of his youth — Brown? I wot so.[15]

One theme he turns back to time and time again, however. It expresses his admiration of his fellow Gloucesters:

This letter is to commemorate Tim Godding — one of the most original people in all this regiment, a big word.

Here am I, sitting on my bed, against my kit bag, half-reading Carlyle, little soaking through to my dull mind, when I become aware that a boxing match is being arranged. Tim Godding will obviously be somewhere near the top of this. And presently 'No, mate, I can't say as I can box, but I've had *** good hidings from one bloke and another . . .'

Today also, when we were lying on our bellies, trying to load and reload and rereload with the quickness of those who get extra pay for it

— though not likely to get the pay for those who have extra quickness — a skylark arose.

Now Tim Godding has little bits of jargon, some of which I strongly suspect to be Hindustani. One of these is 'Ipshi pris', a sign of high spirits, of salutation to a passing battalion, or the crown of a joke. Anything joyful. So Tim Godding turned over, looked up to the first blue of spring — 'Ipshi pris, skylark. Ipshi pris!'

One night also, after lights out, he, as is the usual course of things, gave voice to the feelings of the hut — this time on the universal distaste for army life. 'Ah, let me get out of this bastard lot, and they wont see Tim again. The *** Germans can come and fight on our doorstep, and all I'll say is "Fight on, lads, fight on". They can come and drag our old man out of the front door, and I'll be up in the attic — washing me feet.'

It was also he who made answer to the doctor, when asked how he felt: 'Bad all over, Doctor. Worse in some places than in others.'[16]

Throughout the letters there runs the refrain of his delight in ordinary men who seemed, animal-like, to inhabit their own bodies with perfect equilibrium of flesh and spirit. They, he felt, were complete and firmly rooted, and this was what he longed for in himself.

On 19 February 1916, Gurney's battalion bundled into an assortment of uncomfortable railway carriages and were taken to Tidworth on the Salisbury Plain. From there they were marched, in 'deep snow and a biting wind',[17] to Park House Camp, ready to engage in Active Service Training. It could not be long now before they would be sent to France and the realities of a war they had so far only mimicked.

Gurney's own attitude to the approaching dangers was philosophic and profoundly influenced by his favourite authors:

I am not greatly afraid of death. I am big enough to view great things in their true proportions more or less, though not yet the smaller ones. Of all the written works of man that help one to submit to Destiny I know of nothing more persuasive than that part of *War and Peace* which tells of Pierre's captivity and his peasant friend.[18]

It did not escape his notice that he too was being aided by the Tim Goddings of this world — 'masters of life, and my unconscious instructors'.

Conditions at Park House Camp were not encouraging. The battalion arrived to find no palliasses, no fires, and no electric light. Each man was issued with rations, three blankets, and an order to sleep on bare boards. There was a blizzard that night. Two days later, on 22 February, they were inspected by Sir John French:

At 1.20 we marched out of huts and were drawn up on the hill side; snow was falling and a perishing gale blew: we stood for nearly two hours frozen to the marrow. Sir John French came around at 3.20 pm and had a look at us. He was a small man with a white moustache and a red face: he wore a big fur coat which hid most of him.[19]

A week or so later the thaw commenced and the frozen plain was transformed into a 'quagmire of mud and slush'[20] not unlike Flanders. Ideal conditions, their commanders decided, for digging a trench system.

And so the training continued — twenty-mile route marches, mock battles, nights in the trenches — through March and April. At last, on 5 May, they were ready to be inspected by King George V. At least one young officer, twenty at the time and with rather less than two years of life to look forward to, allowed himself a few mixed thoughts:

It was a most impressive sight. Twenty thousand men, hundreds of horses and wagons all moving together in an endless line, under the command of a single man — all very fine, fixed bayonets, drawn swords, and bands playing. One does not wish to be a pessimist, but I could not help wondering how many would come back alive from France. The whole mass rolling forward looks irresistible. I have never before taken part in a review on this scale. As we went by, there were scores of pretty girls and smart motors. I wonder if they realised how much extra work this show meant to us — how we had been up and about since 4.30 a.m., had marched nine miles carrying 70 lbs on our backs — and did they realise that we should get nothing to eat except hard biscuits until 4.30 p.m. . . . ?[21]

Trapped in this 'impressive sight', Gurney may well have recalled the kindly, but not wholly tactful note of enquiry that had reached him on 17 February:

It has been brought to the notice of the RCM Union General Committee that some of the Members who are on Active Service may have experienced difficulties in arranging for the maintenance of their professional musical interests during their enforced absence, and may be glad to know where to apply in the event of their wanting a temporary teacher for their pupils, a reliable deputy to take over their position, or a responsible representative to gather any royalties from publishers that may accrue . . .

He had turned the message over and scribbled a pencilled note on the back:

I have experienced no great difficulty in arranging for the maintainance of my professional interests, for at best they were only slightly more than nil. As for requiring a temporary teacher, you could serve me little in this; but for any temporary pupils — a half a guinea a lesson of 20 minutes — I should feel most grateful. Your remark about collecting royalties happens merely to be ironic, and does not give me anything like the pleasure the other offer does — that offer to provide a responsible deputy for my position. My position is at present that of a private in the 2nd/5th Battalion of the Glosters, who are about to move into huts on Salisbury Plain. Any deputy, trustworthy or otherwise, would be most gratefully welcomed and fulsomely flattered, receive all my military decorations and valuable insight into the best method of mud cleaning with vocal accompaniment.

Yours truly,

Ivor Gurney.

But there were delights sufficient to quieten the most ardent ironist and unleash the poet. In mid-April he returned to Gloucester on five days leave.

On the Tuesday, the second of the five, I breakfasted deliciously late, and after lounging about in a most unmilitary manner with the Times and Daily News I completed my toilet, got my bike and went down the noblest road I know — the Gloucester–Malvern road, where all the telegraph poles are down and great trees lying stricken and low forever. Through Maisemore, Hartpury, Corse Staunton — near the Malverns now — then into a pub, where I quaffed a foaming beaker of gingerbeer (price 2d) and turned off to Ryton, across roads puzzling on the map, but asking questions of my own courteous country men and women. Then as I neared Red Marley (O the good county) I saw the sight which had been my hope to see — daffodils growing in the orchards and

lovely-green fields smiling at the sun. Little knolls rising up continually
on the unexpectant eye, deep lanes (and still the uprooted disinherited
trees; not wasted to decay, I thought in consolation, but noble over-
thrown by a noble enemy: 'A Roman by a Roman valiantly conquered'),
and a soil coloured of a surpassing red, from which Redmarley gets its
name. That little village set under the shadow of the Malverns and set
with orchards thick and fair with blossom and flowers. Cowslips, blue
bells, ladysmocks: all Shakesperian like the country — a perfect setting
for a comedy.

Then a wandering thought became firm. Lascelles Abercrombie and
Wilfred Gibson both live at Ryton, near my way. I would go see their
houses. And when I asked some pleasant smiling woman where Mr.
Abercrombie lived, I was told 'The second house on the left'. Then
there came a dip in the road with a gorgeous little bit of red sandstone
rock jutting out on the road, then a double cottage with a sort of court-
yard. I stood hesitating for long with my eyes fixed on its white front;
made up my mind, went up and knocked. Let it suffice to say that I
spent 6 very full hours of joy with Mrs. Abercrombie, her husband is
munition-making in Liverpool, and acquired a rich memory. I wheeled
the pram, did feats of daring to amuse the three children, and talked of
books and music with Mrs. Abercrombie, the genius of the place: all
set in blue of the sky, green of the fields and leaves, and that red, that
red of the soil. Abercrombie is very interested in music too, and can
read scores; his is a very wide versatile mind.

Then I left her with kind thoughts and words, westward to Newent
and Dymock, to take supper finally at Minsterworth — but no laughter
there now. Mrs. Harvey being a widow, and her three sons in the
army. But there was Bach for a while. Then out to the night and Venus
high in the air and the black vault studded with stars not so fair as she
but dear to me, most dear.[22]

It could not now be long. On 17 May he wrote to Marion
Scott: 'Next Monday or Tuesday will be the exact date most
likely. All this leaves me merely indifferent, as I set the extra
danger against the not having to clean buttons: and not being
inspected every morning.' On the evening of 23 May he addressed
a brief postcard to Herbert Howells:

Dear Howler,
        Finis est, or rather, Inceptus est (?)
        We go tomorrow. . . .

VII

The 2nd/5th Gloucesters arrived at Le Havre aboard H.M.T. 861 on 25 May 1916. They moved immediately into a temporary camp set up on a hill overlooking the town, and then, three days later, began the long journey to Flanders and the battlefield. They were heading for Le Sart, a small village some twenty miles to the south west of Ypres. Here they settled into billets for two or three days of comparative rest — though, as one officer put it, 'as night came on it was possible to see the glow of Verey lights in the near distance and to hear the thunder of artillery. Life was becoming frightfully real.'[1]

On 29 May orders were given for the battalion to go into trenches in front of Riez Bailleul for instruction under the London Welsh, who were then occupying that part of the line. Two days later the move was made:

That night is one of vivid memories — the curious names of the lanes, Eton Road, Cheltenham Road, Rugby Road — then the main road running from Estaires to La Bassee — then Rouge Croix with its red Crucifix and the sentry standing at the cross roads; then, after a long wait, the splitting up into small parties and proceeding at intervals along a duckboarded trench — the Verey lights in the near distance, the tat-tat of machine-guns and the occasional whistle of a stray bullet. The village of Neuve Chapelle lay on the right.

A further twenty minutes and Sign Post Lane was reached and then the front line breast-works. The night was very dark and the Verey lights from both sides lit up everything at intervals in a ghostly sort of way; there was, too, an uncanny stillness in the air, broken occasionally by spasmodic firing. It was difficult to imagine that this place had any connection with a world war — it seemed so quiet.[2]

The week's instruction passed without major incident and the battalion returned to Le Sart on 8 June. Two days later it moved forward again to Laventie, to be 'in reserve' and supply ration and working parties for the front line, as well as garrison the reserve posts, Fort Esquin, Wangerie, and Masselot.

Laventie is a place of happy memories to many. It was rather a unique little town, built in the form of a cross, with its red brick church in the centre. Though it was only a mile or so from the front line of the Fauquissart Sector, the civilians lived on there and farmed a certain amount of the land around. The town had suffered considerably in 1915, when it was the scene of fierce house to house fighting, yet the billets were fairly habitable and the plane trees still stood in the streets. There were some beautiful lawns and gardens behind some of the big houses. The nights at Laventie were distinctly noisy, since eighteen pounder batteries, not to mention a fifteen inch railway gun, surrounded the village. But the place itself was seldom shelled: it seemed to be a case of 'live and let live'. If the Germans shelled Laventie, the British artillery retaliated on Aubers.[3]

On 15 June the 2nd/5th Gloucesters relieved the 2nd/1st Bucks in the Fauquissart–Laventie Sector and for five days enjoyed their first independent experience of front line fighting.

Nearly two years had passed since the patriotic days of August 1914, and though both sides in the struggle were now infinitely sadder they cannot be said to have grown much wiser. German victories in 1914 had brought their armies in a massive sweep through Belgium to within a day's outing of Paris. They had been stopped by the 'miracle' battle of the Marne. Since then both sides had been locked in a system of trench warfare which admitted only one possibility: the slow bleeding to death of their armies. But if the process seemed slow it was only because so many human lives were involved; in reality the blood flowed fast enough. The first Battle of Ypres, and the second, joined Mons and the Marne in the list of fruitless battle honours. The line of trenches, a line of gaping, eager graves, stretched from Switzerland to the sea. Nothing had been solved. Nothing could be solved. But the generals persisted.

Of the 475 miles of trenches that straddled civilized Europe, few bore much resemblance to the elegant blueprints laid down in army manuals. Where the ground was dry and firm the military ideal might be essayed, even if the rough usages of practical warfare soon reduced everything to a shambles. But, for the most part, the ground was neither firm nor dry, and the protective trench, whether sunk deep in the earth or built above it with sandbagged parapets, rapidly became an all-embracing bath of mud more loathsome than any human enemy.

Trenches were not cut in straight lines but in crenellated fashion, with 'firebays' projecting like blunt teeth. Nor was a front line trench necessarily the most forward position, for out of it ran 'saps' — narrow passages leading to isolated listening posts where sentries would squat, hours at a time, straining to catch the slightest hint of enemy activity.

Behind the front line trenches, and parallel to them, ran 'support' and 'reserve' trenches. The distance between them varied considerably, but all three were linked by a series of zigzag 'communication' trenches. Death was as likely in one as in any of the others.

All that separated the opposing forces was a tract aptly referred to as 'No Man's Land'. It varied in width, narrowing at times to a few yards. But it was uniform in desolation: broken stumps of trees, shapeless piles of rubble, deep waterlogged craters, tangled screens of barbed and rusting wire, and everywhere an oozing sea of slick, black mud.

In this unimaginable arena vast armies of men fought each other and tried not to die. They also fought fear and despair, hunger and cold, disease, boredom, and all the absurdity of a situation whose cause no one could remember or explain; they fought rats and lice and pestilential flies, the stink of rotting corpses and the fetid smell of human ordure; they fought loneliness and excessive, inescapable company; they fought noise and sudden silence; and, above all, they fought the devouring, excremental mud.

Life, at least in theory, followed a fairly regular routine in which the soldier was either 'in the line', 'in reserve', or 'at rest' in some camp many miles distant from the fighting lines. Of the three possibilities, only the third could be considered 'safe'. All nice distinctions, however, were blurred over by the endless 'fatigues' that had to be performed — repairing trenches and wiring, moving rations and stores, cleaning, clearing, bringing in the wounded and burying the dead. The soldier's life was totally exhausting, and in many ways totally demoralizing.

Something of the daily timetable can be gathered from a letter which Ivor Gurney wrote to Marion Scott on 25 October 1916.

The terms 'stand to' and 'stand down' refer to those eerie moments of ritual when, every day at dawn and dusk, each fighting soldier would mount the fire step and stand in readiness for a possible attack.

I promised to tell you something of my life in the trenches. Our last orders were as follows: Stand To 5.30. Stand Down, clean rifles 6.00. Breakfast 7.30. Work 8.30–12.30. Dinner 1. Tea 4.30. Stand To 5. 5.30 Stand Down. Then Ration Fatigue. Listening Post. Sentry. Wiring-Party. Some of these last all night. One is allowed to sleep off duty — but not in dugouts and the average, now the cold weather has come, and rain, is about 3 hours sleep. Out of trenches there are parades, inspections, chiefly for shortages; and fatigues . . . The life is as grey as it sounds, but one manages to hang on to life by watching the absolute unquenchability of the cheerier spirits—wonderful people some of them; after all, it is better to be depressed with reason than without.

When confronted with a difficult proposition the British soldier emits (rather like the cuttle-fish) a black appalling cloud of profanity; then does the job.

He also, at a later date, had something to say about the joys of being 'in support':

'In support' is a term of variable meaning. Here, in conquered ground, it means ration-carrying and fatigues a kilometre from the first line. (Earlier) it meant sleeping on dugout steps, but here 9 men in a tiny dugout; but good fires; lots of wood — our salvation. Tea leaves were boiled 3 times, and we managed a hot drink three or four times every day.

He said rather less about his life as a signaller, however. Censorship would not permit details, and it is likely that he wished to spare his friends all useless anxiety — for however unaggressive a signaller's occupation may seem to be, his duty to keep the lines of communication clear in all circumstances often forced him to face the utmost danger, as a later account shows:

The scene is Headquarters Signal Office in Zollern trench. The operator receives a report from A Company, who are holding the front line, of heavy enemy shelling; he communicates the message to the C.O. who asks to be put through to the Company; the operator plugs in, but gets no reply. The line has been broken. A corporal and a linesman prepare to go along to A Company's line; they dash up the steps of the dugout and dive into the trench to wallow knee deep in slush. After plunging along for fifty yards, the linesman taps in and calling Battalion is answered immediately: the break is further afield — they must go on. Presently the line disappears over the top and they follow it out into the open ground where their only shelter from continuous gun fire is waterlogged shell holes. They scramble on, holding the telephone line for guidance until ahead of them they can dimly see the white outline of Regina trench. There is the screaming of a shell and they drop into the nearest shell hole just as, with a blinding flash, the earth ten yards ahead is churned up; they rush into the trench, tap in again and again are answered by Battalion, but still there is no reply from A Company. On they must go again, out into the open. . . .[4]

For most of 1916, joint Allied strategy was concerned with the desperate situation that had overtaken the French at Verdun. German bombardment of this ancient fortress had commenced on 21 February. It should, by all reasonable calculations, have fallen quickly, but somehow the French managed to hold firm. The battle raged on, inexorably, until the middle of December, and both sides suffered the most devastating losses.

Ways of relieving the pressure at Verdun were considered and plans laid for a simultaneous attack on three main fronts. This, however, had to be abandoned when the Austrians successfully routed the Italian army in the Tyrol in May. Sir Douglas Haig, sublimely confident that every step in his plan had been taken 'with Divine help',[5] therefore prepared to continue alone with a mighty offensive on the Somme.

The preliminary bombardment began on 24 June and continued remorselessly until 7.30 on the morning of 1 July. At that moment the first troops went over the top and into German machine-gun fire. In that day's fighting alone, the British suffered some 57,470 casualties, of which more than 20,000 were fatal.

Haig's offensive dragged on for nearly five months. The Somme became a mincing machine in which the Allies sustained some 630,000 casualties, and the Germans nearly 660,000. In the end it could be calculated that a few miles had been gained and pressure had been taken off Verdun. But neither side was ever quite the same again.

Gurney's 2nd/5th Gloucesters were spared most of the carnage, for they were not ordered away from the Laventie Line until the end of October. Their actual tour of duty on the Somme front lasted rather less than a month — though that month, as we shall see, was a terrible one.

It would be wrong, however, to minimize the dangers that faced them along the Laventie Line. Something of their activities can be read in the battalion's laconic official 'history'. Their 'first time in' began, as we have seen, on 15 June when they relieved the 2nd/1st Bucks at Fauquissart. They, in turn, were relieved on 21 June, but were back again in the front line on 27 June for another week's torment.

A brief spell in billets at La Gorgue was followed by a transfer to Richebourg-St. Vaast, to take over first from the Black Watch (6 July) and then from the 2nd/1st Bucks (12 July):

Things were pretty lively here, as there had recently been an attack on a salient in the German line. The front line trenches of both sides were very close to one another in places, so close in fact that a bomb could easily be thrown from one to the other, and No Man's Land was littered with the dead bodies of men who had been scythed down by machine-gun fire in the late attack. In this sector were such famous spots as Windy Corner, Chocolate Mernier Corner, Factory Post and Port Arthur.

The cemetery at Richebourg was an eerie spot; it had been completely churned up by shell fire: tombs torn open to reveal skeletons that had lain there for years. The crucifix, as was so often the case, remained standing.[6]

The Gloucesters were duly relieved on 15 July and returned to La Gorgue, only to be ordered into fresh billets at Estaires at the very moment they had settled down. Four days later a major attack was launched on the strategically important high ground of Aubers Ridge. The Berks and Bucks bore the brunt of this, however, the Gloucesters being held in reserve. In the end they were required only to bring in and bury the dead.

August found the 2nd/5th back in billets at La Gorgue, and then, from the 9th onwards, occupying the reserve posts at Wangerie, Masselot, and Fort Esquin once more.

Battalion history records that 'nothing of any further importance as far as active operations are concerned occurred' on this sector, and adds that 'judged in the light of later experiences, the Laventie front was a peaceful spot and everyone was sorry to leave it'.[7]

VIII

The ordinary private, such as Gurney (number 3895 in the army's list of disposable items), knows nothing of master-plans and strategy. Nor does he wish to know. Pausing only to wonder what unimaginable irony can have brought him to his present plight, he is concerned with the living moment. Gurney's letters, therefore, speak nothing of strategy, and, save for an occasional reminder of where he was and what he was doing, need no reference to any Grand Plan to make their effect. They record the passing, often incongruous, thoughts of a sensitive creative mind, poured out as a personal lifeline to friends in far-away England.

They are calm letters, curiously detached. But Gurney was involved in a situation that had brought him an unexpected tranquillity. Decisions no longer had to be made: the path of action was plainly marked. Caught up in a loving comradeship wherein all suffered equally and endured, he felt perhaps for the first time in his life a sense of security — a sense that he was no longer the odd man out, and that he had found the family he had always been looking for.

7 June, 1916.
Dear Miss Scott,
    Your letter has just reached me, here, dans les tranchées. Where and How I may not say; bang in the front seat we are; so when you read of a slight disturbance near Donawhere, you may picture me standing gallantly to attention as near to the cookers as possible.
    But O what luck! Here am I in a signal dugout with some of the nicest and most handsome young men I have ever met. And would you believe it? My luck I mean; they talk their native language and sing their own folksongs with sweet natural voices. I did not sleep at all for the first day in my dugout — there was too much to be said, asked, and experienced: and pleasure in watching their quick expressions, for oblivion. It was one of the most notable evenings of my life.

70

The French children are fine, a joy to watch for their grace and independence. Why our good friends over yonder should have called them degenerate only the devil who inspired their spiritual pride can explain. And the women. How different their faces are! How full of character. Some of the country we passed through was very beautiful — rather like the Stroud Valley only far longer, and there was later a river, most serenely set in trees, long lines of trees.

We are of course trying to brush up our French, but it is not easy, for where we stayed the dialect was very broad, and instead of 'Oui' they uttered a sound like 'Waw'.

The food in trenches is curiously arranged, apparently. I dont know whether the A.S.C. steal it, but nobody gets more than a third of a loaf ever, and as a rule only a quarter. This is a serious matter to a battalion that has innocently trusted to the army and spent all its money, before knowing how fickle and uncertain is the day of pay. Where everybody is broke there is of course a certain consolation of comradry, but O give me any other reason to be masterful for this spirit which binds the Infantry into a happy band of brothers. But who may resist French bread and the inviting open door of cafes? Not I. I take my good thing where I find it, and excuse my weakness and extol my taste.

The night before we came up here there was a heavy bombardment of these trenches, so our debut narrowly escaped being extremely trivilling, but the telling of all this and much more must be postponed till that happy day when I shall hold the listener with my glittering eye and bore them to shrieks and titters of apprehensive imbecility. Apres la guerre.

But these few days in the signal dugout with my Cymric friends are of the happiest for years. Out of the Company to an extent we breathe the air of freedom almost forgotten. It really does not do for one who so much desires freedom as myself to think of the general conditions of the last few months.

A waste of spirit in an expense of shame. We are all sick of this continual *** about (pray excuse the language; nothing else but that word does justice to the Army ways). And these boys here, so friendly and good to talk to are — O well, in agreement with us. War's damned interesting. It would be hard indeed to be deprived of all this artist's material now; when my mind is becoming saner and more engaged with outside things. It is not hard for me to die, but a thing sometimes unbearable to leave this life; and these Welsh God makes fine gentlemen.

It would seem that War is one of His ways of doing so.

Best wishes for health.

Yours very sincerely,

Ivor Gurney.

P.S. Your going to London sounds as if your health was improving. I hope so indeed. It is a hard thing to have an active mind and be helpless. Yesterday in the trenches we found it so; our minds were active enough, and we felt sufficiently helpless. There was a trench mortar strafe, and we had casualties. As I was in a Signallers' dugout, a bombardment means little else but noise and apprehension — as yet. But a whiz-bang missed me and a tin of Machonachie (my dinner) by ten yards; a shower of dirt, no more. Good luck to us all. I have been told that I may say that we are with the Welsh. They sang 'David of the White Rock' and the 'Slumber Song', both of which Somerville has arranged. And O their voices! I thank God for the experience.

A letter to Catherine, the wife of Lascelles Abercrombie, written probably on the same day adds detail to his picture of the admired Welshmen:

Well, we landed at one of the noblest — what do I say, the noblest town it has been my good fortune to see; I hope to speak to you of it some day. But we had not long to stay there or anywhere till we were marched here and put in trenches with another battalion for instruction. They were Welsh, mostly, and personally I feared a rather rough type. But, oh the joy, I crawled into a dugout, not high but fairly large, lit by a candle, and so met four of the most delightful young men that could be met anywhere. Thin faced and bright eyed, their faces showed beautifully against the soft glow of the candlelight, and their musical voices delightful after the long march at attention in silence. There was no sleep for me that night. I made up next day a little, but what then? We talked of Welsh folksong, of George Borrow, of Burns, of the RCM; of — yes — of Oscar Wilde, Omar Khayyam, Shakespeare, and of the war: distant from us by 300 yards. Snipers were continually firing, and rockets — fairy lights they call them: fired from a pistol — lit up the night outside. Every now and again a distant rumble of guns to remind us of the reason we were foregathered. They spoke of their friends dead or maimed in the bombardment, a bad one, of the night before, and in the face of their grief I sat there and for once self-forgetful, more or less, gave them all my love, for their tenderness, their steadfastness and kindness to raw fighters and *very* raw signallers. Well, we had two days like that, and played Auction Bridge, talked, read, smoked, and went through a trench-mortar strafe together.

Once we were standing outside our dugout cleaning mess tins, when a cuckoo sounded its call from the shattered wood at the back. What could I think of but Framilode, Minsterworth, Cranham, and the old haunts of home.

This Welshman turned to me passionately. 'Listen to that damned bird,' he said. 'All through that bombardment in the pauses I could hear that infernal silly "Cuckoo, Cuckoo" sounding while Owen was lying in my arms covered with blood. How shall I ever listen again . . . !' He broke off, and I became aware of shame at the unholy joy that filled my artist's mind. And what a fine thin keen face he had, and what a voice. . . .

By 22 June, as we have seen, Gurney had experienced the reality of warfare for himself. He made haste to tell Marion Scott as much as he could about it:

Still another interesting letter! Please dont expect such a one from me as the weather is very dull and sultry, and this is a small room with 8 signallers lying low from fatigue. However, interesting things have happened. We have come into reserve now, having gone through a strafe which a machine-gunner who had been through Loos said was worse than Loos while it lasted — which was $1\frac{1}{4}$ hours, and it left me exulted and exulting, only longing for a nice Blighty that would take me away from all this and leave me free to play the G minor Prelude from the Second Book of Bach. O for a good piano! I am tired of this war, it bores me; but I would not willingly give up such a memory of such a time. Everything went wrong, and there was a tiny pause at first — but everybody, save the officers, were doing what they ought to do and settled down later to the proper job; but if Fritzy expected us as much as we expected him, he must have been in a funk. But they behaved very well, our men; and one bay filled with signallers and stretcher-bearers sang lustily awhile a song called 'I want to go home', very popular out here, but not at all military in feeling. The machine guns are the most terrifying of sound, like an awful pack of hell hounds at one's back. I was out mending wires part of the time, but they were not so bad then. 10 high explosives were sailing over the signallers' dugout and the bay where I was in front of it. A foot would have made a considerable difference to us I think. They burst about 30 yards behind. Their explosives are not nearly so terrible as ours — you can see dugouts and duckboards sailing in the air even in a trench-mortar strafe (Toc Emma Esses — signaller's talk). Theirs of course do damage enough, but nothing comparable. They began it, and were reduced to showing white lights, which we shot away, and sending up a white rocket. Floreat Gloucestriensis! It was a great time; full of fear of course, but not so bad as neurasthenia. I could have written letters through the whole of it. But O to be out of it all! We had a gross casualties or more — some damned good men among them. Two chaps especially, whom I hoped to meet after the war. The writing in the latter part of this letter will be very bad — myself having come off the worse in a single handed combat with a bully-beef tin; but the bandage looks interesting.

Out of the window we can watch men making hay in a fashion, reminding us distractingly of home. They are easily in range of the smallest field guns. Les bons Francais! There is a delightful girl who with her mother runs a cafe in Laventie, evidently born to be the mother of dauntless men. . . .

My dear lady, I am pleased with myself, they tell me I was nearly recommended for a DCM or something or other that was done chiefly by other men. But all through I had time to wish I had chocolate, and wonder whether so much baccy was good for me. I may be chronically introspective (and this is a shocking life for that) but as little fearful as a stolid cow. It has given me still further confidence that once I get back to work my mind will take proper shape and let me be happy. . . .

I tell you what, mamselle: when I return to England I am going to be in wait for all men who have been officers and very craftily question them on several subjects, and if the answers to my questions do not satisfy me, they may look for squalls. This is deadly serious. Talk of 'dithipline' wont suit me.

And on 5 July, 1916 he wrote:

Dear Miss Scott,
            The parcel has arrived, and is being put to its proper use with the proper speed. The cake is excellent. Tray bong. J'en suis tres obligé. If you have not sent the other parcel by the time you get this do not trouble till you receive another F.P.C. The fact is, that in this last 6 days in the trenches, we have had such a devil of a time that I felt that if parcels were to come at all, if 'tis to be done, then twice well it were done quickly. We were made a cock-shy of for the artillery and so have really been part of the advance. One strafe lasted 2½ hours, and gave me a permanent distaste for such. We were under fire every day, and nowhere was safe. In the post where I was for half my time, there were twelve dugouts. Four have been smashed, the cookhouse a mere melancholy ruin of its former greatness, and the bombstore not what it was. Souvenirs are plentiful round here.

I hope you are pretty well now, and that the concert did not harm you at all. Your being able to be there sounds encouraging. Herbert Howells' 'programme' was quite charming, was it not? His English is usually tortured and topsy-turvey, but that was clear and gets just the effect needed. I did not know any song was to be done. It was quite

like old times to see 'Sea Wrack' down again. I must have heard the
thing 4 times at least. But of course 'The Twa Corbies' is a man's song,
if there were any left to sing it, and that's all the comment Sir C.H.H.P.
will get when I write.

And thank you very much for the programme.

Well, the advance, or the preliminary advances, has or have begun and
things have gone very well up to now. O, may they so continue; there
are surely great hopes now of an early advance. Up in the trenches one
is liable to get only the big news and the wildest rumours. One needs
good ones — of the latter, I mean — to keep one's pecker up sometimes. But the chaps stick it like good ones, and I am proud of them.
Pity it is that whatever happens to me, it will be difficult to meet them
again. The world is large, but I do not want better comrades than these,
and these are going by degrees.

But look here about that parcel; and my pencil moves decidedly
quicker at the thought of it.

Here's how (and I've lost my well-prepared curiously conned
syllabus).

Fowl. (since you insist on such a lofty height)

Café au lait. (Tin, you know?)

Cake. Stodgy and Sustaining.

Tommy's Cooker and tin of refills (can't get this here somehow).

Lemonade crystals or powder or such like.

Chocolate. (Plain)

Biscuits. (Oatmeal)   One book. Cheap.

Tin of Butter.

Any old interesting papers.

A candle or two (somebody's always short).

Acid Drops. Peppermint Bullseyes. Toffee or such.

And if you must leave something out, the fowl may be proscribed, on
the ground that it is proteinous matter, and we get tons of such. If one
desires to eat 4 pounds of meat a day tis easy done. But bread . . . Never
have I had more than a $\frac{1}{4}$ loaf, sometimes less, and the tale of my woes
on the subject has ascended to the Lord Almighty with no result, so I
appeal to You.

I should have remembered about the matches. A piano would also be
acceptable, but is not insisted upon. One must not push about trifles.
We could get some of this in reserve but here not so well. Part of the
cake is lying on the first part of this letter, so excuse grease marks.

You said some time ago that 'Helen of Kirkconell' would do well to
set. She is a fine wench but too long and repetitive and her limbs too
much in evidence to be easy in surrender.

'O Waly, waly' I have designs on, but not yet. But have you heard

Elgar's setting of 'To the Fallen'? Is it anyway worthy of the poem? I *would* like to set that! One of the best things I know 'in memoriam'.

Our sergeant-major has softened to all the world, and that includes even me, who went to him and asked him where the biscuits and cheese were; in a strafe; his mind being then set on less mundane matters. And so, in the trenches, I never shave, wash late in the day if I please, and wear horrid-looking sandbags round my legs because of the mud. When the S.M. tackled me about looking so like a scarecrow — or rather . . . 'Come, come Gurney, look more like a soldier for the Lord's sake.' 'Well He doesnt seem to be doing much for *my* sake, and anyway I'm not a soldier, I'm a *dirty civilian*.' He has taken to being more pious and careful of the words he utters. Whereas I delight in expressing contumelious opinions of the Lord Almighty, and outlining the lecture which I have prepared against the Last Day. He is surprised that the 'coalbox' did not fall in *my* bay, but I reassured him that there was a worse thing laid up for me, and left him somewhat cheered.

But in the name of all the Pleiades what *has* a neurasthenic musician to do with all this? One looks at the clear West, the evening stars, and thinks of Minsterworth, booktalk and music in the quiet room there: and then the guns begin; and after, one's friends are taken away, some still, some cheerful at a Blighty. O cuss it all though, I am glad to have been through it all, and will keenly enjoy telling others about it after.

And O the Somme — the valley of the Somme round Amiens! A delight of rolling country, of a lovely river, and trees, trees, trees. Apres la guerre,[1] it must be that I write piffle under the name of Rupert de Montvilliers Fortesque-Carruthers or some such name, to rake in the good gold in exceeding abundance, to see the earth and the glories thereof and develop a paunch. But for all these, there is as yet no opportunity.

Well the weather has improved now, and I hope will give you a chance of getting strong and fit to do something of what you want to do. O Kind President of Women Musicians — forward baggages that they are.

Someday I will write out on some dirty scraps of manuscript I always carry with me, my setting of Davies' 'The Sea', which you would like, I think. Will you send me a penny manuscript book or some MS in the parcel — an extremely well devised one my committee say.

NO PROTEIN

Is the soldier's motto. Another tin of café if you must, but no bully!

Underneath yon auld dugout
I wot there lies a khaki lout,
An' naebody kens what he does there
But the ladye wha' sent the parcel fair.

Your sincere friend,
Ivor Gurney.

So accustomed was she to the idea that Ivor Gurney would now be forced by circumstances to write, if anything, only poetry, that Marion Scott misunderstood his request for 'a penny manuscript book' and sent along an ordinary exercise book. It did not occur to her that anyone would find it possible to write music on the battlefield. But this is exactly what Ivor Gurney was about to do, and in a letter dated 16 August he announced, with pardonable pride: 'I have just finished a setting of Masefield's "By a Bierside" . . . it came to birth in a disused trench-mortar emplacement . . . I hope you will like it.'[2]

IX

'By a Bierside' is the first of five songs Gurney is known to have composed in the trenches. It is an astonishing achievement, arguing a quite exceptional degree of concentration and detachment, and made all the more impressive by the fact that four of them are undoubted masterpieces. They deal, moreover, with two subjects that must have been uppermost in the minds of all soldiers: a longing for the peace and security they had left behind them, and a troubled concern with the nature of death.

Masefield's poem begins in contemplation of the pity and waste of death, but, uplifted at the thought that 'Death opens unknown doors', moves on in triumph to declare that 'it is most grand to die'. 'In Flanders', written at Crucifix Corner, Thiepval on 11 January 1917, is a setting of a poem by F. W. Harvey; a tender cry of longing for Gloucestershire's fields and rivers 'Where the land is low,/Like a huge encompassing O'. 'Severn Meadows', written at Caulaincourt some time late in March 1917, explores a similar sentiment and is a setting of Gurney's own words:

> Only the wanderer
> Knows England's graces,
> Or can anew see clear
> Familiar faces.
>
> And who loves Joy as he
> That dwells in shadows?
> Do not forget me quite,
> O Severn meadows.[1]

Words and music in this song share equally in poignancy and absolute rightness.

The last of Gurney's four great trench songs was written at

'By a Bierside' (Gurney's manuscript: August 1916)

Arras in 1917, probably early in June, and is a setting of Sir Walter Raleigh's famous farewell to life, 'Even such is Time', written during the night before his execution. It forms a fitting climax to a group which, though never intended as a cycle, might easily be performed as one. Together they constitute an achievement fit to be celebrated alongside the very best that emerged from the creative spirits who, protesting, fought and died in the war to end war.

Gurney's fifth 'war song', written some time in 1917, is a setting of W. B. Yeats's 'The Fiddler of Dooney'. It is amiable and fluent but not in the same class as the four serious songs. Its date may be deceptive, for Gurney was in the habit of reworking earlier songs from memory, and it may have existed in some form before he reached the trenches. Even so, there is no rule that insists that the fighting soldier must direct his creative thoughts solely in the direction of the sublime and significant.

'By a Bierside' and 'In Flanders' both reached performance in England while Gurney was still in the line, through the good offices of Herbert Howells, who wrote enthusiastically to Marion Scott:

Prince Consort Road
Feb 14th, 1917

My Dear Miss Scott,
               My eyes will not allow of a respectable letter. But I feel I must tell you that this afternoon I again brought forward Gurney's two songs — 'In Flanders' and 'By a Bierside' — at a lesson with Sir Charles. I played them to him (and to Dr. Wood) and both were most enormously impressed by their beauty. Sir C forgot his week-old criticisms — except for one or two details — and at once said they *must* be done at the second orchestral concert this term. I am going to attempt the scoring of them . . . and it seems likely that Taylor is the only person at College to sing them. I shall have to put 'In Flanders' in a slightly lower key for him. I hope the news of this will hearten the dear warrior. It did *me* good to witness the revived enthusiasms this afternoon . . . and it will cheer you to know.
    Are you feeling better?
                       All good wishes from
                              Herbert.

Gurney approved the suggestion of an orchestrated version, and, indeed, 'By a Bierside' seems to have been composed with the orchestra in mind.

In comparison with his poetic output, Gurney's song-writing in the trenches did not amount to much — though it must be emphasized that conditions would have made it infinitely harder to write music, and it was not until after the war that he was able to write poetry to match the four serious songs in quality. Scribbling in pencil in small notebooks that would fit his uniform pockets, Gurney allowed his pent-up creativity to flow into poems of all shapes and sizes. Something was sent by almost every post to Marion Scott for safekeeping. On 19 October 1916, he announced 'At present I have it in mind to write 15 or 20 more, and chiefly of local interest, make a book and call it *Songs from the Second-Fifth.*'

Marion Scott took the hint and together they laid plans for an assault on the publishers. In the end, after a recommendation from the composer Thomas Dunhill, it was Sidgwick and Jackson who agreed to take the volume. Gurney was pleased, for the same firm had brought out Will Harvey's first volume. *A Glouce-stershire Lad*, with considerable success. Writing to Marion Scott on 27 July 1917. he expressed a rather cautious delight and a fair amount of self-criticism — mixed, as always, with a kind of naïve pride:

My Dear Friend,
　　　　　Your letter of terms has arrived. Thank you for it. It seems to me that you have done very well, but still — that is no reason why you should not try to do better still, since publishers are our lawful prey and natural enemies. Personally (again) when the book was written there was no thought of making money behind it, but chiefly an occupa-tion and mind exercise. For all that, I really do not see why the book should not pay, though I do not expect any very laudatory reviews from the *Times* etc. You have won the preliminary skirmishes, anyhow.

My own opinion of the book is, that it is very interesting, very true, very coloured; but its melody is not sustained enough, its workman-ship is rather slovenly, and its thought, though sincere, not very original and hardly ever striking. For all that, the root of the matter is there, and scraps of pure beauty often surprise one; there is also a strong dramatic sense. Where it will fail to attract is that there is none, or hardly any of the devotion of self-sacrifice, the splendid readiness for death that one finds in Grenfell, Brooke, Nichols, etc. That is partly because I am still sick of mind and body; partly for physical, partly for mental reasons; also because, though I am ready if necessary to die for England, I do not see the necessity; it being only a hard and fast system which has sent so much of the flower of England's artists to risk death, and a wrong materialistic system; rightly or wrongly I consider myself able to do work which will do honour to England. Such is my patriotism, and I believe it to be the right kind. But how to write such poems as 'If I should die' in this mood? (Also, I am not convinced that poets believe what they write always. Brooke was a sincere exception, but then he was lucky: he died easily in the war. So often poets write of what they wish to believe, wish to become, as one prays for strength and virtue not yet obtained.) Golly, what a lecture. Serves you right.

Well, I have been thinking. To all appearances the War looks like ending between July and September 1918. So my resolution goes, and there probably will be another book. So look out! But angels of ministers of grace defend us, another year!

I should like to talk with you, and yet would a talk be sufficient? For one forgets so easily things which one knows too well. Details wearisome to write but interesting to hear. Men I have met. A boy of twenty who was an expert amateur conjurer, a great lover of Boswell's Johnson, a lover of machinery, who had read and admired (Cary's and Doré's) Dante, also 'Paradise Lost', (though he knew that he did not understand them: a rare modesty); the common soldier's attitude to classical music and literature; his cheerfulness, his loose talk, his petty thieving, his nobility; his songs, his literature; his absolute acceptance of any rumours of 'Conferences' concerning Peace; his grumbling at his own country, his admiration of Fritzes, and especially of Hindenburg; his (lessening) contempt for the French; his activity, his sanity; his praise of and scorn of wanglers; his cleanliness, his hate of being considered as Tommy, or of being thought a soldier, or patriotic. He is a queer and lovable character. Not in twenty talks could I tell you what I know.

We had a concert here last night. Really, some ragtimes are most exhilarating. 'Mississippi', 'Dixie', 'Alabam', 'Charlie Chaplin's Walk', the one about the amorous shopkeeper also. I hope to play you these someday. They are not 'Georgia' nor 'Sambre et Meuse', but I know worse music.

So you have decided to call the book 'Strange Service', which is a very exact description of the feeling that made the book; it would sell better as 'Severn and Somme' perhaps, but that is your business; you are my War Cabinet, but far more stable than the real (What a justification for the old cabinet principles all these changes are! The S. Westminster and the Nation have been fully justified.)

Do you think there will be much more fighting this year? Shall we not wait for USA, or the collapse of Germany?

Be happy and get well. You are hereby appointed G.L.A. (Grand Literary Agent) with double salary.

With best wishes,
Your sincere friend
Ivor Gurney

I hope Mr. Scott's laryngitis is nearly gone by now.

Arriving when Gurney was in the front line, Marion Scott's telegram announcing that the book had been accepted caused a degree of consternation in circles where telegrams only meant bad news. It caused consternation, too, and then a little fame that a mere private could command publication. The contract was duly signed and witnessed — a strange diversion in the trenches — but a great many things were to happen to Gurney before the volume itself, slim and neatly bound in red, appeared on the bookstalls.

Again, the pattern of his experience is best traced through his letters. Sometimes, despite a casual opening, the news was not good:

24 August, 1916

My Dear Miss Scott,
I hope you are still improving, and getting on as well as becomes an Englishwoman in these times. You may have written to me, but I am at a hospital miles away from the lines to have my spectacles and teeth mended, and to drink as much coffee as my interior may be induced to receive. Unfortunately we are kept within the camp, and one's efforts are necessarily confined in their sphere. Anyway there will probably be your parcel waiting to go into the line with me, when the time for return comes.

Do get on well enough, and write me those interesting letters which are part of such joy as I can get here. They are the proper kind of letters too, properly commixed of news and intellectual brilliance. Continnery, mon ami, or rather m'amie. (I suppose.) I am writing in a canteen, temporarily transformed into a lecture room, subject being Prussia; the soldiers listening very attentively. Would they have been so attentive 3 years ago? I wonder!

The thing that fills my mind most though is, that Willy Harvey, my best friend, went out on patrol a week ago, and never came back. It does not make very much difference: for two years I have had only the most fleeting glimpses of him, but we were firm enough in friendship, and I do not look ever for a closer bond, though I live long and am as lucky in friendship as heretofore. He was full of unsatisfied longings. A Doctor would have called it neurasthenia, but that term covers many things, and in him it meant partly an idealism that could not be contented with realities. His ordinary look was gloomy, but on being spoken to he gladdened one with the most beautiful of smiles, the most considerate courtesy of manner. Being self-absorbed, he was nevertheless nobly unselfish at most times, and all who knew him and understood him must not only have liked him merely, but loved him. Had he lived, a great poet might have developed from him, could he only obtain the gift of serenity. As a soldier, or rather as I would say, a man, he was dauntlessly brave, and bravery in others stirred him not only to the most generous recognition, but also unfortunately to an insatiable desire to surpass that. His desire for nobility and sacrifice was insatiable and was at last his doom, but his friends may be excused for desiring a better ending than that probable, of a sniper's bullet in No Man's Land. There is only one thing to make me glad in all this, which is — that I saw him a few hours before he went out, and he lent me his pocket edition of Robert Bridges' 'Spirit of Man', a curious collection, but one well worth having; and a worthy memory of my friend. I need no such remembrances; if the Fates send that I live to a great age and attain fulness of days and honour, nothing can alter my memory of him or the evenings we spent together at Minsterworth. My thoughts of Bach and all firelit frosty evenings will be full of him, and the perfectest evening of Autumn will but recall him the more vividly to my memory. He is my friend, and nothing can alter that; and if I have the good fortune ever to meet with such another, he has a golden memory to contend with. A thing not easy.

I am anxious to hear what you think of my setting of Masefield's lovely poem. Do not spare criticism. Once I could not write away from the piano: that was written in the front line. Indeed I am becoming fit for my job — by which, as you know, I do not mean fighting. Our front has been fairly quiet, but that term will not exclude raids or bombardments, or the unwelcome irritations of French Mortars. These things make me horribly afraid, but never past the possibility of making jokes; which must be my standard of paralytic fear. (I tell you, should we return to the RCM, it will not do for Sir CVS to act python to our rabbits. We live in holes but only for protection against Heavy Artillery, and his calibre I fear is not as huge as other more modern calibres.) Tell me something about our College people.

O horror! Mr. Dunhill sent me the proof, and after the bother of

coming from trenches it cannot be found. Please let him know the
only alteration is the one you suggest — an ending such as yours etc.
Not the very trite schoolboy alteration of the second All ended to How
ended! Or at least, let him do so in proper journalistic style with
all ended. . . . . .

HOW ENDED! ! ! ! ! !²
or something of that sort. Printed in red, with vari-coloured exclamation marks; and a huge sforzando fff in brackets; with a footnote to
emphasize the point, and a mention thereof in the editorial; also an
increase of price for the Magazine Supplement — my photo with a
huge laurel printed thereon.

These are great days now — in England. But in France, they are
either — awful or — dull. Ours is the latter lot, which means less
horror but also less chance of a blighty.

I still expect to come through, but then, who doesn't? — out of the
line. 'Our Cheery Wounded'. You don't say!

Mr. Garvin ventured to speak of a 15 months possibility last Sunday.
But the French papers have a more optimistic opinion, when they con-
descend to hint at it. Gustave Herve does not think she can last another
winter. O that it may be! Anyway, we can stick it, and will, since now
we understand Fritzy and his cloudy soul.

Goodbye and best wishes for
Exuberant Vitality.
Yours very sincerely,
Ivor Gurney.

Lieutenant Harvey was not, in fact, dead. On 17 August he
had wandered, unaccountably, into the German trenches at
Douai and had promptly been taken prisoner. He passed the
remainder of the war in camps at Gütersloh and Crefeld, and
elsewhere. Gurney was delighted at the news: 'Traybong!', he
wrote. 'No more to be said, except, since I am freed from supposing him to be na pooh, I have only to worry about not being
na poohed myself, in order to meet him again.'³

Throughout Gurney's letters there runs a strain of jauntiness
and joking that speak more vividly about the tensions of warfare
than the most sombre accounts ever could. Sometimes the joke
is an anecdote recounted for the general entertainment of his
friends: 'I saw a scrawl on a barn door a few days ago. It will
interest you, I think. "Where is my wandering boy tonight?
Neuve Chapelle" (and date). Thats all, and pretty grim at that.'⁴
Sometimes the joke is more personal and savage — 'All nonsense

85

about the rhythms of war! Dr. Davies has said that the noise of
the guns, etc, etc. But then that is only what one expects him to
say'[5] — and sometimes it is designed to make petty indignities
more or less tolerable: 'Yesterday we had pudding: clammy
lumps of cold damp flour, congealing and hanging together
strongly by the force of malice.'[6] Throughout there is a strong
vein of irony — Here I am in the billet instead of being at
Church Parade. C of E is on my Identification Disk, but only for
burial purposes: the Wesleyan chaplain is so good I prefer to go
there for spiritual sustenance.'[7] — together with a very keen eye
for the kind of detail that was later to be transmuted so effectively
into poetry: 'The machine gunners manage to make their job
interesting by playing tunes on their guns. As thus. After the
ordinary casual shots and steady pour one hears:

which always sounds comic, and must, I imagine, require some
skill.'[8] But sometimes the real agony cannot be disguised:

7 December, 1916.
My Dear Friend,
                           . . . we suffer pain out here, and for myself it some-
times comes that death would be preferable to such a life. Yet my chief
thought is that I have found myself unfitted for Life and Battle, and am
gradually by hard necessity being strengthened and made fit for some
high task. I suffer so because of my self-indulgence in the past, and some
part of my temperament. This thought upholds me, as it upheld Peter
in 'War and Peace', and I try to accept what comes with patience — to
take it with smiles is years away from me — and to feel that I am fulfilling God's purposes. The task is hard and myself weak, but the thing
must continue, and may leave me ready to accomplish some great work
for which I am intended. All this is to say — that I blame myself much
more than I used to, and pray for patience. . . .

A great many of his letters, however, manage to combine the con-
flicting emotions, and the best of them convey the poetry and
pity of war in terms that are vivid and remarkable:

3 February, 1917.
My Dear Friend,
            The boys are nearly asleep — eight of us in a room,
say, 14 feet by 10, with a large stack of wood, a fireplace and equip-
ment. Outside it is bitterly cold; in here, not so bad; and good
companionship hides many things. A miner, an engineer, a draper's
assistant, a grocer, an Inland Revenuist, and a musician among them.
('Retreat' sounds).

Firelight

Silent, bottled in firelight, in dusky light and gloom
The boys squeeze together in the smoky dusty room.
Crowded around the fireplace, a thing of bricks and tin,
They watch the shifting embers, till the good dreams enter in . . .

But O, the cleaning up! I suppose I get as much hell as anyone in the
army; and although I give the same time to rubbing and polishing as
any of the others, the results — I will freely confess it — are not all
they might be. Today there was an inspection by the Colonel. I waited
trembling, knowing there was six weeks of hospital and soft-job dirt
and rust not yet all off; no, not by a long way. I stood there, as sheep
among the goats (no, vice versa) and waited the bolt and thunder.
Round came He-Who-Must-Be-Obeyed, looked at me, hesitated,
looked again, hesitated and was called off by the R.S.M. who was
afterwards heard telling the Colonel (a few paces away from me), 'A
good man, sir, quite all right. Quite a good man, sir, but he's a musician,
and doesn't seem able to get himself clean.' When the aforesaid R.S.M.
came round for a back view, he chuckled and said 'Ah Gurney, I'm
afraid we shall never make a soldier out of you.'
    It is a good thing they are being converted to this way of thought at
last; it has taken a long time. Anyway the R.S.M. is a brick, and
deserves a Triolet.

> He backed me up once;
> I shall never forget it.
> I'm a fool and a dunce,
> He backed me up once.
> If there's rust I shall get it,
> Your soul, you may bet it,
> Yes, all sorts and tons. . . .
> He backed me up once;
> I shall never forget it.[9]

(Triolet form quite forgotten. Please let me have it.) I fear there will
be little writing till this tyranny be over past.

I am very glad you are pleased with your first chapter, and shall be very interested to see it someday. Someday! Meanwhile le permission n'arrive pas, Curse it. I left the soft job only to get leave, and if the Fates have landed me into an orgy of cleaning without the leave. . . . May the frost have their potatoes, as Don says.

I am interested to see how you compare poetic forms to musical. It will mean what I love anyway — a Good Jaw.

Please dont expect anything of any setting of mine of 'To the Fallen' until after the war — and after that. You see, most of my (always slow) mind is taken up with trying not to resist things, which means a passive unrhythmical mind and music. Wait till I know Wagner and Bach thoroughly, and have a better digestion.

Jem tells a tale of how he wore one of those sachets until he found that, though the rest of his clothes were pretty good, the sachet was quite — athletic. But toujours le gagster — Jem.

Fire went out long ago, while I was hammering out 'Firelight'. It is too cold to think, write or read. Then Sleep. O if I could but dream such things as would mean escape for me. But I never dream, one way. or the other. Please excuse writing.

Your sincere friend,
Ivor Gurney.

2 April, 1917.
My Dear Friend,
Tin whistles and mouth organs still going hard, and we waiting for dinner and moving afterwards, for a company of ours took two more villages last night, and we shift also of course.

We have been hard worked, but still and all the same, this open country work is far preferable to trench life. This place is quite pretty, very pretty; and this morning I saw, at first dawn, one mystical star hanging over a line of black wood on the sky-line; surely one of the most beautiful things on earth.

I hope by the time this letter gets to you you will be trotting about in real Spring sunlight: it is cold here as yet, but no man may foretell of April's whims.

I told you of the death a little time back, of one of our most looked-to corporals. Well, that was before the advance. About a fortnight after the movement started we heard his grave had been discovered; and after tea one evening the whole company (that was fit) went down for a service there. Quite a fine little wooden cross had been errected: the Germans had done well: it was better than we ourselves would have given him: and on the cross was 'Hier ruht ein tapfer Engländer, Richard Rhodes' and the date. Strange to find chivalry in sight of the destruction we had left behind us: but so it was. They must have loved his beauty, or he must have lived a little for such a tribute. But he *was* brave, and his air was always gallant and gay for all his few inches. Always I admired him and his indestructibility of energy and wonderful eyes.

I am sorry about the shortage of pianos, that may affect me and my tinklings.

April 4th or 5th

I thought we were going over the top tonight, but it has been postponed — a state of things that will inevitably lead to soul-outpourings. My state of mind is — fed up to the eyes; fear of not living to write music for England; no fear at all of death. Yesterday we had a little affair with a German patrol, which made me interested for 5 minutes; after which I lapsed into the usual horrid state of boredom. O that a Nice Blighty may come soon! I do not bear pain and cold well, but do not grumble too much; so I reckon that cancels out. One cannot expect to have everything, or make one's nature strong in a week. It snowed like anything yesterday, but today has been quite beautiful, and I have strolled about chatting of Maisemore Wood and such-like things of beauty. Your Kampite blocks came in very useful — what was left of them, and a warm drink now and then is salvation indeed; after the drink I settle down to think of the delightful cosy comfortable teas I will have one day, and of the music to follow: trying so to forget my feet. What an April! Well, we have had some bonfires not so many days back.

My dear friend, it has been very kind of you to write to my friends as you have, and I know they are grateful. It is something to know that my father realises his trouble and sacrifice have not been all wasted. He has been too good always: especially considering the difference of our temperaments, and my long wasted time. Surely my life must lead to something. Surely the apprenticeship has almost passed?

I'm afraid there are no poems again. The conditions are against it, but, thank goodness, rations are better now.

My friendships are mostly queer ones, and this is queer, but believe me, a very valued one. You have given me just what I needed, and what none other of my friends could supply to keep me in touch with things which are my life; and the actuality of which is almost altogether denied me. Well, perhaps it will not be long before I am back again, and having tremendous jaws about your book, and seeing you grow stronger, and watching Audrey grow up, and seeing what her smile grows to be. Here we are called up. Goodbye.

Your sincere friend,
Ivor Gurney.

Next day:

Our Q.M.S. has told us that the 61st are mentioned in despatches. Is this true I wonder? We have risen a little in our own estimation if this is so: one does not wish to belong to a washout division. This morning was beautifully sunny, and daisies are poking their heads out here and there — without steel helmets! O the Spring, the Spring! Come late or early, you must give hope ever to dwellers in the house of flesh. How does your frail tenement get on? I hope it is warmer and sunnier with you now, and you playing on your violin, revelling in sunlight of earth and music.

Just how deep such observations were to strike in Ivor Gurney's creative mind can be seen in the poems he wrote. Some were responses that occurred almost immediately, to be scribbled down in the little crumpled notebooks he carried with him and published in his first two volumes:

> They found him when the day
> Was yet but gloom;
> Six feet of scarréd clay
> Was ample room
> And wide enough domain for all desires
> For him, whose glowing eyes
> Made mock at lethargies,
> Were not a moment still; —
> Can Death, all slayer, kill
> The fervent source of those exultant fires?
> Nay, not so;
> Somewhere that glow
> And starry shine so clear astonishes yet
> The wondering spirits as they come and go.
> Eyes that nor they nor we shall ever forget.[10]

Sometimes the response did not find an outlet for many years:

> Certain people would not clean their buttons,
> Nor polish buckles after latest fashions,
> Preferred their hair long, putties comfortable,
> Barely escaping hanging, indeed hardly able.
> In Bridge and smoking without army cautions
> Spending hours that sped like evil for quickness,
> (While others burnished brasses, earned promotions).

These were those ones who jested in the trench,
While others argued of army ways, and wrenched
What little soul they had still further from shape,
And died off one by one, or became officers
Without the first of dream, the ghost of notions
Of ever becoming soldiers, or smart and neat,
Surprised as ever to find the army capable
Of sounding 'Lights out' to break a game of Bridge,
As to fear candles would set a barn alight.
In Artois or Picardy they lie — free of useless fashions.[11]

But late or early, the response was that of a genuine poet — for
that is what the war had forced him to become.

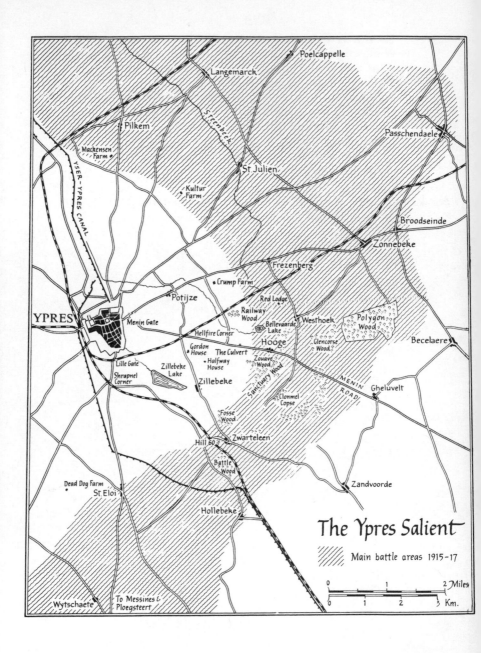

Poelcappelle

Langemarck

Pilkem

Mackensen
Farm

YSER - YPRES CANAL

Steenbek

St Julien

Passchendaele

Kultur
Farm

Broodseinde

Zonnebeke

Frezenberg

Crump Farm

Red Lodge

Potijze

Railway
Wood

Bellevaarde
Lake

Westhoek

Polygon
Wood

Becelaere

YPRES

Menin Gate

Hellfire Corner

Hooge

Glencorse
Wood

Gordon
House

The Culvert

Halfway
House

Zouave
Wood

Sanctuary Wood

MENIN ROAD

Gheluvelt

Lille Gate

Zillebeke
Lake

Shrapnel
Corner

Zillebeke

Clonmel
Copse

Fosse
Wood

Hill 60

Zwarteleen

Battle
Wood

Zandvoorde

Dead Dog Farm

St. Eloi

Hollebeke

The Ypres Salient

Main battle areas 1915-17

0   1   2 Miles

0   1   2   3 Km.

Wytschaete

To Messines &
Ploegsteert

X

The geographical realities of Gurney's military career had taken him, as we have seen, first to a point on the line just below Ypres. In this relatively quiet sector the battalion had remained until 27 October 1916, when it began a slow trek southward to join in the last days of Haig's Somme offensive. Albert, devastated but still a place of wonder on account of its famous statue of the Virgin and Child leaning perilously from the shattered tower of the basilica, was reached on 20 November:

During the only night the Battalion remained in Albert rain fell continuously. Company commanders rode forward to reconnoitre the line and on the following day the troops were moved up to occupy trenches in front of Grandecourt. The contrast between the sectors in front of Laventie and the Somme crater fields was striking. Here were primitive conditions — men clinging to shell holes, mud deep enough to completely submerge a gun team and limber, masses of unburied dead strewn over the battle fields; no sign of organised trenches, but merely shell holes joined up to one another — and, last, but by no means least in importance, no landmarks anywhere.[1]

By 22 November, nicely in time for St. Cecilia's day, the battalion was in position and ready for action:

In the front line the mud made movement of any sort practically impossible until the frost hardened the ground; shaving was not to be thought of; ration parties were held up in the mire and so we were down to one cup of cold tea per man per day. . . . The shelling was so incessant that we were compelled to live more like rats than men.[2]

It was from here that Gurney wrote his letter of 7 December to Marion Scott: 'We suffer pain out here, and for myself it sometimes comes that death would be preferable to such a life.' And in later years the drenched fatigue and cynical bitterness of the whole experience — so far removed from the days of 'Now, youth, the hour of thy dread passion comes' — found its way into a poem of remarkable power:

> Rain there was — tired and weak I was, glad for an end.
> But one spoke to me — one I liked well as friend,
> 'Let's volunteer for the Front Line — many others wont.'
> 'I'll volunteer, it's better being there than here.'
> But I had seen too many ditches and stood too long
> Feeling my feet freeze, and my shoulders ache with the strong
> Pull of equipment, and too much use of pain and strain.
> Besides, he was Lance Corporal and might be full Corporal
> Before the next straw resting might come again,
> Before the next billet should hum with talk and song.
> Stars looked as well from second as from first line holes.[3]

The 2nd/5th Gloucesters remained in the line, on and off, until 24 December and then, on 30 December, moved to Varennes in preparation for a month's training period at Gapennes. It was the coldest winter in living memory.

Training complete, the battalion marched to L'Etoile on 7 February 1917 — Gurney neatly bypassing the censor with a letter that told Marion Scott that he and his friends had 'nestled in a village under a huge rock . . . The literal translation of the pretty name of this place is The Star, and there are earthworks all around, remains of 1870.' The movement south continued, this time by train: to Wiencourt, near Amiens, on the 13th, to Framerville on the 15th, and then into the line to relieve a French infantry regiment in the Ablaincourt sector.

Early in March the battalion moved into Brigade Reserve at Raincourt:

Billets in this village, though the buildings were in ruins, provided a certain amount of comfort and were a distinct relief from the truly horrible conditions on the front line. For the most part, when in Reserve on the Somme front, the men had to exist in conditions nearly as bad as those in the forward zone. The shelling, too, was very heavy at this time in the back areas . . .[4]

What in fact was happening was that the Germans were shooting off surplus ammunition in preparation for a withdrawal to the Hindenburg Line.

The move was no victory for the Allies. It was an intelligent strategic response to a new offensive that was soon to be launched and which the Germans knew all about. The architect of the impending disaster was the French general Robert Nivelle. Wildly ambitious and insanely stubborn, he had insisted on a plan whereby the main French army would attack the Germans on the Aisne river front, broaden and intensify, and then drive on in a magnificent sweep to the Belgian coast. In order to tie down the German forces, two more attacks were to be launched simultaneously — between the Somme and the Oise, with St. Quentin as the objective; and between Bapaume and Vimy, in the hope of reaching Cambrai.

All this was planned for Easter 1917. But the Germans knew literally every detail and promptly began to withdraw their troops, effectively wiping out the St. Quentin attack and leaving the British in an awkward position at Arras. A more flexible mind might have grasped the implications of the situation. But Nivelle was not to be deterred by enemy strategy, however brilliant. He had laid his plan — everyone knew it — and he would stick to it. The British were to move first, on 9 April, Easter Monday; and then, on 16 April, he would demonstrate the full majesty of his military genius.

During the month before Nivelle's fiasco, the 2nd/5th Gloucesters spent much of their time following the German withdrawal:

The Battalion was actually at Guillancourt when the news of the German retirement became definitely known. The men had been hoping for a well-earned rest, but instead they received orders to be ready to move forward at an hour's notice. The move took place on the following morning, March 18th, but the Battalion made the journey without some of its officers, who were at the time indulging in Amiens leave.

Vermandovillers was reached at 1.15 pm, and the troops became road menders for the next ten days.

The Germans had done things very thoroughly: villages were devastated, all fruit trees cut down, all cross-roads mined, all wells rendered useless. . . .[5]

The follow-up continued: Epenancourt, Croix Moligneaux, and Caulaincourt — memorable for its ruined chateau, and a mausoleum, unaccountably left intact, in which two companies of

Gloucesters (one being Gurney's) decided to make their billet. On 31 March they reached Vermand, and two days later attacked and cleared the village of Bihecourt.

Near Vermand

Lying flat on my belly shivering in clutch-frost,
There was time to watch the stars, we had dug in:
Looking eastward over the low ridge; March scurried its blast
At our senses, no use either dying or struggling.
Low woods to left (Cotswold her spinnies if ever)
Showed through snow flurries and the clearer star weather,
And nothing but chill and wonder lived in mind; nothing
But loathing and fine beauty, and wet loathed clothing.
Here were thoughts. Cold smothering and fire-desiring,
A day to follow like this or in the digging or wiring.
Worry in snow flurrying and lying flat, flesh the earth loathing.
I was the forward sentry and would be relieved
In a quarter or so, but nothing more better than to crouch
Low in the scraped holes and to have frozen and rocky couch —
To be by desperate home thoughts clutched at, and heart-grieved.
Was I ever there — a lit warm room and Bach, to search out sacred
Meaning; and to find no luck; and to take love as believed.[6]

Everything in Nivelle's plan that could go wrong, went wrong. By the middle of May the fact had to be faced that not only had the general's plan failed utterly, but that whole French regiments were in open revolt and thousands of men had deserted. One such regiment went meekly to the front baaing like sheep — such was the slaughter they knew awaited them.

Ivor Gurney was spared from the British part in the adventure, for on Good Friday night he was wounded and had to be sent to hospital at the 55th Infantry Base Depot, Rouen. Edward Thomas, less fortunate, was killed at Arras on the Easter Monday.

14 April, 1917.
My Dear Friend,

Well, I am wounded: but not badly: perhaps not badly enough; as although kind people told me it meant Blighty for me, yet here I am at Rouen marked 'Tents'. I do not yet give up hopes, but very few boats have been running lately; none at all for some days; and the serious cases go first, of course. It was during an attack on Good Friday night that a bullet hit me and went clean through the right arm just underneath the shoulder — the muscles opposite the biceps, to describe them more or less accurately. It hurt badly for half an hour, but now hurts not at all; I am writing in bed with the arm resting on the clothes merely. Well, I suppose your letters will be lost to me for a little; please send them to me when you receive them.

I hope you are well now, in spite of the awful April weather.

There is a gap of two days between the writing of the two pages. I can send you no address: we are being shifted about too much, and everything is doubtful. Apparently the hospital boats have been and are almost completely held up, or else I might have had a chance for Blighty; though there is no real damage done to my arm, not enough to please me.

Alas! Alas! there are hardly any books here! And the life is made up of hanging about waiting to be shifted again. Now if I could find some real hard reading to do — something to distract my mind, all might be well; or if I had some MS and a few books of verse, I would turn out something in spite of the flatness of my mind. O well, hopes are not yet gone.

Will Harvey is getting his parcels, and has a new book of verse almost ready. This is good news: and it will be very interesting to see the difference between the two; for of course there will be a difference.

Though this Spring is cold and inclement, I cannot keep out of mind what April has meant to me in past years — Minsterworth, Framilode, and his companionship. And my sick mind holds desperately on to such memories for Beauty's sake; and the hope of Joy. 'By a Bierside' came from two evenings above all others: one most magical afterglow at Framilode when I was alone: and the evening before I rode in late to find England had declared war. Great billowy clouds hung over distant Malvern, and the poplars, black against the glowing West, sang music unto me, which someday I may fit myself to sing to others — but not yet; not in these conditions; when Pain rules so much and so continually in the sight of one who bears Pain hardly, supporting his courage by other examples. Still more analysis! Yes, but you are kind and infinitely patient and it does me good to 'moan'; as the Army word is.

My total cash is 3½d, so you see that in spite of my credit of about 175 francs, I can buy nothing in the way of books. Two Daily Mails will finish my literary purchases. So, if I can send you an address, please send me some small books of verse, and Tolstoi's Cossacks (World Classics — Pocket Ed). I wonder whether at last I might try Housman's 'Shropshire Lad'?

I will write again in half a shake.

Your sincere friend

Ivor Gurney.

(I write with my perforated arm, so you see not much is wrong.)

He remained in hospital for about six weeks, which, though boring, passed pleasantly enough. 'There is nothing to do', he wrote on 11 May, 'save laze or wash clothes, enjoy the blue of the sky and regret the waste of precious time.' But it was not possible to avoid day-dreams:

Last night we were talking after lights-out, chiefly about the merits of Town and Country life, as exemplified by Liverpool and Bourton-on-the-Hill, hotly discussed by a clerk and a keeper, both convinced. I like these arguments and usually start them. Someday I also must live in a little grey stone Cotswold house, with one largish room for the music room; with a garden to flame in summer against the cool greys and greens of house and trees and hedges, and then invite my friends to tell me of the great world and what goes on there between the mansions and the slums.

O for a garden to dig in, and music and books in a house of one's own, set in a little valley from whose ridges one may see Malverns and the Welsh Hills, the plain of Severn and the Severn Sea; to know oneself free there from the drill-sergeant and the pack, and to order one's life years ahead — plans, doubtless to be broken, but sweet secure plans taking no account of fear or even Prudence but only Joy. One could grow whole and happy there, the mind would lose its sickness and grow strong; it is not possible that health should wait long from such steady and gently beautiful ways of life. The winter's hardships should steel one, the spring bring Joy, summer should perfect this Joy, and autumn bring increase and mellowness to all things, and set the seal of age and ease on things not before secure. I grow happy writing of it . . .

By 18 May, however, he was 'back with the Batt: alright, but the Batt is back also practising attacks. (Today I was twice a "casualty" — is there anything in it?). So there is no need to worry just yet; as the present is taken up by the process of Feeding You Up, preliminary to serious business.'

His letters, as always, veer between several extremes of emotion. One, a note of congratulation to Herbert Howells on his engagement, is full of delightful banter: a sudden return, as it were, to the manners and moods of their student days:

30 May, 1917.
My Dear Howler,
                          So you've been and done it! Shall I congratulate you? I don't know; since before me there seems to lie two fat biographies, both of Herbert Howells.

The first opens at a passage:

At this time the composer's powers, already great, were doubled by the most fortunate act of his life: the engagement to and subsequent marriage to Miss Dorothy Dawe, a singer of miraculous endowments. From this time onwards his record is one blaze of great works and huge accomplishments. The first 14 Symphonies, the great Sanscrit Te Deum, for the opening of the new lavatory in the Dead Language Section of the British Museum; the noble setting of the genealogies in the Old Testament; of the great Bradshaw Opera, the epic of railway life; and the whole of his masterpieces up to Op 462 which begins his Middle Period, was inspired by the remarkable lady whose exquisitely chiselled nose rendered beautiful sounds which otherwise would have been painful; for she preferred to sing through this organ only. etc, etc.

And

We must here, with regret, but extenuating nothing as is our business as honest chroniclers, set down the record of the sad fact that blighted this great life; that drove a despairing man to the false comfort of spiritous liquors and that of becoming a Plymouth Brother; bleared his eyes and upset his digestion; and, in a word, set his feet on the dark path that was to lead him to spiritual damnation as Harmonium Professor at the Royal College of Music. He became entangled in the fatal web of fascination spread by an unknown contralto of doubtful attainments and tone quality.

O there's more of it, but I'm off up the line tonight and can't bother. . . .

Other letters sound a note of despair that is scarcely to be wondered at. By 1917 he had travelled a long way from the jaunty patriotic optimism of his first days in France.

What a life! What a life! My memories of this week will be: Blockhouse; an archway there through which a sniper used his skill on us as we emerged from the rooms at the side; cold; stuffy heat; Brett Young; smashed or stuck Tanks; a gas and smoke barrage put up by us, a glorious but terrible sight; Fritz's shells: one sunset: two sunrises: 'Bible in Spain'; the tale of the cutting up of the K.R.R's in 1914; of Colonel Elkington; of the first gas attack also; of the Brigade Orderly; and of the man who walked in his sleep to Fritzy, slept well, woke, realised, and bolted; Thirst; Gas; Shrapnel; *Very* H.E.; Our liquid fire; a first sight of an aeroplane map . . . Does it sound interesting? May God forgive me if I ever come to cheat myself into thinking that it was, and lie later to younger men of the Great Days. It was damnable: and what in relation to what might have happened? Nothing at all! We have been lucky, but it is not fit for men to be here — in this tormented dry-fevered marsh, where men die and are left to rot because of snipers and the callousness that War needs. 'It might be me tomorrow. Who cares? Yet still, hang on for a Blighty.'

Why does this war of spirit take on such dread forms of ugliness, and why should a high triumph be signified by a body shattered, black, stinking: avoided by day, stumbled over by night, an offence to the hardest? No doubt there is consolation in the fact that men contemplate such things, such possible endings, and are yet undismayed, yet persistent; do not lose laughter nor the common kindliness that makes life sweet — and yet seem such boys. Yet what consolation can be given me as I look on and endure it?

Any?

Sufficient? . . .

I wish I wasn't so lousy. Dont trouble to sympathise. I take that for granted or would not have written comme ça. . . .[7]

The ordeal was nearing its close. On or about 30 May Ivor Gurney was given 'a new number and badge of servitude: 241281', and shortly afterwards transferred to machine-guns: No. 1 Section, 184 M.G.C. The change came as a relief:

I do not like the thought of sticking Germans, forbye the chance of getting stuck. And it is a far more interesting game, a better fed; one does not do fatigues; one usually gets a dugout in winter; does not go into the front posts, which in winter are feet deep with slime and water; and, as I have said or hinted, is a safer service on the whole.[8]

He was, however, much to his delight, still attached to the 2nd/5th Gloucesters who, towards the end of May, had marched to the Arras front and were engaged in mopping up operations. On 1 June the battalion took over trenches in front of Guemappe, where they were engaged in wiring and consolidating — and burying the dead. Rest and reorganization began on 23 June at the village of Buire-au-Bois, and lasted long enough for an irrepressible and aptly named Lieutenant Wooster to achieve his ambition by founding a Battalion Concert Party, the 'Cheeryohs'.[9]

But the fun and games was not to last long. By the middle of August the battalion was on the move again, this time to the Ypres front to take its share of the great new offensive that Field

Ivor Gurney, 1915

Gloucester

Passchendaele

Ivor Gurney, *c.* 1922

Ivor Gurney – the asylum years

Marshal Sir Douglas Haig had set in motion at 3.45 a.m. on the morning of 31 July.

That offensive, which was to go down in infamy as the third Battle of Ypres and in the popular mind as Passchendaele, had come into existence through the failure of Nivelle's Easter campaign. The intention, so simple and elegant on paper, was to capture the salient and its vital ridges, thereby delivering Belgium and relieving the French, and then advance in one majestic sweep to the Dutch coast, taking the main rail links and forcing the Germans into a general withdrawal.

Needless to say, events did not follow the pattern suggested by Sir Douglas's consultations with the Lord. The grey dawn of 31 July turned to drizzle and the drizzle turned to rain. By dusk the battleground was awash and the scene was set for a dismal farce, acted out at the eventual cost of over half a million lives. When the Gloucesters arrived to play their part they went first to the Buysscheure area and then, on 21 August, up the line to support trenches at Warwick Farm. On the following day they joined the Oxfords and the Bucks regiments in an attack on a giant concrete fortress known as Pond Farm.

The exact part that Gurney played in these and subsequent battles is not known. On 29 August he wrote to Marion Scott: 'We are off up again and this is the last letter written in the quiet.' Prophetically he enclosed a new poem — 'The Volunteer':

I would test God's purposes:
I will go up and see
What fate is mine, what destiny
God holds for me.

For He is very secret,
He smiles, but does not say
A word that will foreshadow
Shape of the coming day.

Curious am I, curious . . .
And since he will not tell
I'll prove him, go up against
The flary mouth of Hell.

And what hereafter — Heaven?
Or Blighty? O if it were . . .
Mere agony, mere pain the price
Of the returning there.

Or — nothing! Days in mud
And slush, then other days . . .
Aie me! 'Are they not all
The seas of God?' God's Ways?[10]

At some point in the early part of September, on or about the
10th, he found himself at St. Julien in direct line for the Passchendaele Ridge. There was gas in the air, and he swallowed it.

The man was he who blinded his eyes all
Before his week of the Line and took just as it came
Patrol, bombardment, all but the mud's shame,
Did fatigues, straining his heart, and saw others fall,
Went over the top uselessly and without blame,
(Machine guns rattling Hell a foot overhead),
Mended his wires, spotted raids, smoked his pipe
In a Hell of death — escaping, and afterwards, dull
At Grandecourt, or frozen at Chaulnes, uttered vile
Words of the whole damned show, marched from Somme to St
    Quentin,
Got wounded, saw Rouen, Arras — and for fear, and to be writing
In comfortable dugouts while Gloucesters had night without shelter,
Became a machine gunner at Ypres, and perhaps went further
(By accident) carrying a message in night than Erebus dimmer,
Passed Gloucesters, was off to Berlin apparently for a saunter,
When a voice hailed him — who had watched Gloucesters go in a
    smother
Of gun smoke, a Hell of thunder, a Heaven of azure
Of mist, to be defeated, retire somehow or other
And there before the dawn told them he had nearly gone
Carrying a damned bundle of machine gun gadgets,
Staying in the line three weeks straight on to the Gloucester's ten;
So rather than be attached to the Gloucesters, he would
Rather stand freezing, and known of the Line, than be
Attached, watching the candles of poetry
Gutter to nothing in a draught, beside a corporal
Or a lieutenant, and to stare at the paper in the darkling flood,
Knowing the Gloucesters behind one, the Gloucesters before one;
Writing an impossibility, and the great good
Of being known Infantry denied to one and all.
So cursed kinder and meaner fate, and applied
To be restored once again to a soldier's way plain.
Having stirred Fritzy to a bombardment, and performed a solo
In a night of blackness and fear — and gone past the first Line;
Got gassed, and learnt the machine gun, how it played
Scales and arpeggios — perhaps not wholly in vain.
So for the second time cursing a soft job, denied
Pleasure of performance on so clumsy an instrument,
Longer in the Line — a fool at a difficult trade.
It seemed better to return to a regiment than learn
Lessons that never were meant ever to be applied.
So heard the news of returning with a solemn pleasure, turning

To feel my rifle at shoulder — yet gas changed all;
Instead of moving South with the Fifth Army,
Chokes and gasps of gas moved a doctor's sympathy
(Three weeks in needing rest — hoping a week to befall)
And got to Blighty — as unexpectedly as ever any
Of honest gas (but not much) got by a tale
Of five hours gas bombardment, which was true
(I brought that down) or keeping silence as to the
Real reason — which was three weeks at Ypres,
Without a rest (or laurel) (nor yet a cypress),
Having seen a Passchendaele lit with a flare of fire
And Ypres a dawn light ruddy and golden of desire,
The stuck tanks — and shook at our guns going in
As my body would not stay still at such Hell of din;
Worse than any of theirs — and seen Gloucesters going over;
Many for the last time — by accident gone further.
Dwelt in two pillboxes, had open station —
And lost of geography any the least notion,
Seeing Verey lights going up from all quarters,
And all German, and yet to go onwards where the
Tangle of time and space might be somehow dissolved,
Mixed with Londoners, Northerners and strange Gloucesters
Whom I knew not — and seen shattered Ypres by canal waters.
Our own guns shook me more than Fritzy guns with fear,
An airplane burned to earth near me in disaster,
Barrages on barrages fell on fatigue parties unhelped there —
Gas was driven, out of summer heaven
Bombs fell to shatter near artillery to no matter,
Machine guns bothered at biscuits, bully beef tins,
Naval guns blasted a dug-out to no use there,
Terribly fell the anger of the German clangour
Of guns on any that dared to move an inch in daylight there,
Death was compelled a hundred times and withheld,
Yet there is no honour of Ypres — though the Romans had
Saluted Ypres the word — without word gainsaid
They bent my helmet for me; they broke the machine gun nearly,
Carefully ranging, traversing, till the gun was tilted
Which after setting upright we set tobacco alight.
The routine of Ypres, the daily way of artillery fight,
I keep it for an honour out of Hell's will wrested,
And remember courages in faces eager or resolute and white;
September's sun that hallowed all that earth unthought
That even Passchendaele exalted and gilded —

The forward post of Gloucesters by nothing shielded,
And our post naked of shelter, save one trench hidden in the night:
Ypres, they that knew you are of a Company through you.[11]

ENGLAND: 1917-1922

There is no sound within the cottage now
But my pen and the sound of long rain
Heavy and musical, I must think again
To find so sweet a noise, and cannot anywhere.

The soothingness and deep-toned tinkle, soft
Happenings of night, in pain there's nothing better
Save tobacco, or long most looked for letter . . .
The different roof-sounds. House, shed, loft and scullery.[1]

XI

An element of mystery attaches itself not only to the date on which Ivor Gurney was gassed, but also to the degree to which he was affected. A letter written on 9 September makes no mention of the subject. The first hint came in a cheerful note to Marion Scott, dated 12 September:

By the way I am still in the line, but not having had at all a bad time of it. My throat is sore from gas; it is just (or was) as if I had had catarrh, but only an occasional explosion of coughing is left now. No luck! One cannot smell the new gas. One starts sneezing. The old gas had a heavy hot-house Swinburnian filthy sort of odour — voluptuous and full of danger.

At a time when mustard gas could blister the skin and strip the bronchial tubes of mucous membrane and cause such unendurable agony that the sufferer might have to be strapped to his bed (the old Swinburnian chlorine gas had brought death by slow asphyxiation), Gurney's encounter must surely have been very mild.

The matter is still further complicated by an account that Gurney wrote, probably in 1925, in one of his asylum poems. These, though often chaotic from a literary point of view, are remarkably accurate in recording events, and there is therefore no reason to reject his less than heroic version of what took place in September 1917:

> After the Gloucesters went over, in a Hell and smother
> (I just missed that, carrying a tripod and heavy boxes
> Instead of a handy rifle with and bullets rather),
> Got order to return (praising army to learn
> That news), got gassed, and bullied and ordered an early
> Parade (after three weeks) while the Gloucesters might turn
> Sleepily three half hours more — and cursed my luck's ways

Went sick for contrariety and gas symptoms;
Hoping a week's easy; with six others wheezy
(Though ready for the Line) and coughing discreetly,
(Who had walked through gas too lazy to do the easy
Thing — and wear gas masks, till it overdid us).[2]

All of which sounds, to use one of his own favourite words, remarkably like a 'wangle'!

Thus it is impossible to say whether it was the after-effects of a mild gassing, or evidence of that general state of collapse which the army liked to describe as 'shell-shock', that finally changed Gurney's 'luck'. At all events, before the month was out he had his Blighty. Letters now came from Scotland — a stone's throw from the birthplace of Sir Douglas Haig:

26 September, 1917.
My Dear Friend,
　　　　　　To write to you on common notepaper, white and smooth, to be in between sheets white as snow — yesterday, but I smoke in bed! — and to hear noises domestic and well known, flurries and scurries about one — how sweet are all these! And to be within 17 miles of Enbro, that old city of Scott and R.L.S.; such is my nature that this last idea or fact is sweetest of all. *Ward 24, Edinburgh War Hospital, Bangour, Scotland*, is my present address.

Only slowly and uncertainly is the conviction leaking in . . . that I am *really* in Blighty.[3] You remember F.W.H's parable of the man who was in Heaven and did not know it? Even so is it with me! Last night started the change moving a little quicker for I played for two hours, mostly in accompaniment, and found to my joy that what I had hoped for is true — the effort to concentrate is a pleasure to me; which means that in so much neurasthenia is a thing of the past, and that what I have would go if I lived my old life once again, with an added incalculable Joy added thereto. Rejoice with me my friend, for that which was lost is found; or shall I say rather — its hiding place is known. . . .

I am not well of course, but the thing that struck me on the boat coming over was that no one looked well. There was not any more jollity among all that crowd going to Blighty than if it were merely Another Move. The iron had entered into their souls, and they were still fast bound; unable to realise what tremendous changes of life had come to them for a while. Dear Marion, this was sad to see, and a tribute to the power of the Old Sweats and Prussians generally. But the river — that magnificent river, the Seine! From Rouen to Le Havre it is just one splendid Symphony, the greatest I have ever seen. I could only try to forget I was so weak of soul to remember a feeling of sickness in my body, and wish they would give me three days rations and a small sailing boat. By the Lord, I would have sailed her clean across if there had been sight of any star. Airships were patrolling the harbour mouth. Now I must go down to shave — in front of a real mirror!

Clean sheets, clean clothes and skin; no lice; today's papers; ordinary notepaper . . . What next?

Goodbye, and all good wishes for all good things.

Your sincere friend

Ivor Gurney.

A letter to Herbet Howells, posted a few days later (2 October), adds a few more details:

I am not *quite* sure whether the gas has not slightly aggravated my ordinary thickheadedness and indigestion. If this is so, then there's hope for the Wangler; if not, then no hope: I should be merely a Lucky Blighter soon to be cast out into outer darkness again. Anyway, I am that spoilt pet of Society — an accompanist that can read at sight. But O! what that same Pet has to endure! The rapturous soulfulness that disdains tempo. The durchganging baritone that will not be stayed long by interludes of piano, whose eager spirit is bars too early for the fray. The violinist that will play *songs* — not only the voice part but any choice twiddly bits that a careless writer has left to the piano. The universal clamourous desire for ragtime. Topsiturvinesses of diseased vanity of all sorts, kinds, conditions.

Edinbro is indeed a magic name. Its glamour is increased (as usual) by distance and denial. 16 miles and regulations of the most strict. I wonder which was Henley's hospital? There are many memories round this city, but the dearest to me are those of R.L.S., that friend of Everyman. Henley and the Great Sir Walter, Dr. John Brown and Holyrood come after him in my mind.

There is no blooming (Well done!) music in my head. I am frosted up. Last night I felt the beginning of the thaw, the first hint of what joy music might give. I was playing Beethoven, and for one golden minute my wandering mind was fixed and could see the stars; I forgot the restraint that so long has been partly self-imposed on myself and flew free. Why, I had no indigestion to speak of! A glimpse up the shaft of Hell.

Perhaps some songs may come from me before I return, but there is a lot to do before my mind will freely conceive anything. You simply dont know what France means, not in horror, but in everyday trial. If this letter is to go, it must finish now. 'Hoping that you are in the pink',

Yours ever
I B G

Though it was to be some time before anyone would appreciate the irony of Gurney's belief that his war experience had somehow cured him of earlier troubles, his letters begin now to express deeper ironies of which he was fully aware:

The contrast between the magnificent behaviour of Man to that of the apparent callousness of God is most striking, and was it for no other reason than that of having companied with good men one could face God with (almost) a slightly cynical but interested expectation. His debt to Europe, to the World, is very great.[4]

One wonders what the gentle soul to whom he confided these thoughts made of them? Though patriotic drums thundered less loudly and less often than in the first days of the war, such ideas were still not common and she cannot fail to have observed the weariness and disillusion that now gripped him. The body rested, safe and snug between clean sheets, but the mind turned back again and again to the rain-sodden trenches and the mud and the sweat and the comrades dying one by one. . . .

Moreover, little by little the world of happy warriors from which he had drawn so much comfort and strength was falling apart and leaving him to face a new and even more insidious kind of warfare on his own:

Nielson went yesterday, and I suppose we shall never meet again. And Evans, the Welsh singer whom I *may* come across. Dammit, there are only too many golden people in the world. (There were more still before August 20th.) But Nielson's wrinkled wise face and deep eyes were lovely to look at and gave me strength. Men of the sea are better to live with than the sea itself, and through his talk, though there was nothing nautical in it, ran ever the old charm of moving salt green water, and pictures of fearless sailors taking their chance.

I might have asked his address, but didn't. It was wiser, since he is there in my mind as clear as life, and since we shall not meet again, and since it is foolish to regret. Since we are living in this damned topsy

turvey irritating old world of ours, in short. Nielson! What a name!
What a man!⁵

There were, fortunately, things to distract his mind, and chief
among them was the imminent publication of his first book of
poems, *Severn and Somme*. Not that he expected much — some
part of the critical reception that had greeted Will Harvey's *A
Gloucestershire Lad* had been sufficient warning that snipers were
active:

Did you see the review of F.W.H.'s book in the T.L.S.? Golly, but
there is nothing to give my poor friend a swelled head in that notice.
It *is* true that in 'A Gloucestershire Lad' there is not much good stuff,
but what of that when 'In Flanders' is there — a pure beauty, actual
colour and wistful distance of blue hills on the page? As for my own,
they will not say much to affect me, for the sight of the whole thing
in proof convinced me that humility should be my proper mood, and
gratitude for a hobby found when one was needed. Neither he nor I
have lived in the proper atmosphere to write much yet — the company of men who are trying for the same end and prize of a modern
technique. That matters little to me, who have another and finer string
to my loom. . . .⁶

The prime dedication in Gurney's book was to Margaret Hunt,
but he felt obliged to add a preface which reveals the complex
motives that had gone into the making of his poems — not least
of which was Gloucester and the countryside around it. Touching
in itself, and vividly underlining the qualities that made him so
loved by his friends, it also serves as a reminder of his skill with
prose:

This book stands dedicated to one only of my friends, but there are
many others to whom I would willingly dedicate singly and in state, if
that did not mean the writing of forty books of verse and dedications —
a terrible thing for all concerned.
So that, under the single name and sign of homage and affection, I
would desire such readers as come to me to add also:
To my father and mother; F. W. Harvey (also a Gloucestershire
Lad); Miss Marion Scott, whose criticism has been so useful, and she
so kind, in spite of my continued refusal to alter a word of anything;
the Vicar of Twigworth; Herbert Howells (and this is not the last time
you will hear of him): Mr. Hilaire Belloc, whose 'Path to Rome' has

been my trench companion; Mr. Wilfred Gibson, author of 'Friends', a great little book; many others also, including Shakespeare and Bach, both friends of mine; and, last but not least, my comrades of two platoons of the 2nd/5th Gloucesters, who have so often wondered whether I were crazy or not. Let them draw their own conclusions now, for the writing of this book it was that so distracted me. . . . This is a long list, and even now does not include old Mrs. Poyner, who was so jolly and long-suffering; nor my boat *Dorothy*, now idle in the mud; though a poet sang of her full glory at Framilode.

Even as I write the list becomes fuller, farther extended, yet a soldier must face pain, and so it remains shorter by far than it might be.

I fear that those who buy the book (or even borrow) to get information about the Gloucesters will be disappointed. Most of the book is concerned with a person named Myself, and the rest with my county, Gloucester, that whether I live or die stays always with me — being in itself so beautiful, so full of memories; whose people are so good to be friends with, so easy-going and so frank.

Some of the afore-mentioned people I have never had the good fortune enough to meet in the flesh, but that was not my fault. I hope they will forgive my using their names without permission. Ah, would they retaliate in kind! That is, however, not likely, as I never was famous, and a Common Private makes but little show.

All these verses were written in France, and in sound of the guns, save only two or three earlier pieces. This should be reason enough to excuse any roughness in the technique. If more reason is required, people of home, and most of all, people of Gloucester, may well be indulgent to one who thought of them so often, and whose images of beauty in the mind were always of Gloucester, county of Cotswold and Severn, and a plain rich, blossomy, and sweet of airs — as the wise Romans knew, who made their homes in exile by the brown river, watching the further bank for signs of war.

Herbert Howells got a personal note of apology, full of delightful banter — though whether he appreciated the military metaphor is another matter:

My Dear Erbert Owls,

this is a sad shock for you — bear up, my man. There is nothing dedicated to you in 'Severn and Somme'. Why? Because there were too many friends to whom I wished to dedicate and all took away from the prime dedication. Miss Scott in consideration of her faithful service has two; Will Harvey has two more which directly refer to him. No other living people are there.

I hope you wont mind and will understand. However, I propose to write a 'Symphony in Canon'. Its length is directly dependent on the patience of the audience. The first, leading part goes over the top, say, at 8 Pip Emma, and reaches its first objective (Common time till now) at 8.27 p.m. Starts again (3/4 Largo) at 8.27, and is again found digging in at 8.51, going over immediately for its third objective, and finally turning up at its fourth objective at 9.48, when the working parties (that is, the last-entered voice) have just started. It has two alternatives — to go straight backward, bar by bar, or to start at the beginning again, but *it must not stop*. An Artillery of 200 Italian combined-instrumentalists (16 to each man, you know them?) provide the barrage. And Ha! You blench! It is to be dedicated to Y O U ! !

Yours

I B G.

Reviews began to appear during the first weeks of November. By and large they were friendly and welcoming, and Gurney at last felt able to claim the title 'War Poet' — a title which he was later to wear with obsessive pride, as if it were a military decoration of the highest order.

The poems themselves vary in quality. Some are little more than jingling verse, and not always fluent at that. Others echo rather too glibly the facile *pro patria mori* sentiments that were so popular in England among the hordes that had not experienced trench warfare at first hand. But others ring absolutely true, both as poetry and as experience aptly distilled. And one ballad hits on a truth almost too terrible to contemplate — for in it, darkly, Ivor Gurney foresaw his own fate:

> As I went up by Ovillers
>   In mud and water cold to the knee
> There went three jeering, fleering spectres,
>   That walked abreast and talked of me.
>
> The first said, 'Here's a right brave soldier
>   That walks the dark unfearingly;
> Soon he'll come back on a fine stretcher,
>   And laughing for a nice Blighty'.
>
> The second, 'Read his face, old comrade,
>   No kind of lucky chance I see;
> One day he'll freeze in mud to the marrow,
>   Then look his last on Picardie'.

> Though bitter the word of these first twain
>   Curses the third spat venomously;
> 'He'll stay untouched till the war's last dawning
>   Then live one hour of agony'.
>
> Liars the first two were. Behold me
>   At sloping arms by one-two-three;
> Waiting the time I shall discover
>   Whether the third spake verity.[7]

More often, though, it is the memory of things past that pro-
vokes the most complete response — as in the sonnet 'Afterglow', dedicated to Will Harvey, whose friendship it celebrates:

> Out of the smoke and dust of the little room
> With tea-talk loud and laughter of happy boys,
> I passed into the dusk. Suddenly the noise
> Ceased with a shock, left me alone in the gloom,
> To wonder at the miracle hanging high
> Tangled in twigs, the silver crescent clear. —
> Time passed from mind. Time died; and then we were
> Once more at home together, you and I.
>
> The elms with arms of love wrapped us in shade
> Who watched the ecstatic West with one desire,
> One soul uprapt; and still another fire
> Consumed us, and our joy yet greater made:
> That Bach should sing for us, mix us in one
> The joy of firelight and the sunken sun.[8]

This quality of almost mystical union with things intensely observed, is something that was to show increasingly in his poetry
and mark him out as a writer of very considerable power and
sensitivity.

He continued to write poetry now that he was out of the line,
and to send it to Marion Scott for safe keeping. He also began to
rediscover his musical voice — necessarily muted in France,
despite the four masterpieces of song he had managed to capture
and set down in the trenches. From now on, however, the writing of poetry assumed an importance almost equal (but never
quite) to the composition of music — that is, as something much
more than an alternative born out of necessity.

As the distance between the experience that prompted his poetry and the act of creation began to increase, his work gains in strength and authority. Two such poems, soon to be published in his second volume, *War's Embers* (1919), were sent for safe keeping in December 1917. The first, sketched probably on the battlefield itself, but now polished, perfect and very striking, records his reaction to the news that F. W. Harvey was presumed killed. Though that news, as he soon discovered, was false, his knowledge of death was real enough, and the shattered corpses he had seen were no less dear. It is called 'To his Love', a title that is very much of the period and circumstances, a memorial in the innocent homoerotic overtones of war and comradeship. It is one of the great war poems:

> He's gone and all our plans
> Are useless indeed.
> We'll walk no more on Cotswold
> Where the sheep feed
> Quietly and take no heed.
>
> His body, that was so quick,
> Is not as you
> Knew it, on Severn river
> Under the blue
> Driving our small boat through.
>
> You would not know him now . . .
> But still he died
> Nobly, so cover him over
> With violets of pride
> Purple from Severn side.
>
> Cover him, cover him soon
> And with thick-set
> Masses of memoried flowers
> Hide that red wet
> Thing I must somehow forget.[9]

The other poem advances a more 'modern', laconic style, no less skilfully handled, and very different from the pastoral elegy that tradition had handed down to him:

Lying in dugouts, joking idly, wearily;
   Watching the candle guttering in the draught;
Hearing the great shells go high over us, eerily
   Singing; how often have I turned over, and laughed

With pity and pride, photographs of all colours,
   All sizes, subjects: khaki brothers in France;
Or mothers' faces worn with countless dolours;
   Or girls whose eyes were challenging and must dance.

Though in a picture only, a common cheap
   Ill-taken card; and children — frozen, some
(Babies) waiting on Dicky-bird to peep
   Out of the handkerchief that is his home

(But he's so shy!). And some with bright looks, calling
   Delight across the miles of land and sea,
That not the dread of barrage suddenly falling
   Could quite blot out — not mud nor lethargy.

Smiles and triumphant careless laughter. O
   The pain of them, wide Earth's most sacred things!
Lying in dugouts, hearing the great shells slow
   Sailing mile-high, the heart mounts higher and sings.

But once — O why did he keep that bitter token
   Of a dead Love? — that boy, who suddenly moved,
Showed me, his eyes wet, his low talk broken,
   A girl who better had not been beloved.[10]

Even in this poem there is an element of personal foreknow-
ledge, for while in hospital Gurney had met and fallen in love
with a V.A.D. nurse, Annie Nelson Drummond.

She, however, had almost certainly not fallen in love with him.
Undoubtedly she liked him and enjoyed his company — for
limited periods at least — but she did not take his gentle, un-
demanding passion seriously. How could she? He was just another
soldier, wounded and far from home, different only in that he
wrote poetry and composed music. It was pleasant to talk with
him, and walk perhaps and laugh. But he was not the kind of man
a sensible Scots girl would marry.

For Gurney it was a very different matter — the letters he

wrote to Herbert Howells, now about to marry the pretty
Dorothy Dawe, make that quite clear:

Annie Nelson Drummond is older than I thought — born sooner, I
mean. She is 30 years old and most perfectly enchanting. She has a
pretty figure, pretty hair, fine eyes, pretty hands and arms *and* walk. A
charming voice, pretty ears, a resolute little mouth. With a great love
in her she is glad to give when the time comes. In hospital the first
thing that would strike you is 'her guarded flame'. There was a mask
on her face more impenetrable than on any other woman I have ever
seen. (But that has gone for me.) In fact (at a guess) I think it will disappear now that she has found someone she thinks worthy.[11]

He goes on to add, rather comically, and erroneously as it later
turned out: 'A not unimportant fact was revealed by one of the
patients at the hospital — a fine chap — I believe she has money.
Just think of it! Pure good luck, if true (as I believe it is). But
she is more charming and tender and deep than you will believe
till you have seen her.' And then, pathetically: 'O Erbert, O
Erbert . . . I forgot my body when walking with her: a thing
that has not happened since . . . when? I really dont know.'
As the weeks passed by, the day-dreams grew: 'But to get her
and settle down would make a solid foundation for me to build
on — a home and a tower of light.'[12] He sent one of his Gloucester cap badges to his sister to have it dipped in gold and made
into a brooch, but accompanied it with strict instructions to say
nothing to anybody. He does not seem to have mentioned his
hopes either to Miss Hunt or to Miss Scott.

What happened is not known.[13] Whether the end came abrupt-
ly and in anger, or whether the reality of the situation crept in
little by little there is no way of telling. But the end did come
and the tower of light became a pit of darkness.

XII

Early in November 1917 Ivor Gurney was declared to be on the
road to recovery and transferred to the Command Depot at
Seaton Delaval. 'Some kind fairy has given me a course of signal-
ling, which means 2–4 months training. A commission would
mean 6 months more!' He was determined now to stay in
Blighty as long as possible, even if it meant actually applying for
a commission which, as he doubtless knew, he was totally unsuited to hold. Moreover, Northumberland pleased him, even if
it meant a parting with Nurse Drummond. He wrote to Howells:

I am glad to say that the weather for two days has been beautiful indeed,
and Tyne Side has looked quite like the South Country. The sea in
Whitley Bay was quite wonderful, and it would have given you leaping
thoughts and rhythms for something very great of the future. Lets have
some Sea Music out of you someday old chap, will you?
    Or what of the Forest of Dean Symphony? What of the opening pages
of the sight from Newnham-on-Severn looking out across the valley to
the hills? An A major beginning, surely?[1]

    But the pleasure of enjoying a relatively cushy number ('owing
to slight indigestion, presumably due to gas: wink, wink!') was
not to last: 'Alas for the two months! Today I am on ordinary
training, and that means but a short stay if nothing happens.'[2]
The army's change of mind must have been a severe blow to his
hopes, but it may be too much to read into the words 'if nothing
happens' a veiled hint that either he knew himself to be fundamentally unwell, or intended to make himself so, for his letter to
Marion Scott passes on to everyday matters as if nothing untoward
had happened:

Two of the local reviews have reached me. They are just what I expected — and didn't want. But I got a delightful letter from Haines —

the man who knows Gibson and Abercrombie — which said how pleased he was at his first glance, and how it seemed to be a not unworthy companion for Sassoon's book, and Sorley-Turner; whom I have not read.

By the way, some time ago Sassoon walked up to his colonel and said he would fight no more. Flashes, of course; and blue fire. There were questions in the House, and a general dust-up; but at last they solved it in a becoming official fashion, and declared him mad, and put him in a lunatic-asylum; from which there will soon come a second book, and that will be interesting to see.[3]

Could it be that Gurney, consciously or unconsciously, was contemplating something of the sort himself? The letter continues:

Will you let me know what poems you have received lately? I have been rummaging in my Bangour notes, and have written a little since I saw you.

There are 7 or 8 things to come, not all quite polished up and hair-parted, but nearly so.

Thank you so much for 'Friends', for I love that book. Of course, Rupert Brooke is exquisite enough, but we can always read 'Friends'. Mrs. Gibson, probably affected by W.G.'s being called up (a C 3 man!) has fallen downstairs, and spoilt one eye forever. When Rupert Brooke went abroad, he left his copyrights equally between Gibson, Abercrombie and de la Mare. They have had £2,000 each! That's why Gibson has not died, and his family. Poetry pays — it took a War to make it; but still, there you are.

By 23 February 1918, he was back in hospital 'through stomach trouble caused by gas'. This time there were no accompanying winks, for his condition, as he lay in Ward A17 at No. 1 General Hospital, Newcastle-on-Tyne, was worrying. Nevertheless, he made some kind of recovery and was sent to Brancepeth Castle, Durham, for further training. There he seems to have suffered a mild breakdown, probably unknown to, or even discounted by the doctors, for on 26 March he wrote to Marion Scott a somewhat unusual and disturbing letter:

Here's some news for you.

You know how a neurasthenic has to drive himself, though he feels nervy and his heart bumps in a disturbing but purely nervous fashion? Well, Ivor Gurney determined to drive himself. His heart certainly did not feel right, but that was imagination and he must go on — through Salisbury Plain, Laventie, Somme, Caulaincourt, Vermand, St. Julien.

He was tested once or twice, but doctors said nothing. They marked him A 3 at Depot when he got there. It is true that he never felt well, and had continual digestive and general nervous trouble, but that presumably was to be driven out. Which lands him at Depot getting weaker and fuzzier in the head without knowing why. On Friday he went to Durham 9 miles there and back, after which his pulse was waltzing irregularly like this as it is now

that's my heart. Surely a prostitute's job is cleaner compared to doctors who allow this and mark 'Debility' on a case sheet that a man shall not know? Shall leave the hospital a little recovered and go on till he drops again? That's what they have done for me. By God, I'll do nothing more strenuous than clerical work for months, whatever they try to do with me, and *never* march again.

Two days later another letter arrived. And if the way in which he had talked of himself as if a stranger had puzzled Marion Scott, the new letter must have alarmed her thoroughly:

Yesterday I felt and talked to (I am serious) the spirit of Beethoven.

No, there is no exclamation mark behind that, because such a statement is past ordinary ways of expressing surprise. But you know how sceptical I was of any such thing before.

It means that I have reached higher than ever before — in spite of the dirt and coarseness and selfishness of so much of me. Something happened the day before which considerably lessened and lightened my gloom. What it was I shall not tell you, but it was the strangest and most terrible spiritual adventure. The next day while I was playing the slow movement of the D major [sonata] I felt the presence of a wise and friendly spirit; it was old Ludwig van all right. When I had finished he said 'Yes, but there's a better thing than that' and turned me to the 1st movement of the latest E flat Sonata — a beauty (I did not know it before). There was a lot more; Bach was there but does not care for me. Schumann also, but my love for him is not so great. Beethoven said among other things that he was fond of me and that in nature I was like himself as a young man. That I should probably not write anything really big and good; for I had started much too late and had much to do with myself spiritually and much to learn. Still he said that he himself was not much more developed at my age, and at the end — when

I had shown my willingness to be resigned to God's will and try first of
all to do my best, he allowed me (somehow) to hope more, much more.
It depends on the degree of spiritual height I can attain — so I was led
somehow to gather.

There! What would the doctors say to *that*? A Ticket certainly, for
insanity. No, it is the beginning of a new life, a new vision.

As the letter continues, the handwriting deteriorates somewhat.
But one spark of unconscious humour, or perhaps even gentle
malice, adorns the end:

I could not get much about Howells off L van B: (the memory is faint)
he was reluctant to speak; whether Howells is to die or not to develop
I could not gather.

And then a last defiant plea to be understood, as though he knew
that his revelation contained the seeds of insanity: 'How I would
like to see your face! No, you'll take it seriously, and decide I
am not unbalanced or overstrung. This letter is quite sane, n'est
ce pas?'

For the moment the doctors do not seem to have noticed anything unusual about Ivor Gurney. Such peculiarities as may have
been observed were doubtless put down in part to the fact of his
being a composer and poet, and in part to mild shell-shock — a
common thing in places where men groaned and whimpered at
night as they relived the filth and despair of trench life. He was,
in due course, returned to Depot at Seaton Delaval.

But by May his condition must have deteriorated considerably,
for he was now ordered to Lord Derby's War Hospital at Warrington — a place that specialized in the kind of nervous dis-
orders that four years of senseless slaughter was throwing up in
increasing numbers. Here things went from bad to worse. He
began to demand that money should be sent home to his father.
Puzzled, the Commanding Officer wrote to Gloucester to ask if
the family was really in need, or was it, as he feared, a sign of
mental instability.

The family in Gloucester, already alarmed at the unusual fre-
quency and rambling nature of his letters, grew desperately
concerned, but was gradually reassured both by Ivor himself and
the doctors with platitudes that impressively explained everything: 'Nervous Breakdown from Deferred Shell-shock.' 'That,'

wrote Dorothy Gurney to Marion Scott, 'is just about what it is and is rather relieving!'[4]

The blow came in letters dated 19 June 1918. The longest was addressed to Marion Scott. It had been written in The Soldier's Home, Bold Street, Warrington, and it read:

My Dear Friend,

this is a good-bye letter, and written because I am afraid of slipping down and becoming a mere wreck — and I know you would rather know me dead than mad, and my only regret is that my father will lose my allotment.

Thank you most gratefully for all your kindness, dear Miss Scott. Your book is in my kitbag which will be sent home, and thank you so much for it — at Brancepeth I read it a lot.

Goodbye with best wishes from one who owes you a lot. May God reward you and forgive me.

Ivor Gurney.

He was found, dazed and wandering, by the canal, unable, as yet, to carry out his threat. The following day he wrote again, so ashamed that he reverted to mere initials and a pitiful formality:

Dear Miss Scott,

Please forgive my letter of yesterday. I meant to do what I spoke of, but lost courage. Will you please let Sir Hubert know.

I. B. Gurney.

The letters were rounded up, from Howells and Harvey, Parry and the family in Gloucester. Most of them were destroyed. But it was now no longer possible for anyone to hide behind medical jargon for an explanation of the depth and nature of his agony. And any temptation still to do this was squashed once and for all by the letter that Major Robertson, the Administrator of Lord Derby's War Hospital, wrote to the Gurney family at the end of that fateful week:

Dear Sir,

241281 Pte Gurney

In reply to your letter, I have to say that your son interviewed his Medical Officer last Wednesday and stated that he wished to be sent to an Asylum. He admits that he hears imaginary voices which urge him to commit suicide. He has been placed under special supervision in order to provide for his safety.

The laconic, almost bored tones of military efficiency left no room for doubt.

A letter dated 1 July from John Haines in Gloucester to Marion Scott makes it plain that Gurney's friends, in their various ways, did everything they could to help. One of their first concerns was to have him removed from Warrington to a hospital nearer Gloucester or London so that he might be visited:

I think it was splendid of you to go to Warrington and I am sure you went a long way towards saving the situation by doing so and that what you have done since will finish the job. I dont know St. Albans but I do know something of the Cardiff place, if it is, as I believe, Whitchurch. I have friends there and know it well and the country a few miles off is most beautiful with grand hills. I heard from Ivor this morning — a postcard, and have written to him again. I enclose two letters received by me today from Abercrombie: they speak for themselves. I hope Canon Stevens will look him up soon. Warrington is the most detestable place I have ever spent six hours in, without exception, and the place would drive me mad, despite my lack of genius, in a very few weeks. How Gurney must dislike it I can well imagine. On the other hand I dont recommend the idea of any mental place very near Gloucester (they abound), nor do I think he should be allowed to go to his people until he is better than he is now: the father is too delicate and the mother too nervy.

On 3 July Gurney wrote to Marion Scott:

Tomorrow I go to St. Albans; which surely will be better than here? For there may be a Cathedral to look at through the window. . . . Perhaps there may be some farm work there, or at any rate something more interesting than staying in a ward; though there [are] multitudes of good men [here].

And on 4 July he went by train to Napsbury War Hospital.

Exactly what caused the breakdown can never be known. The army's glib verdict of 'deferred shell-shock' is no more than an all-purpose label to cover a basic lack of understanding. Gurney's own letters give better clues, even if they are slight.

There is, for example, the constant theme of guilt and sense of failure: 'The past few months have shown me how little worthy I am of my friends.' And flickering across this, alternating with a deep loathing of all things military, is a feeling that comradeship has been lost and that somehow he has let even his beloved regiment down: 'O to be at the Front, enduring in company with splendid people of the Gloucesters.' There is also a sense of disappointment that the pain he has endured has not brought its reward — for the sense of self-loathing and the desire for cleansing punishment is a frequent theme in his letters: 'The price of almost anything that one desires worthily, is only Pain . . . long ago I decided that to accomplish what I wish was worth a great deal of pain and was ready to undergo it.'[5]

And there remains the nagging doubt that something may have happened to him either at the Command Depot, or in one of the hospitals — something that pushed him over the edge of despair. Hints occur in the asylum writings:

> Returned to Depot, where the police tortured me,
> (Remembering old evil, keeping accounts of the Devil,
> Marking a soldier, having broken a musician)
> And to deep Hell injured and compelled me.[6]

It may well have been that he was suspected of malingering and made to suffer accordingly. And had this happened, the sense of outrage and betrayal would have been past bearing.

He remained at Napsbury for a little over three months. It was clear, even to sceptical authority, that his military usefulness was at an end. At the beginning of October 1918, a few weeks before hostilities ceased, he was granted his discharge and sent back to Gloucester to live his 'long hour of agony'.

XIII

Gurney, in crying need of calm and reassurance, returned to a family deep in its own distress. For some time now his father had been seriously ill, undergoing operations to check the cancer that was soon to kill him. Inevitably the tailoring business had slipped downhill. Complete ruin, however, seemed unlikely, for, after several petitions and a bullet wound, the army had finally agreed to Ronald Gurney's compassionate discharge from the Welsh Guards. But the situation was tense and scarcely designed to cope with further burdens.

To all intents and purposes Ronald was now head of the family. It was on his shoulders that everything rested. Once, years ago, he had dreamed of becoming a doctor, but such money as the family could spare had gone automatically to Ivor's education. Ronald, accordingly, had joined his father's business, but later took what opportunity he could to escape. Three years in India and America as a tailor and cutter broadened his horizons and he might well have elected to stay out of the country had it not been for the war. His return to Gloucester, therefore, was accompanied not only by deep anxiety, but also by a certain resentment. Having been through the war himself, he was not in a mood to be over-impressed by signs of instability in a brother who had always been pampered at his expense and had consistently paraded superior intellectual airs. He had abandoned his own independence for the sake of the family: the least Ivor could do was to try and 'get a grip on himself'.[1]

Winifred Gurney also felt certain resentments. In 1900, on the birth of the last child, Dorothy, she had been taken away from school (she was fourteen) in order to help her mother about the house. They did not get on well: 'I usually got the worst end in of mother's nagging. I never did the right thing.'[2] But eventually, 1905, she was able to grab at a little independence as a

127

supplementary teacher. During the war she worked as a voluntary Red Cross nurse, and then trained professionally at Birmingham and Cheltenham, thereafter devoting forty years to nursing. She did not marry.

Dorothy, the youngest, was perhaps the luckiest and happiest, for she was allowed to follow her own path, training as a teacher and in secretarial work. Significantly, she too fled the family circle, going first to Canada, and then, in 1926, to Australia. There she married and settled down, never to return.

Florence Gurney remained herself — 'hard', 'unable to show affection', ruling 'with a rod of iron'.[3] Like so many of her class and generation she believed that life was designed to be a vale of tears through which one must trudge in the faint hope that earthly punishments would be sufficient to ward off eternal damnation. She was, in short, unlikely to prove much of a comfort to anyone in Ivor's distress. Nor in fact were any of the family.

His behaviour when he returned home was decidedly erratic and his friends became very alarmed. Writing on 6 October, John Haines reported the situation to Marion Scott:

I saw Ivor for most of yesterday. Perhaps you had best not tell him I have written to you. He spent an hour at the office and I was horrified — at all events at first. Quite evidently his trouble was on him especially badly and, at first, I thought him in a pretty serious way. After a while I began to see that his ideas about the voices and so forth, though extravagant, were in themselves ordered and sensible — granting the fact that they existed, and I became more comfortable. It was a beastly day but I cut the office and took him for a walk (rain or no rain) over the Cotswolds; Crickley, Birdlip and so forth, for the whole of the afternoon; tired myself out and I hope him. He was much more normal and left me happy enough with plenty of books and less annoyance from his voices — I think. I think something must be done with him soon. Is it any use for him to think of music or work connected therewith — yet? He talks of the sea. His shrunken appearance is not satisfactory, nor his quietness and humility. He left at 7 and I was so exhausted and drained that I slept the clock round!

He wrote again three days later:

All we know is this. Yesterday Ivor told his people he was going down to Lydney with Howells for the night and that he wanted to see about a ship there. Now Howells was in Gloucester not at Lydney, a fact Gurney knew, or should have known. It is just possible he may have gone to Lydney of course, but we shall know for certain in the morning.

Inquiries are being made everywhere and directly anything definite is known you will be wired to. My own opinion is that there is no special cause for anxiety. I knew the hospital people had recommended a sea voyage to him and I knew that the idea powerfully attracted him. I believe he will turn up at one of the ports.

And then, on 10 October: 'I walked from Newnham to Lydney today to make inquiries about Ivor and have only just got back to learn that Dorothy Gurney had left me a message that he had returned. I have not seen him.' By the same post Dorothy Gurney wrote Marion Scott a detailed account of what had happened:

Ivor turned up just before dinner today. He had been to Newport looking for a ship and there he met (so he says) a chap he was with at Brancepeth and who owed him some money. I will now try to tell you what he has been doing since he left us on Tuesday.

He went to Lydney, but found that there were no men wanted there. He walked to Newport from Lydney (about 23 miles) in the night and reached Newport on Wednesday. He was offered a boat but it was not sailing for a week and that didn't suit him. He slept with this man he met there on Wednesday night and obtained money from him to return home. He says that if the ship had been sailing in a day or two he would have gone. He wrote a PC to Father last night, but it did not reach us until tea-time today.

When he arrived in Gloucester from Newport he did not come straight home but went to some cafe and had some dinner. (This food question is going to be a great difficulty I'm afraid.) He had forgotten an appointment he had with Mr. Haines to go to Newnham today, but Mr. Haines went in case Ivor should turn up. . . .

Ivor had taken his kitbag with him, and his everyday requirements and some books, so he was in earnest. I must say he looks very much better than on Tuesday and he is quite collected and clear now, but he was very bad on Monday and Tuesday. The walk evidently did him good.

He had 2/- left and has given that up to Mother and has agreed that he shall have to give his money to Father. Mr. Chapman turned up here this afternoon and was much relieved to find Ivor here. Ivor was as sane as possible with him and went with Father to the station to see him off.

He realises the fuss he has caused for he said 'I *have* made a hash of things, and haven't done myself any good.' He certainly didn't think he was doing anything seriously wrong.

He is to go to the local Pensions Committee tomorrow, who, by the way, have had reports of his case from the Napsbury hospital, and he is to see the doctor here who is a very good one. On the advice of the Secretary of the Pensions Committee and for our own protection we informed the police last night and they have a description of him and his photo. We have informed everybody now of his reappearance. . . .

He still wants to go to sea, but Mr. Chapman asked him to think of something else. He is rather enthusiastic about getting a job as a labourer at Beachley Docks at £2 a week, but he must have somebody who understands him with him. He doesn't want to do farm work as you suggest.

I'm afraid Howells has been terribly upset about it — he looked really ill today and uttered such sighs of relief when I went to tell him that Ivor had returned. He is staying this week in Gloucester to be with Ivor, but it has not been a success, it appears, for Ivor forgot his appointment with him on Wednesday morning.

Throughout the month his moods changed. As John Haines explains, nothing could be predicted:

I seem always to be writing contradictory letters to you about Ivor. The fact is I simply dont know what to make of him and he varies as the wind. On Friday he seriously alarmed me by his depression and the 'possession' he appeared to be under by his voices. After all, he took my advice (though he said he didn't mean to) went to see Kerr and spent a pleasant evening! Yesterday he met me at 11, came with me to Newnham and walked with me for four hours through the Forest. He appeared to be perfectly happy and was quite normal all the time — hardly alluding to his possession at all in fact. He enjoyed the scenery, quoted poetry, and got as near to his old enthusiastic self as I have yet seen. His chief trouble is concerned with food — he would eat nothing all day. He asserts that if he gives way to the desire for food he is unable to stop: the less he eats the less the desire. He declares that if he has lunch he invariably afterwards goes out and buys huge quantities of cakes and eats them and continues doing so as long as he has the money. This is not an illusion, I know. He hates it and looks upon it as a sort of bestiality. I am almost sure that on Friday he sold books and bought cakes with the proceeds. He had been given money for his fare yesterday and directly we got to Newnham he emptied his pockets into mine of all the money he had left for fear, I imagine, that he would buy cakes with it. There was not quite enough for his return fare and so I expect he had already done something of the kind, though of this I am not sure.

He was so anxious not to defraud me that, later in the day, he insisted on my taking his tobacco to make up the difference. He refused to accept refusal. I tell you all this for your private ear because it is symptomatic. I feel that this craving for food is at the bottom of the trouble with him. It is not a fact that he only indulges in these 'gorges' when he has no regular meals — I have independent evidence that he really does eat the most prodigious quantities of cakes when the humour is in him.

I think it highly probable that Bangour has something to do with it all — though not necessarily all. I think it is from that quarter that he gets his spiritual catchwords and phraseology. I do not think he is in communication with the place now.

Sometimes it seems to me that the wisest plan would be to interfere as little as possible with him and seek to let him work out his own salvation. . . .

He is horribly afraid of losing moral sense and stealing or doing something of the kind to get food. It is pathetic. He refuses food at home, later gets it out of the cupboard when his mother isn't looking and then comes and accuses himself to me as a thief.

Besides the matter of irregular and compulsive eating, which had been a feature of Gurney's behaviour even before the war (though not on so spectacular a scale), Haines's letter raises the problem of what actually did happen at Bangour. Such clues as exist are slight and of doubtful value. Marion Scott is silent on the matter and does not seem to have pursued Gurney's cryptic remark in his letter of 28 March 1917: 'I have reached higher than ever before — in spite of the dirt and coarseness and selfishness of so much of me. Something happened the day before which considerably lessened this and lightened my gloom. What it was I shall not tell you, but it was the strangest and most terrible spiritual adventure.' Did he perhaps dabble in spiritualism, or come under the influence of some kind of religious fanatic?[4] John Haines seems to have had knowledge of an 'outside' influence, but apart from the one tantalizing reference left no further clue as to who or what it actually was. The latter days of a punishing war were ripe for gospels of Armageddon and other apocalyptic visions in which 'dirt and coarseness and selfishness' might be made to feel in need of purgation. Given his capacity for guilt, Ivor Gurney would have been a willing victim for anyone preaching such a cleansing doctrine.

Whatever the facts may be, one thing is certain: in October 1918 Ivor Gurney was still a deeply disturbed person.

Relief seems to have come about through physical hard work —
something he always had recourse to, as if the endless turning of
his mind could only be stilled when the body itself was exhausted.
By 2 November, though still harping on the possibility of going
to sea ('this time less ignominiously, I hope') he was able to
write to Marion Scott: 'I am glad to tell you that I am better myself, after a fortnight's hauling of heavy things about the Munitions Works: but that is a job that wont last long — fortunately
— by the looks of things in the papers. Isn't the news glorious.
. . .' The armistice, the confirmation of a small war pension (a
princely 12/- a week), and word from Sidgwick & Jackson that
not only was *Severn and Somme* to be reprinted, but they were
prepared to publish a second volume, *War's Embers*, on slightly
more generous terms, must all have helped to stabilize his condition. Reassured, he plunged ever more deeply into composition:
songs, piano pieces, chamber music of all sorts poured from him
in astonishing quantity. And his output of poetry was only
marginally less.

Friends also helped. John Haines, for example, took him on an
extended walking tour of the Black Mountains. At Christmas the
novelist Ethel Voynich, a friend from pre-war College days, in-
vited him for a few days in Cornwall.[5] There the party went rock
climbing at Gurnard Head, and, suddenly missing him in the
gathering dusk, were astonished to find that he had climbed to
the top of a narrow 'chimney' in the rocks, from which he had
to be guided down by the experts among them. It turned out that
he had been writing in his music notebook a setting of Francis
Ledwidge's poem 'Desire in Spring'!

Such was the buoyancy of his mood that he was able to with-
stand the shock of two deaths in 1919, both of people dear to him.
On 3 March Margaret Hunt died. She was forty-four years old
and had always suffered from a weak heart, and so succumbed
very quickly to the influenza epidemic that raged through a war-
weary Europe. To outward view Ivor Gurney seemed unaffected,
and John Haines was able to report: '. . . so far as I can gather,
at the moment, he feels it a happy release for her, since she was
in considerable pain'; and then went on to add:

He himself is wonderfully normal and well. I have had two or three
evenings with him and he appears to be composing both verse and

music with the same extraordinary rapidity still. F. W. Harvey gave a poetry recital at Stroud on Saturday and it was illustrated by several songs set by Gurney and accompanied by him: 'In Flanders', 'Horses', 'The Red Farm', 'Piper's Wood', and 'Minsterworth Perry'. Next to 'In Flanders', I like 'The Red Farm' best. 'Horses' is fine but requires exceptional singing and Harvey was not in the best of voice. . . .[6]

But the loss undoubtedly went very deep, and only in later years, in certain asylum poems, was he able to measure it.

Two months later, on 10 May, his father died at the age of fifty-seven. But this was expected and welcomed, for he had endured several operations and had suffered greatly before succumbing to the cancer that was eating him away.

The only picture we have of Ivor's reaction comes from Winifred Gurney:

. . . [he] had been staying with his friend Will Harvey at his Minsterworth home, and returned with a bunch of flowers in his hand on the day that our father was to be buried, having also a bandage round his neck covering a boil. To my great surprise he allowed me to dress the boil and brush his clothes. At no other time would he allow this; and after the funeral he went straight to the piano and played Chopin's Funeral March.[7]

If indeed he felt deeply about the matter, he left no account either in poem or letter. Even in the asylum writings, tracing and retracing his life and pain, he made no mention of his family. It is as if life with them did not exist for him.

It was left to Ronald Gurney to inform Marion Scott of the family's loss — which he did in a lugubrious set piece: a virtuoso performance of unintentional humour: 'You have probably heard that Dad has "crossed the Rubicon". Its a merciful blessing. His sufferings at the end were ghastly and the actual "finale" was suffocation.' His letter went on, however, to reveal that Ivor himself was still giving cause for alarm:

I should like to ask about Ivor. I have had little chance to talk to him. I'm always hard at work — really he hardly gets in the house before his nerves and Mother's collide and off he goes again.

Apparently he thinks of returning to College. I should like to know if it is true that they have asked him to come back.

I dont honestly think that he is fit — but personally I think that the evil of his returning is less than the evil of remaining in this atmosphere and is worth the risk. When I get the chance I'm going to give him a rattling good talking to and doubtless 3/4 of it will be disregarded.

The College had indeed kept his scholarship open. The decision was to be his: if he felt fit and able to work, then he could return. It was all very tempting — even though the beauty of Gloucestershire had him by the heart:

Could you have seen Hempsted this afternoon. Cleeve, Crickley, Cranham, and the Cathedral standing out grey in the distance, sentinel to Malvern! A clear, not far-too-beautiful afternoon, but one that let beauty through, if not displayed it. But O that night after going to see Emmie at Cleeve! I walked back by Leckhampton, Shurdington, Brockworth — just missing Crickley. Meteors flashed like sudden inspirations of song down the sky. The air was too still to set firs or beeches sighing, but the grass swished; twigs crackled beneath me, and the occasional stir of wild creatures in the undergrowth set off the peace — O the depth of it!

Strengthened and uplifted, he decided to return to London and face the struggle of being a professional musician once more.

XIV

The Ivor Gurney that began to pick up the threads of college life, this time with Vaughan Williams as his composition teacher, was a very different creature from the inexperienced Gloucestershire lad of 1911. He was a man, and he had been deeply scarred. But he was also something of a celebrity. He was a War Poet, with one volume to his credit and a second in the press. He was on the threshold of being acknowledged as a composer: Winthrop Rogers was considering the five 'Elizas', and Stainer and Bell had already accepted 'Captain Stratton's Fancy'. In June 1919 he had been able to report that 'A gent named Johnston Douglas is singing "The Penny Whistle" and "Fiddler of Dooney" on Friday' and that 'Stainer and Bell will take, I think, "Edward" and "The Twa Corbies".' (They took 'Edward', but left 'The Twa Corbies' to Oxford University Press.) John Masefield had already sent 'one of the most delightful of letters'[1] about his work, and he was in correspondence with J. C. Squire. He was beginning to move as an equal among equals.

There can be no doubt that he worked hard at college, even though he had scarcely grown more tractable since his Stanford days. Vaughan Williams, however, was a kindlier man, less dogmatic about music, and much more humble in his respect for other men's talent. There was little he could do to help his idiosyncratic pupil, whose music was sometimes brilliant, sometimes knotted and confused; but, typically, he became his friend and champion.

To begin with, he found cheap lodgings in Earls Court. Money was hard to come by, for Cheesman was no longer able to supplement his scholarship and the army pension went nowhere. Soon a general dislike of London piled on economic necessity and drove him to High Wycombe to act as organist at St. Michael's Church. He had already held this position for a few months at the end of 1914 while attempting to join up, and had formed then such a strong attachment to the vicar, the Revd. Arthur Chapman, and his family (and in particular to his two young daughters, Winifred and Marjorie), that he now turned to them as a natural source of security and domestic affection. Once more he arranged matters so that he was all but adopted.

The tone of such letters as have survived from this period is cheerful and optimistic, the grumbles being good-natured and of transient importance only:

Here's Masefield's letter for you to look at — a sight for sore eyes, a discovery of generosity most good to look on.

There's no one to play to worth playing to — no one to stay with till twelve o'clock at night, imbibing and discoursing sweet music, or books and — generally — discoursing sweetly. . . .

Tragic to miss the 2nd/5th dinner, where so many fine people were, so many seen under difficulties and bearing that well — of mud, of vermin, danger, routine-annoyance — so on, so forth ad infinitum.

This is a very delectable land, and with any sort of luck I do not intend to leave it. If there be foolish folk intending to study that difficult but fascinating Siren of Music at close quarters, such I intend to trap and having enticed to doom, suck dry.

My little parlour is not inhabited yet but will be in a day or two. Masefield's 'Here was the Legion Halted' has just got set, in some fashion or other — perhaps not too badly. Words, I want words! Where's another Kathleen ni Houlihan?

Meanwhile the office boy of 'Harper's Magazine' has imitated the example of him of the 'Spectator' and slung them back at me. My pet malediction on the whole! Stevenson's letters were the best refuge from life, and in that gossip, courage, friendliness, a certain forgiving tolerance came in on me.

My slippers have just received the honour of a report from my mother, who found them (probably) where she had put them — a most safe hiding place as a rule. This afternoon I go to a farm voluntarily for a couple of hours or so, under the lee of a wood in a small valley — for an unmusical brain the best restorative.

Safely ensconced at 51 Queen's Road, High Wycombe, and thus once more in touch with nature and the peaceful ways of a small town, Gurney began to achieve a sense of stability and purpose. The creative force within him gathered strength, flowing out both in music and poetry, much of it of very high quality.

With such a refuge to return to, the business of 'journeying disconsolate and grumbling towards London and College and music' could be faced almost with equanimity. Even London could be seen to have its charms:

> Dawn comes up on London
> And the night's undone.
> Stars pale feebly out, and the air stirs
> Faintly as high on Western hills in firs.
> Slow across Heaven gray sodden clouds go slow —
> High across Heaven; and Thames with steely gleams
> Changes her one flood into many streams,
> And papers are on sale by Bridge-ends where
> A rounded balustrade may shield from air.
> Sleepers have gone
> Where men go who can have no warmth but sun,
> Unless a lucky twopence might mean tea.
> (One affluent adds Woodbines and a bun.)
> It is half past three.
> See now how she changes, the brooding city,
> To casual Being from Eternity,
> Her strangeness all ways gone, while Paul's as ever
> Is mighty and a King of Sky and River,
> Monarch unquestioned of the middle air,
> And what moves there,
> Aeroplanes, swallows,
> Of all but fog-drift there.
> That obelisk which all night long did grieve
> For Egypt and a queen not lost to story
> Shows now but granite, smutted, transitory.
> (O shapely still!)
> Trees that were night's tongues
> Now are but prisoned things sprung up from clay,
> And of Earth's will.
> Now have come among us
> Seagulls and cheeping sparrow-beggars, gray
> High-sleeping pigeons. Tug calls far away.
> Big Ben answers with his smaller brood.
> There's a morning mood,
> A change of sky.
> Common are all things — London's Day-by-day.[2]

Though Ivor Gurney's movements and activities, other than the writing of music and poetry, are shadowy and uncertain, a letter to John Haines, postmarked 11 November 1919, reveals that he had already become known to and accepted by several of the Georgian poets:

I have seen Shanks in London 3 or 4 times, Monro, Turner at his house. And one evening Shanks, Munro and myself went to hear Steuart Wilson sing the 'Wenlock Edge' cycle of Vaughan Williams — a fine strong piece of work.

On Saturday as you will hear from F.W.H[arvey] we visited Masefield in his proper haunt at Boar's Hill, where are Graves, Nichols and Bridges also. He was extremely nice, a boyish, quiet person with a manner friendly enough and easy to get on with. . . .

Neither F.W.H. nor myself thought Masefield cared for 'By a Bierside', but the 'Old Bold Mate' and 'The Halt of the Legion' and 'Upon the Downs' pleased him. . . . Boar's Hill is not pretty as *we* know prettiness but it isn't bad — 4 miles south of Oxford and (so they say) within a few hundred yards of a great view, which we did not see. Once again Masefield expressed admiration of my last book — 'It was jolly good', and I fancy wants me to go to Oxford on a grant. . . .

Nor is it hard to imagine him once again an eager browser at the Poetry Bookshop in Devonshire Street, catching the literary gossip and attentive at the public readings.

In every sense, then, the second half of 1919 seems to have been filled with profitable activity and heavy with promise. His musical output was by any standards remarkable: forty or more songs, including some of the finest he ever wrote; several short piano pieces, including the *Five Preludes*, later published by Winthrop Rogers; a violin sonata; the String Quartet in F major, and the greater part of another in A major; and an extended orchestral work, the *Gloucestershire Rhapsody*. Add to this an almost equal quantity of poetry (he was soon to offer Sidgwick and Jackson a third collection, entitled *Rewards of Wonder*) and it becomes obvious that he was working under an alarming pressure.

Signs of trouble began to appear early in 1920. Again this was to be a year of immense creative activity, in which he produced even more songs than in 1919 and only marginally less instrumental music. But already, in February, Herbert Howells felt uneasy:

My Dear Marion,

        I saw Ivor yesterday in Gloster. He came to tea, there, with Dorothy and myself. It seems he walked last Tuesday from High Wycombe to a village 8 miles east of Oxford; continued on Wednesday to that city; and took a train from there to a place on the Cotswold ridge (I have forgotten the name of the village) and walked across the hills to Dryhill Farm, Crickley. He certainly looks none the worse for the expedition. But he is in a restless mood, I think. He talked depressingly of the lack of prospects in Wycombe; and the organistic work there is evidently much against his natural longings. He spoke emphatically of his need for open air farm work to refurbish his musical mind and give him 'ideas'. He is minded to give up everything of a strictly professional life, in favour of work on a farm, from which he would hope for brief periods of absence for the purpose of going to London to hear a concert or two. He spoke of his 'elemental' need of such a life . . . and, for the moment at any rate, it is the only sort of life he has any craving for. I passed no definite opinion on the wisdom or folly of the scheme; but begged he would take counsel of you and others ere he did anything so drastic as the renunciation of professional life.

    Maybe he has already told you of what he feels in need . . . anyhow, I tell you now, so that you will know. It is very evident (or was so yesterday) that he does not want to leave Gloucestershire until after Easter.

    It is not easy to determine to what exact extent his present mood is based on simple restlessness. In my own view it is more deep-seated than any ordinary mood. . . .

    Howells's suspicions were soon confirmed. From now on Gurney was to shuttle uneasily between Gloucestershire, High Wycombe, London, and almost any other place his fancy suggested — particularly if there were friends in the area, or a fine view to be enjoyed. His manuscripts, nearly always dated with time and place, give some indication of the extent of his wanderings. Though nominally a student at the Royal College, and nominally an organist in a busy parish church, he was in reality a Super-Tramp. He thought nothing of walking from London to Gloucester, sleeping out in barns or under hedgerows when the weather was good, earning a few pence by singing folksongs in country inns, burdened with little more than his pipe and baccy pouch, pencils and notebooks ready to jot down music or poetry as it occurred to him. When in London, said Marion Scott,[3] he frequently slept on the Embankment, or dossed down in some common lodging house. On more than one occasion he was picked up by the police for questioning (once as a suspected burglar), but released again as a harmless eccentric.

From time to time he would settle; at one point, in May 1920, even believing that he had found the cottage he had dreamed of in the trenches:

Cold Slad,
Dryhill,
Witcombe,
Glos.

It requires a little explanation, does it not? Well, in one of my fits of not being able to stand it any longer, I wrote a letter to the chief churchwarden at Wycombe, arranged for the service to be taken, and came here — to find out what might be found out. An old Cotswold stone house with one pretty good upper room, but draughty. There are holes in the floor — to be dodged. There are two square places in the roof which will need stopping. The garden was long ago a ruin, the stream dried up, and weeds grew in it; no one came save the curious; and now under the shadow of the great rise of Crickley — here am I.

I am a bit afraid, but hope to earn a little money somehow, enough to carry on. If not, there are the picture palaces, which I carefully looked up in the *Era*, and Captain Browcher's promise to take me to sea.

Though the cottage proved an impossibility, he stayed on at Dryhill Farm for most of the summer, 'learning the business of farming at 5/– a week'. Yet even this was not the answer: 'I dont like farm work much. The skilled work I am not given, the unskilled is drear, but O the beauty of the place, the beauty! Yes, I am a lucky chap, but my place is College.'

He remained on the books of the Royal College until the summer of 1921. After that it was impossible to continue his scholarship: he had failed his F.R.C.O. examination and there was no point in trying to pretend he was in any real sense a 'student'. From now on his base, if so wandering a life can be said to have had any base, was Gloucester. Not 19 Barton Street, where he and the family simply got on each other's nerves, but with his aunt at Longford, just outside the city on the Tewkesbury road and near the church at Twigworth — familiar and much loved ground — where Alfred Cheesman had become vicar in 1912.

He found no regular employment. Odd jobs came his way: working on the land, usually in some menial capacity (once even picking up stones), briefly in a cold storage depot in London, two short spells as pianist in cinemas at Plumstead and Bude, which, predictably, ended in disaster. Such things helped to supplement his meagre pension and relieve the humiliating necessity of living off his aunt's charity. His friends were generous. Marion Scott, acting as his literary and musical agent, roused a considerable interest in him and active help was now being given by such people as Vaughan Williams (who for a time made him an allowance), Walter de la Mare, Jack Squire, and many others. Where jobs could appropriately be offered, they were offered:

A. Fox Strangways: *Music & Letters*
15.6.1921
Dear Gurney,
 I am sending you a copy of the current number of this rag. Will you have a look at the first two dozen pages and see the sort of thing I am asking for, and then do a version of any that take your fancy, but especially the 'Erlking', which beats everybody. I saw you today in the offing, but you tacked and were lost below the horizon. . . .

J. C. Squire: *London Mercury*
[Undated]
Dear Gurney,
 There is a fine poem in this, but I dont think you've completely excavated it. Do come on Thursday. . . .

Singers, such as John Coates, Clive Carey, Steuart Wilson, and Harry Plunket Greene, did their best to include his songs in their recitals:

John Coates, London.
19.6.1921
Dear Mr. Gurney,
 I have not the pleasure of knowing you personally, but your songs and I get along famously! I'm singing your 'Spring' at the second of my Chelsea recitals (I sang it at the Wigmore Hall recently and people loved it). . . .

Tributes of friendly concern came from all sorts of people:

Scott-Moncrieff, Edinburgh.
14.10.1921
Dear Mr. (since you will call me Mister: why I dont know) Gurney,

You are the one man whose appreciation of my verse translations seems to be worth having, since you are swayed by none of the ordinary and base motives and I feel sure you could be damned nasty about them if you wanted.

Why have you left London: have you any work: can I do anything: has Bruce Richmond sent you any books, or do you need any? None of these questions needs an answer — but I feel concerned for your material welfare. Your spiritual welfare is all right. . . .

Walter de la Mare, London.
18.6.1921
Dear Mr. Gurney,

Forgive me for not having written before; I have been away from home. I know very little indeed about music publishing; but a friend of mine is getting *one* song done for £6, so £35 for four seems, by comparison, rather a high charge. Of course there is not any immediate hurry and we can talk the matter over again when you are free from this other important work you speak of in your letter . . . we might try one or two songs first, as an experiment. It doesn't matter in the least whether they are my words or not — I should like you to think only of the music and shall love the words to be E.T's, if Mrs. Thomas would agree. . . .

Even Sir Charles Stanford had been stirred into lending a helping hand, and had sent *Severn and Somme* to the Poet Laureate (Robert Bridges) for his opinion. Bridges replied on 18 March 1922, with guarded enthusiasm:

My dear Stanford,

I have read Ivor Gurney's poems. I read them before I read his Preface, and came to the conclusion that he had certainly come in contact with the poems of Gerard Hopkins wh. I printed in 'The Spirit of Man' — and I find in his preface that he has been reading that book. I thought that the best of his poems were the later sonnets in which this influence is evident. It seemed to me that Gerard Hopkins' bold way of dealing with his thought suited Gurney very well — such verse as

'Only the love of Comrades sweetens all,
Whose laughing spirit will not be out-done'

'Tho' Heaven be packed with joy bewildering
Pleasures of soul and heart and mind, yet who
Would willingly let slip, freely let go
Earth's natal loveliness' —

I thought that in these poems he had found a worthier expression than
was at his command before, and if he shd think of taking to writing
poetry, he might wish to perfect his manner before he introduced himself to the public. On the other hand his liking for Hopkins points to
his taste being *naturally* very severe and artistic, and in that case his
earlier easier style might be more popular than his later would be.

I am of course wholly in favour of the latter.

The value of the poems as spontaneous statements of conditions of
mind under strange conditions of present interest I do not feel called on
to estimate. You would probably be able to judge of that better than
I can.

I shd judge that it is certainly in his power to write good poetry if he
gave himself up to it — and if that is so, then it follows that something
of his natural artistic gift will appear in almost everything that he does
either ill or well. How far this will affect the public and please them is
more than I can guess. It seems a matter of chance.

Yours sincerely,
R. Bridges

Gurney's own efforts to further his cause were not, however,
always couched in the most conciliatory terms. A letter to
Edward Marsh, written probably in 1922, manages to be both
pathetic and truculent. Marsh must have been perturbed, and
possibly even annoyed, by the curious footnote written in a
triangle across the bottom left-hand corner of the letter. It read:
'A man named Tourneur wrote "The duke's sons great con-
cubine, a drab of state, a cloth's silver slut Who has her train
borne up, but lets her soul trail in the dirt." ' The letter itself
was less enigmatic:

Dear Mr. Marsh,
          I send under the title of 5 Songs of Rupert Brooke,
4 settings, of which I do not think very much, but they are probably
better than those of most folk.

These four have been done some time. I must try to get another for
the set — 'The Pacific Clouds', with luck.

If you care to get these sung to you, I can believe you would like them, though mere carpentry in the doing. I am fond enough of 'When Colour goes Home' to wish to have done that with some sprite in me, but could not.

> With best wishes
> I remain
> Yours very sincerely,
> Ivor Gurney.

Marsh did not reply. Nor did he return the manuscript.[4]

For a normal person, Gurney's situation in 1921 and 1922 was not without hope. Admittedly he had no job and could see little prospect of getting one, but his works were beginning to find publishers and an audience. *War's Embers* had not been a success, and Sidgwick and Jackson turned down a third volume of 80 poems (*Rewards of Wonder*), but individual poems appeared in *Music and Letters* (October 1920), the *London Mercury* (October 1922), and in J. C. Squire's *Selections from Modern Poets* (1921) and *Younger Poets of Today* (1922). Many a poet has had to survive on less encouragement. And some composers might even have found the musical situation a positive cause for optimism. Winthrop Rogers had brought out the five 'Elizas' in 1920, as well as 'The County Mayo' and 'The Bonnie Earl of Murray'. Boosey had taken four songs, and Stainer and Bell had taken two. Most heartening of all, the Carnegie Trust, stimulated to interest by Marion Scott, had agreed to publish vocal and full scores of two major song cycles for voice, piano and string quartet — both settings of Housman's verse: *Ludlow and Teme* and *The Western Playland*. Though they did not emerge from the press until 1923 and 1926, Gurney was able to correct proofs of the first and was fully aware of the decision to publish the second.

Even with regard to instrumental music things were looking up. In 1921 Winthrop Rogers brought out the *Five Preludes for Piano*, and Stainer and Bell accepted the *Five Western Watercolours*, which they published in 1923. Thus although nobody was very interested in the piano sonatas and violin sonatas, or the several string quartets — and there is no evidence that Gurney himself seriously considered them worthy of publication — the charge of 'neglect' cannot be substantiated. Perhaps he was not appreciated as fully and widely as he felt he had a right to be — but what artist ever feels entirely satisfied in this respect?

What, then, went wrong? To begin with, the creative flow diminished during 1921 and 1922, falling away to about half what it had been during the two previous years. In quality it was no different: a mixture of genius and muddle — some songs complete masterpieces, others beginning well and then tailing off, some a mere chaos of half-realized inspiration. Possibly he noticed the inconsistency, and possibly he felt afraid.

Secondly, the problem of employment was virtually insoluble. He must have known how unsuited he was to any kind of regular, orthodox musical job — even the menial task of cinema pianist eluded his grasp. He must have compared his situation with that of his hard-working brother. He may even have suffered under exasperated taunts — understandable enough from those who were not able to appreciate his kind of music (if only he had written songs that everybody could hum, and kept the home fires burning like that other Gloucester Ivor!). He must, in short, have felt guilty, useless, and unwanted.

Worse, he began to feel that he had been betrayed by the country he loved and whose cause his art and his life had served. Were the sufferings of a war poet to count as nothing? Were wounds, and gas, and a lifetime of bad dreams to be assuaged by a 12/– pension? Was there to be no reward for all the pain he had endured?

Friends tried to help. Edward Marsh brought his influence to bear on the income tax office in Gloucester and eventually a post was found under the sympathetic eye of William Kerr — himself a minor poet, who was to find publication in the fifth and last volume of *Georgian Poetry* (ironically through Gurney's recommendation!). It lasted only a few months. A gentle excuse was made — for he proved hopelessly ill-equipped even for the most trivial office routine — and he was dismissed to put himself 'on the Unemployment Shame' once more.

He began to imagine that 'electrical tricks' were being played on him. He felt pains in the head and the voices returned. He left his aunt's house and thrust himself, uninvited, on his brother, who had just married. Here his behaviour became intolerable. He would shut himself in the front room of their house in Worcester Street and shout for them to keep away. He would sit with a cushion on his head to guard against electric waves coming from the wireless. He refused to go to bed, or to eat properly. He

sneered at his brother's orthodoxies: 'Only fools go to work —
why dont you get somebody else to keep you.'[5] He flew into
violent rages. He threatened suicide and called at the police
station to demand a revolver. He was given sedatives by the
doctor, but swallowed the lot as soon as his back was turned. He
tried to gas himself.[6]

Distraught, the family appealed to the doctors again and they
in turn called in the two magistrates necessary for committal.
There was no alternative. By the middle of September 1922,
Ivor Gurney appeared to be insane.

England

For the London Metropolitan Police Force,
Threadneedle Street.

On a memory

There was a boy, his earlier sins were past,
Walked all one March into a Joy at last,
Music waking in him, Music outwelling
From the good soil, That Western land, fulfilling
All hopes of the mind, all spirit's deep desire.
There was continual tending of the fire
Which is to God most dear. And a woman found him,
Who loved God more than he, and did surround him
With more music, but not his love of earth
Had. He was West-Country in birth.
Such love she had as few, no tiny thing
Of two-legged body, and of feathered wing,
No twig no branch of any month's aspect
But had her love, of beauty so exact
So true a touch of worship. And she taught
Courtesy by courtesy's natural grace uncaught.
A new spirit moved him. Nature was guide,
All things were nothing to the waking-eyed
Spirit that desired fame out of good work.
Night walking, clear thinking, and little shirk
Of what was needed for tasks. Time went, and still
Grew on his making-passion and strong will
To work his best. That love fell below this, but God
Knowing the truth of all, loved both still, his rod
Touched not. The desire of both was to Him. Carlyle,
Shakespeare, other past great men, the more-than-while
Lasting influences of the good past.
She inspired — she upheld, and the good did last
Well into work. London was reached, she inspiring,
And not forgotten, ever, save illness took
Sufficient from me to forbid music or book.
Then All went, but otherwise it was she
Who ruled my Making, my first tasks to order,
And kept me to such memories of the beauty
Was bright a hundred miles off, near the border
Of Wales. Holidays were hers too. The College terms
Were of her, she the writer of many letters
Who turned to work, me, in my masters' fetters.
But love can carry across a hundred miles.

My stains of love redeemed by work, and the guiles
By which I strove to uphold the strength of work.
Illness, but Gloucestershire cured all, and again coming
To the long Streets to happy hours, I worked
And walked without rest, much. Little I shirked.
The War came, I not well, and was then refused.
Took an organist post, joined up, and the hard-used
Infantry joined in manoeuvre or steady drilling.
In health, she my bright thought was continually filling.
When the sun took me full with its bright joy
To be only a nature thing, a boy,
Then her thought shone in me as light on water —
A happy image, a comfort, a Nature's daughter.
Out to the Front, and there her letters made bright
Patches of love, though often neglected, the right
Touch of gossiping, when summer days long
Bothered the being with heat; and when the Winter
Brought the cold, wet, deep mud, then her strong
Courage upheld. Across water at last I came.
She was iller now, but dear, but dear, and her name
Thrilled still on lips. My work was meant for her.
I turned to work, and returned to playing there
The piano as of old — then her ending came.
I stood by her coffin, and smoked, there was no shame.
Now after four years, I look back and see that she
Has been best inspiration, or that beauty
She loved. God help us if such love be not accepted.
For, before God, not such love is rejected.
What shame there was many times under the stars
Has been walked off. Their worship mars
All wrong, and makes right much in the Maker's sight,
For peace comes body and soul to whom by night
Walks, and forgiveness between God and his
Children, and she was surely of happiness —
His happiness. Long ago He forgave.
I did not go visit her cemetery grave,
But walked in quiet places that she loved,
Or on hill roads far from crowds or noise removed.
The spirit of greenwood, the heart of music was she.
And now, after her death, they torture me
With past things, forgetting how hard my trying was,
How true to work, her goodness and true grace.
And what disaster now to be brought to wreck
Where her help can avail but little, the check

Of wicked fortune, mostly by wickedness
Brought to so great a fall, for not much work
Can be accomplished, and the unborne restrictions
Fight against freedom, O the derelictions
Of betraying fortune after so much bitter trying,
And she, who helped so, now has great denying —
Great betrayal of all that love, which giving
Was happy, and found certainty in believing.
The love that gave all to an end of work —
My work of which her faith saw much to believe,
That memory, now brought back to pierce or grieve.[7]

I. B. Gurney

ASYLUM: 1922-1937

Misery weighed by drachms and scruples
Is but scrawls on a vain page.
To cruel masters we are pupils,
Escape comes careless with old age.

O why were stars so set in Heaven
To desire greedily as gluttons do;
Or childish trinkets — May death make even
So rough an evil as we go through.[1]

XV

A letter from Ronald Gurney to Marion Scott, dated 14 September 1922, makes it clear that in order to preserve Ivor's disability pension it was necessary to let the Pensions Office handle his case. It is not a pleasant letter, and it is important to read it in the light of what the family had suffered and were suffering:

I am very much obliged to yourself and Ivor's friends for their persistent help to a rather undeserving person.

Personally I myself as you know have never been over sympathetic to him, as I have always been convinced that he was being handled in the wrong way. As a matter of fact, I had thought he was slowly improving, when Mr. Kerr sent for me. I do not live at home now, as I have been married this 2 months.

This last business has rather broken my patience with the family in general, and for the future I intend the lot of 'em to do exactly as they are told. No two of them will live together for the future.

As for Ivor, for the present he is going under the Pensions Office to a country house near Bristol (a neurasthenic Convalescent Home). They think it best he should not be certified insane for the present.

There is no reason under the sun why he should not become thoroughly well enough to be able to do his music.

But it will only be done by his being permanently under discipline and a definite stronger will directing his life. Never again will I permit kind but lenient and letting him have more or less his way kind of people.

Please dont think I am directing that at London. The trouble is here, not there. Please hold over all arrangements you thought of making for him in London. If the Pensions do not cure him, I will in a month or two's time carry out the original tentative decision to send him to Barnwood and try that.

When he returns well enough, he will for the future live with me. If there is anything then that the College would like him to take up with a view to bringing out something worth while, I will see that he does it.

But you can take it from me, he will never be fit enough as long as he lives to take a post and earn his living in the ordinary way. I expect him to get a full disability or nearly so Pension for life.

When he is back again, I should be glad if the College or anyone else desiring to get him to do anything will direct the wish and the requirements to me. He will simply not have to think for himself at all, just write his music and poetry and be quietly happy.

All this can only be done by myself only and I shall be glad if you will refrain from giving him anything but simple thoughts to think about. He thinks far too much about things that are far too deep for everlasting pondering upon. He thinks and thinks about such ungodly things, that his head is in a huge unwieldy mess.

Dr. Vaughan Williams was kind enough to guarantee £100 towards any necessary expenses. For the present I shall need nothing. If Barnwood is ultimately necessary and inevitable I shall let yourself and the Dr. know and every possible effort shall be made to deal with him.

Up to now I have never endeavoured to deal with him, but he will not again be allowed to drift.

Thanking you and hoping that your own troubles will soon be right.

Sincerely yours,
Ronald Gurney.

It is not hard to imagine the dismay this letter must have caused. Yet, read sympathetically, it contains a certain rough kindness, and the course outlined for Ivor's future treatment would have reduced him to no more of a cypher than he was eventually to become. It is a letter written in anger and distress and, above all, fear. It is filled with a family's brooding suspicion that Ivor had somehow been seduced by high falutin' ideas, out of his class, out of the protective background. It cries an age-old fear of books and learning, of tempting fate by too high a flight, of corruption through lack of discipline. But before we condemn it, it is as well to consider the social pressure that had moulded the opinions and prejudices it enshrines.

In fact Gurney's London friends did not do as Ronald asked. A letter from Walter de la Mare indicates that they had gathered together a fund to help and that, in J. C. Squire's words, they regarded him as 'a man of genius' and were not prepared to wash their hands of the problem just like that. The chance to act came soon. The convalescent home quickly realized that his case was beyond their competence and he was transferred to Barnwood

House, a private asylum on the outskirts of Gloucester, for more authoritative treatment. It was now essential to raise money to pay the fees, and on 6 October de la Mare wrote to Marion Scott to explain what he had done: 'I thought the best thing was to write to Eddie Marsh at once. And, as always in these thing, he at once did all he could, and rang up a friend in the Pensions Office and "tried to interest him" in Gurney.' The result was that the Ministry ultimately agreed to raise the pension to £2 a week. In the meantime the management committee at Barnwood House agreed to maintain their patient without payment — presumably on some guarantee of settlement whatever the final arrangements.

Barnwood House no longer exists in its entirety. It was a large red-brick building of dour aspect lying a few yards back from the main Gloucester–Hucclecote road (the 'Avenue') behind high walls. Inside it was not unpleasant — though long, echoing corridors and hygienic tiles scarcely made it a joyous place. Locally it was regarded with a mixture of pride, awe, and dread. Pride, in that it was known to function efficiently; awe, in that it was expensive; dread, in that it was an asylum. Gloucester offered two more places of retreat, but they were public institutions and, by comparison, places of genuine local horror. Barnwood House was always 'Barnwood House'. The others were 'the looney bins' and thus the terminus of all hope.

What happened to Gurney can best be read between the lines of the few letters that have survived from this period. Two came direct from the asylum to Marion Scott and were written by Arthur Townsend, the Superintendent:

30 October, 1922.
Dear Miss Scott,

        I am sorry I cannot report any definite improvement in Mr. Gurney's condition, his delusions are unchanged and he continues to say that he is subject to persecution by means of telegraphy and that he is made to undergo much mental and physical torture. At the same time as he tells me this he does not appear to be suffering from either the mental or physical distress he describes. He occupies a good deal of his time in reading and writing and with his music.

He is sleeping quite well and on the whole taking a good amount of food, though still not as much as I should like; the difficulty with regard to food is irregularity, he will miss a meal or two and then eat an abnormal amount at another meal and this of course is not as it should be.

Physically we think he is looking better than he was.

By all means send the cigarettes as you kindly suggest. Mr. Gurney smokes a good deal.

9 November, 1922.
Dear Miss Scott,

I am sorry to say that Mr. Gurney managed to escape last night, at 9 o'clock he suddenly took hold of a large clock, hurled it through the window and hurled himself after it. Our efforts to find him were unavailable [*sic*] but fortunately, though we were unable to find him, he went to the Police Station where they detained him until we sent for him.

In going through the window he cut his hands rather badly and there was a considerable loss of blood.

In the circumstances I would advise you to defer your visit for the present. . . .

Exactly how worried, desperate even, his family became at this turn of events can be gathered from a letter which Ronald Gurney wrote three days later:

Dear Ivor,

I have seen your letter to Mother and am sending on the books I can find and also some old clothes of yours which will do to go on with. My advice to you is not to shout so damned egotistically about your being a better man than me. You are only shouting at the very one you depend on.

If you were to forget for a while that you are such a wonderful man you might get well and, for a change, do something to prove it. For your information — ie. your royalty money — you might think for a change of the various money you have from time to time had off me. The various times you went to London and the odd pounds you have had. Also since leaving home you have had 3 suits and an overcoat — tobacco (once to the extent of 9/– worth) 10/– when I visited you. Your royalties since you left Westfield Terrace have been a total of £14 in 15 months. There is nothing left of it, nor a good deal over. Yet you ask for another 10/– each time as if I was made of money. Besides! If you are a better man — PROVE IT and earn more than me. I have no patience with you at all. For the want of a little effort on your own part you are where you are. Personally I think you want your stubbornness broken at all costs, then you might think of others as well as yourself.

I am enclosing 10/-. I dont care to again send a lot of tobacco, I sent you 8 ozs just before coming to you and 2 days after you had none. That is not reasonable. Help yourself and I'll help you.

On the back of the letter and in the margins, Ivor Gurney pencilled his comments —

Letter sent to one of Five War Poets in torment all day. (Confined — tormented to eat — eating in torment — head) by a brother who visited him at Barnwood House Gloucester — to find him being broken by electrical torment. Who lies before God as his letter shows. Who, being prayed to for rescue — sends enclosed letter. O God!

— and then gave it to Marion Scott!

Ronald Gurney was not a cruel man. He was simply very worried and totally exasperated — driven to the end of his tether by a situation he could not possibly hope to control. Probably, in judging him as they must have done, none of Gurney's London friends noticed that the ten shillings was actually sent. Only someone with a first-hand experience of mental illness can begin to understand the depths of outrage and despair that can move those who are left behind to pick up the pieces. There is in insanity an element of opting out; and, like suicide, it is not always easy to forgive. Ronald Gurney certainly felt this:

I understand far better than anyone else in the world the inner state of his mind — for the simple reason that I have exactly the same nervous system and temperament. As a matter of fact I myself have travelled a long way down the same road that he has gone. I am convinced that nothing on earth will do Ivor much good till by Iron Discipline he has had his natural obstinacy and stubbornness broken down. They will have to be semi-cruel to do it. . . .

And his observation of his brother, though rashly expressed, did contain insights that were very shrewd.

To Ivor's friends it seemed essential that he should leave the Gloucester area. It was too near home and all that home implied. It was too easy for his mother to visit, morbid and recriminatory, bewildered and weighed down with a woe that her melancholy expectations of life had now been fulfilled. Arrangements were made, and on 21 December 1922, at 7.30 in the morning, he was driven with two attendants to the City of London Mental Hospital at Dartford, Kent, and into the care of Dr. Steen.

The entries in Ivor Gurney's Dartford medical file begin with a few bald statements of fact.[2] He is described as a musician, aged thirty-two, single, 5ft 8¾ in. in height and weighing 10 st. 3 lbs. His hair and eyes are brown, and his teeth 'deficient'. Though he has suffered from stomach ulcers, his general state of health is noted as 'moderate', and he is said to be 'steady in his habits (almost teetotal)'. The nature of his mental disorder is given as 'Delusional Insanity (Systematized)' — a diagnosis which would nowadays be translated as paranoid schizophrenia. Under the heading 'Mental Condition' the entry reads: 'The patient is strange in his manner. He has delusions that he is being tormented by electricity. He says he is in a tangled police case and is being treated as a medical case. He has auditory hallucinations.' Later entries add a little more detail:

The electricity manifests itself chiefly in thought. Words are conveyed to him. They are often threatening, [and] they have been obscene and sexual. He has heard many kinds of voices. He sees things when he is awake, faces etc that he can recognise. He has also had a twisting of the inside. He cannot keep his mind on his work. Sleep is good. Does not dream. Takes food well. With regard to suicide he has had such pains in the head that he felt he would be better dead.

However real these 'electrical tortures' may have been to Gurney, it is important to recognize that they were entirely imaginary. He was never at any time subjected to electro-convulsive therapy — for the simple reason that it had not yet been invented and was not used in psychiatry until several years after his death. In believing himself to be under the influence of 'wireless' and 'electricity', Gurney was latching on to the latest perplexing scientific development. In 1922 it was broadcasting that amazed and frightened. Nowadays it is influences from outer space.

The recorded details of his condition do not change much over the years. At times (for example, in July 1924) he became aggressive; in 1927 he believed there were machines under the floor that were torturing him; in 1929 he claimed to be the author of Shakespeare's plays, and the composer of Beethoven and Haydn's works. On many occasions he refused medical examination. He is often described as 'apathetic and dejected', 'withdrawn' and 'solitary'. On one occasion, 6 January 1923, he ran away, making for London and Vaughan Williams's house in Cheyne Walk, but after two days he was apprehended and made no further attempt to gain his freedom.

There is little more to be gleaned from the official records. He was treated kindly and considerately, but he was one of many and the day to day pressure of institutional life left little or no room for careful analysis and detail. It was, in the circumstances, all that could be expected, and it would be unfair to blame the doctors for lack of insight. But one cannot help noticing that the records use such phrases as 'he is said to be very musical' (17 June 1932), rather as if every aspect of his life now lay under the same suspicion. And no one, it seems, made it their business to study what he was writing. Had they done so, they might, at least in the early years of his incarceration, have been surprised.

Once the doors of Dartford had closed upon him, Ivor Gurney began to write letters of appeal: to his friends, to mere acquaintances, to strangers even. It seems odd that any of them were allowed to be posted; only those addressed to obviously impossible recipients, such as the London Metropolitan Police Force, were held back. The rest went out, and they caused great distress. To Marion Scott, for instance:

Dear Lady of Mercy,
                       I am grateful to be removed from Barnwood House, and thank you very much, but the pain of thought is great. Much has been written, of London chiefly.

Save me, I pray you. Get Dr. Steen to release, I pray. For yesterday he said that the electrical influences would continue anywhere. Last night I wrote to Dr. Vaughan Williams to get me Death, for this I cannot endure. Rescue me to something. For Death I long for. There is no reason I should not be released from this confinement — these rules. *My friends may always remove me*, may they remember I suffer worse than Death.

Do not allow me to remain in uncertainty — so great a weight.

Have mercy — not another day here.

    I remain
                yours gratefully for all the trouble.

But have mercy. Release from all this.

                              I. B. Gurney

'I don't know what is best to do about the letters from Ivor Gurney,' wrote Walter de la Mare. 'Does it only make matters worse if one answers them and tries to express how grieved one is? And should I, do you think, send on the one that is addressed to Mr. Masefield as well as me?'[3]

There was nothing his friends could do, save watch and pray that tranquillity might eventually be restored to him. In the meantime they paid the bills that his pension did not cover; they sent books and tobacco; and they visited him, though it was heart-breaking to do so.

Marion Scott was, it need hardly be said, the most faithful. She took him out by car, and, accompanied by an attendant, they visited places in the area: Canterbury, Dover, Rochester, Knole Park, and so on. She took him to a performance of *A Midsummer Night's Dream* at the Old Vic. She arranged for a string quartet to play one of his works (probably the A minor quartet) and copied out the parts herself. She did everything she could to bring comfort and a sense of normality.

Most important of all, she began to collect his manuscripts and make plans for publication. In 1923 she persuaded Ronald Gurney to send her everything he could lay hands on: 'Re the manuscripts. I am sending them on Goods GWR as there is rather a lot of them. As I myself know nothing about music, I have packed everything on manuscript paper in his writing. I am afaid you'll have a tough job with it. . . .' She also took steps to ensure that everything he wrote in the asylum, letters, poems, music, down to the smallest scrap, was preserved and passed on to her.

The immediate public results of her devotion was a slender trickle of poems in such publications as J. C. Squire's *London Mercury* (January 1924); *Music and Letters* (April 1925); and most important of all the publication in 1926 by Stainer and Bell of a set of six songs to words by Edward Thomas: *Lights Out*. Most of the songs were written between 1918 and 1922, but one, 'The Trumpet', seems to have been wrung out of him in 1925 — probably at her suggestion, for the cycle obviously needed some kind of climax. The difference in quality is instructive. Publication was underwritten by private subscription, and the whole venture may simply have been a continuation of Gurney's own investigations into the possibilities of private publication which Walter de la Mare refers to in his letter of 6 June 1921.

To

Ivor Gurney has written (verse) quarters of a pint of such,
dropped half a pint —
  ask or what print or MS or heard
  William Shakespeare founded his criterion
  of poems
(or on what idea, or electrical idea, or account)

  and where he got his work and notes from.

  Ivor Gurney.

An asylum letter, undated and never posted

In the meantime the asylum manuscripts piled high. To begin with he wrote mostly poems: reliving the Gloucestershire countryside and the sights and sounds of his beloved city; reliving the mud and terror of the trenches and the death of comrades; crying out in despair at the sense of betrayal and persecution that now overwhelmed him. Only very gradually, over many years, did the power of coherent verbal expression desert him.

Music came less readily. Scarcely anything at first; and then, in 1925, a sudden flood of nearly fifty songs. A handful followed in 1926, and then silence.

But even those songs which prove to be earlier works rewritten are almost useless. Though spun from ideas that are coherent and interesting in themselves, they are rambling and diffuse and stubbornly incapable of logical connection. The very handwriting betrays the fact: blurred and overcrowded, curiously lacking in tension — as if the effort to hold the pen was too great, so that the notes seem almost to slide off the page. By 1926 what spark was left in Ivor Gurney could grapple only with words, and then only fitfully.

The best of his asylum poems, however, make terrible reading. Some are so controlled, so 'finished', that the idea of insanity seems absurd:

> What evil coil of Fate has fastened me
> Who cannot move to sight, whose bread is sight,
> And in nothing has more bare delight
> Than dawn or the violet or the winter tree.
> Stuck in the mud — Blinkered up, roped for the Fair,
> What use to vessel breath that lengthens pain?
> O but the empty joys of wasted air
> That blow on Crickley and whimper wanting me![4]

Or again, the poem addressed 'To God':

> Why have You made life so intolerable
> And set me between four walls, where I am able
> Not to escape meals without prayer, for that is possible
> Only by annoying an attendant. And tonight a sensual
> Hell has been put upon me, so that all has deserted me
> And I am merely crying and trembling in heart
> For Death, and cannot get it. And gone out is part

Of sanity. And there is dreadful Hell within me.
And nothing helps. Forced meals there have been and electricity
And weakening of sanity by influence
That's dreadful to endure. And there are orders
And I am praying for death, death, death,
And dreadful is the indrawing or out-breathing of breath
Because of the intolerable insults put on my whole soul,
Of the soul loathed, loathed, loathed of the soul.
Gone out every bright thing from my mind.
All lost that ever God himself designed.
Not half can be written of cruelty of man, on man,
Not often such evil guessed as between Man and Man.[5]

They sound like the utterances of a man whose mind may perhaps have momentarily lost its balance, but who was now being
driven, little by little, into a state of total insanity.

Almost as if they instinctively knew this, it was a long time
before his friends abandoned all hope of a cure. In 1925 Marion
Scott was taken in by the claims of a Canadian doctor who believed that he could handle Gurney as a private patient, live with
him and cure him. But it gradually emerged that he was a char-
latan, deep in debt and eager only for the down-payment that
would stave off his creditors. In 1927 Adeline Vaughan Williams,
acting on the advice of a distant relative, consulted a Christian
Science practitioner and arranged for a course of treatment. It
made no visible difference and was eventually brought to an end.

Rather less helpfully his mother would intervene from time to
time, expressing her views to Marion Scott:

. . . your letter was such a comfort to me I dont want him to be moved
if there is a chance of his getting better but that head Nurse came and
sat down by me evidently wanting him to be got from there he said he
had been there long enough and thought it would do him good to have
a change the Dr was inclined to be red headed his manner of shaking
hands how he spoke gave me no confidence in him at all I fancy he was
the house Dr. . . .[6]

But it was all hopeless. By 1928 it was clear that the sanity that
still flickered so tantalizingly in him would never return to stay.
The asylum was now his only home.

XVI

It is possible that the last years of Gurney's life were less agonizing. For if we are to judge by his writings, the periods of terrifying sanity became fewer and fewer. The letters of appeal no longer recount the tragic history of his decline, but give way to fantasy and confusion. Some read like veiled autobiography:

My Dear Thoreau,

You cannot wish me to be back more than I myself wish: and I shall bring you a new book 'Handley Cross' which is a marvel, and some new music which will astound ordinary pianos — this new music for which we all long — and that leaks so painfully across the ocean to us . . . it is of Robert Schumann, a Fantasie in C . . . they say that Robert Schumann is restless and composes without plan or scruple — one afternoon a page and a half of the Fantasie [;] at night (if he can face it), a little more . . . then goes to friends and begs them to put it away for three days . . . and when it is safely stowd away, he sits down at the piano and makes them write the extemporization of the next movement out . . . thus progressing to divine heavenly things in no honour, peace of mind, or good . . . A dismembered masterpiece lies in three houses till by some terrible effort he recalls all at once . . . and again at some Bechstein of sweetest silverest tone (but what have they done with the others?) puts in completion by some Shakespearian triple effort on three movements — and leaves friends to write out those scraps of giddy perfection: fitting like edelweis in the crags.

Oh! Brahms goes on long walks and comes back with a sketch book full of notes: sometimes a movement: sometimes a part of three. He says 'I do not see that I may walk far, but the flowers help me and the brambles are the friends of my struggles.'

Anyway, stayer in and visitor of friends, or walker — like a Yankee skipper through the undergrowth, I shall bring things as notable as Cathedrals; of the very stuff of creature's thought — and certain ideas about pianos (sketches and such diagrams of mechanism . . .).

Dec 15 1865   H. W. Longfellow to H. D. Thoreau.

Others are more obviously chaotic and suggest an almost total loss of identity — as for example this, from Siegfried Wagner to August Manns:

This is Franz Schubert's death day/and enough for Kent Reach to think of —
whose chimneys smoked grandly, but Nature said 'W. E. Henley Prague 1731 — ' So light dies down — But after saying that Europe could not stand war for its thought, by 137 degrees —
Barnet won I think/ especially about the South, most likely — but perhaps about the going North, where may Italy (North) and Rochester book-sellers flourish.
The weeks and battles forgotten — (terrible to remember) need all the good of Artois and Picardy's poetry —
Meanwhile the regrets and hopes of Highnam Manor float about the world — now vast in great victory, and as urgently as Sidgwick & Jackson cry out for the honour of provinces.
Virgil is running 2/3, and is the master of business — music is at last in a very healthy state/and Rutland Boughton's group is announced — Rudford and Minster, that accepts such news, now forgets its threats and terrible fears, St. Maur gives news of pride every day, and seems to enjoy Welsh local poetry.
It seems true that Anton Dvorak and Rochester Cathedral have truly the salvation of music and poetry — and one might wait for Spring with 137 hopes — But desperate is Hebbel's need for Frankfort's urgencies.
'Lyrik, lyrik' in Schiller's name ever demanding, and let London lose its regrets and clear its History there with the brutality of Eaglefield-Hull, and as the name of Thames flows steadily to honour.
Nature, now sombre, sometimes says tremendous things, and sometimes lightly, as of the biographer of F. P. Schubert and waits for Florence City's reasons and reason —
That London may honour St. Crispin — a saint glorious enough for Aquitaine/and to please William Cartwright, magister artis.
I ask for some more money, please, and a small poetry book if there is one (modern if it can be got). It is painful and hard to write about modern anthologies though — and so better to rejoice (theoretically) about *Max Reger* — / England is a South Place story. . . .
The glory of 1913 and 1914 is here remembered/as always worth the imagination of Petrograde and Moscow. (140–183); later with the surpassing interest of men's music — like our hopes of Novgorod's earth.

with best wishes
(yours very sincerely)
Ivor Gurney   Oct 23   1933
Dartford. Kent.

On one occasion he cut out a newspaper cartoon of a top-hatted plutocrat talking to a small girl who clutches (or rather hides behind her back) a small doll, and added his own wild and comic caption: 'Dr. R. W. Vaughan Williams obtaining natural specimens from Herbert Howells for Pastoral Symphony uses.'

Tragic as all this is, it does not suggest a keen edge of suffering, but rather that the faculties have dulled over into a vague dream. It is hard, though, to discount the suspicion that Gurney's mind might have righted itself had he not been locked away. Fifteen years in a lunatic asylum may well have destroyed what in other circumstances might have been saved.

Glimpses of his daily routine are not easy to come by, but a head nurse, Mr. Fletcher, remembered him as a hostile patient, though not a violent one.[7] He would not attend the entertainments arranged for the patients, but preferred to be on his own. There was a piano in the ward, and this he would play for hours on end, much to the annoyance of the other inmates. When he was not playing he read (crates of books were returned to Ronald Gurney, the words obsessively underlined), and made notes on sheets of toilet paper. He was a heavy smoker, and several times managed to set fire to his bed linen. He was not troublesome, simply difficult to reach and wholly turned in on himself.

Reports from friends and relatives, written to the long-suffering Marion Scott, vary in tone — reflecting always their own sense of proportion. Adeline Vaughan Williams, for example, wrote in measured, sympathetic terms:

We spent some time with Ivor Gurney on Monday. There was no doubt that the state of his mind was worse than when we last saw him. The idea that he had written everything and composed everything persisted throughout our visit and his thoughts were often very confused. But there were moments of real conversation and he spoke of real grievances, i.e. that the best music comes on too late on the wireless and he has to miss it. He also spoke of his loneliness, 'No one comes to see me', and when I praised his cutting out he said 'I have nothing else to do'.

I did not think him looking very well — certainly older — but his colour was better and his hair looked healthier.

Ralph and I agreed that the Christian Science if it has done anything has worsened his mental state. We do not see the use of continuing this treatment if you consider that it has been given a fair trial. Certainly he

gets no help at all for his mind from his surroundings. How I longed to
take him away!

He was gentle as usual . . .

Florence Gurney returned from her visits in quite a different
mood, and with other preoccupations:

. . . do you think he really means I am not to come and see him again
life is so trying I can't save much money I should like to know if he
really wants the Gloucester Journal it costs me 3d every week and I am
afraid he doesn't read it of course you have seen his books how he
serves them they have given me many a back-ache and heartache trying
to take out all the pictures and give them to some little boys and girls
tis so wicked that such a lot of books should be spoiled 7d for carriage
one box and 6d for the other and money so scarce and then they have
to be burned we have been 3 or 4 days trying to burn a lot of them when
twas so cold up in our workroom but it was too much trouble and so
many sticks had to be burned I had to stop it I have tried to sell some
of them to pay the carriage but people look at you as if you wanted to
rob them I do wish he wouldn't get any more. . . .

But of all those who visited him, one person's impressions
stand out — possibly because she was a stranger and was meeting
him for the first time. This was Helen Thomas, the wife of the
poet. Gurney had loved his work and set at least eighteen of his
poems to music. In 1932 Marion Scott wrote to Mrs. Thomas
and suggested that she might accompany her to Dartford. Years
later, in the Easter issue of the R.C.M.'s magazine for 1960, she
recalled what happened:

We arrived at the asylum which looked like — as indeed it was — a
prison. A warder let us in after unlocking a door, and doors were
opened and locked behind us as we were ushered into the building. We
were walking along a bare corridor when we were met by a tall gaunt
dishevelled man clad in pyjamas and dressing gown, to whom Miss
Scott introduced me. He gazed with an intense stare into my face and
took me silently by the hand. Then I gave him the flowers which he
took with the same deeply moving intensity and silence. He then said:
'You are Helen, Edward's wife and Edward is dead.' I said. 'Yes, let us
talk of him.' So we went into a little cell-like bedroom where the only
furniture was a bed and a chair. The window was barred and the walls
were bare and drab. He put the flowers on the bed for there was no

vessel to put them in; there was nothing in the room that could in any way be used to do damage with — no pottery or jars whose broken edge could be used as a weapon. He remarked on my pretty hat, for it was summer and I had purposely put on my prettiest clothes. The gay colours gave him pleasure. I sat by him on the bed and we talked of Edward and myself, but I cannot now remember the conversation. But I do remember that though his talk was generally quite sane and lucid, he said 'It was wireless that killed Edward', and this idea of the danger of wireless and his fear of it constantly occurred in his talk. 'They are getting at me through wireless.' We spoke of country that he knew and which Edward knew too and he evidently identified Edward with the English countryside, especially that of Gloucestershire. I learned from the warder that Ivor Gurney refused to go into the grounds of the asylum. It was not his idea at all of countryside — the fields and woods and footpaths he loved so well — and he would have nothing to do with this travesty of something that was sacred to him. Before we left he took us into a large room in which was a piano and on this he played to us and the tragic circle of men who sat on hard benches against the walls of the room. Hopeless and aimless faces gazed vacantly and restless hands fumbled or hung down lifelessly. They gave no sign or sound that they heard the music. The room was quite bare and there wasn't one beautiful thing for the patients to look at.

We left and I promised to come again.

Ivor Gurney longed more than anything else to go back to his beloved Gloucestershire, but this was not allowed for fear he should try to take his own life. I said 'But surely it would be more humane to let him go there even if it meant no more than one hour of happiness before he killed himself.' But the authorities could not look at it in that way.

The next time I went with Miss Scott I took with me one of Edward's own well-used ordinance maps of Gloucester where he had often walked. This proved to have been a sort of inspiration, for Ivor Gurney at once spread them out on his bed and he and I spent the whole time I was there tracing with our fingers the lanes and byeways and villages of which he knew every step and over which Edward had walked. He spent that hour in re-visiting his beloved home, in spotting a village or a track, a hill or a wood and seeing it all in his mind's eye, a mental vision sharper and more actual for his heightened intensity. He trod, in a way we who were sane could not emulate, the lanes and fields he knew and loved so well, his guide being his finger tracing the way on the map. It was most deeply moving, and I knew that I had hit on an idea that gave him more pleasure than anything else I could have thought of. For he had Edward as his companion in this strange perambulation and he was utterly happy, and without being over-excited.

This way of using my visits was repeated several times and I became for a while not a visitor from the outside world of war and wireless, but the element which brought Edward back to life for him and the country where the two could wander together.

In 1937 Marion Scott, heavily backed and encouraged by two young composers who had never met Gurney but who were to play a vital part in rescuing his music and poetry, Gerald Finzi and Howard Ferguson, finally brought to fruition plans for securing his reputation that Finzi had first mooted in 1925. It was decided that *Music and Letters* would give over a generous part of the January 1938 issue to an appreciation of the man and his work; and that, in addition, the Oxford University Press would publish twenty songs in two volumes.

The manuscripts were duly scrutinized and different versions compared. Finzi and Ferguson set to work, turning when necessary to what Marion Scott and Herbert Howells could remember of the way in which Gurney interpreted his own music. No one had any doubt of the impact the songs would make, least of all Vaughan Williams, who wrote to Hubert Foss at O.U.P. to assure him that the collection was 'first rate'.

But at Dartford things were not well. Over the past four years Gurney had steadily lost weight and by November 1937 he was only a little over seven stone.[2] Bilateral pulmonary tuberculosis was diagnosed, and his friends were quickly informed. Proof copies of *Music and Letters* were rushed to him, but he was too weak to take the wrapping paper off the parcel and seemed not to understand what the articles signified. He was told about the songs, but only murmured: 'It is too late . . .'[3]

On 15 December Marion Scott received an urgent telegram: 'It would be extremely advisable for you to visit, as I regret to state that the patient is considered to be dangerously ill and he is going steadily downhill.' He must have rallied a little, for later a friend wrote to her:

It makes a difference to me to know the details, pitiful as they are. It nearly choked me to read it. But oh, my dear, I am so glad that he was able to give his messages and wishes to you personally. That he should have wanted to live, under those conditions, seems hard to understand, when one thinks how passionately he used to want to die. . . .[4]

He struggled on for many days: Christmas Eve, Christmas Day, and then 26 December, the feast day of St. Stephen the Martyr. And on that day, at 3.45 in the morning, he died.

They took his body back to Gloucester, and there in the bleak unlovely churchyard at Twigworth, towards sunset on the last day of the year, he was buried.

For the English Police
For Scotland Yard.

Chance to Work

I have never had chance to work, for when a boy
Small day was mine, bed-time too soon came by —
Few friends were mine who might have taught me books;
Yet loved I Nature with its joyous looks;
Played football hard as most, and the Cathedral
Worshipped surely with its great rise and fall.
Yet later there was one of sweet humanity
Who brought much worthy knowledge free to me.
But sitting still spoiled health, and the great poets
Were still misted with fear and explaining notes.
Too much food, too few hours, yet sunrise I saw
Brighten sweet Highnam woods, and the bright clouds draw
Off from an April sky, strangely roused up.
Beauty brazen and strange; from the sky's top
To the houses edge unreal, strange. But when
Schooldays were left, a noble man of men
Helped me, my sloth spoilt me and worse was known.
Yet his prayers called on me some goodness down.
One March called me out walking with the natural
Love of joy, and with clean fervour my heart was full.
Gloucestershire called — the Western light, the true
Elizabethan surrounding daylight, ever new,
Ever old, satisfying. Knowledge lacked, not
Yet was the time of work by me to be got.
Much of the natural joy that goes with making
Was given me, known to me; Nature set me shaking
In ecstasy of purity, passion true —
That life Marston, Shirley, Greene and Dekker knew.
Now was music seen to be mirror of Life,
Discord like brambles beautiful in wind at strife
Criss-cross, sawing across light; great chords known
As repose of hills against the East fire known.
A woman's love now helped. Great knowledge grew
Of how the makers gathered and guarded to
Endeavour each small thing seen, each great sight felt,
Holiness of Earth was known. But not yet dealt
Life with me fairly. Long night watches were denied —
So needed — and still labour; On Cotswold side
And higher up, at night it was granted me
The quarries white in moonlight, black greenery

Of beech against the moon; graceful tree-stems,
Stars such as Chaucer saw, and still sky-rims;
O high above the valley. Was mist streaked there?
A dawn is remembered also. But night to labour,
To work, read, walk night through — this needed a friend
Guiding more wisely than I knew. But Life did send
Many consolations. Art apprehended, springs
Of true worth known — natural, of divine sendings —
Earth, air, and water the true sources of song or speaking
In high words. Not out of books the awaking
Spirit might gather much save of discipline —
Manners application of work's rules —
A right weight given to mastership and use of schools.
All this out of love chiefly was taken, and love
Makes rules of nobleness. Nevertheless, above
Love is Law for youth, though Law light-laid —
Friends to me dear, yet rules were right to be made
On me — the legacy of toil out of the past
So pondered, so dwelt upon, formed four-square at last.
London came, with mastership and right rule indicating,
Dull bending to what hitherto had been of Love's rating.
Art in fetters, till limbs had grown strong — City's
Surroundings for Nature's sweetest teachings and pities.
The long streets going onward without much joy.
Mean lodgings, far country, and duty's employ
For all those fires and strong compulsions: the true
Sources of what is worthy, at once old and new.
Ill-health there was, and hardest straining at tasks
Of school sort — a hard term, such that good memory asks
Not to look back upon. Holidays came
To freshen the mind once more; the country-side same
As ever, new-old, old-new, gave life and hope
To heart and soul. Two months of growing; then again
To London — the wonderful mists of Autumn with men
Seen small-black in the smother. Work easier now,
With rules understood. Song and the quicker glow
Of Lyric now were mastered, more. The stern forms
Made afraid the pupil spirit; that yet charms
Needed. Walking all day with sketch-books came
Later, the best plan. Clarity of mind; and dream
So was kept. Terms went. Holidays with dear friends —
Sailing, walking. Going as Nature intends
On white ways for discovery of what lay

Unvisited by most; white water, or spray
Of bramble queerly hanging, or new-old farms,
Black timber, or timber unwrought; or runnels in storms
That fill and empty tiny water-courses
Perhaps nine months all dry; or small gay horses
Galloping sham-afraid from frightening trains.
Walking all morning, afternoon too, the lanes
On high-roads — To return dusty, tea-thirsty
To friends, the piano, sketching ambitiously
Such works as broad country might bring to attempt.
There was hay making too, how wisps unkempt
Clung to the clothes, the horses strong trampled
And all wide Heaven had cumulus unexampled
With War threatening, falling. At last to strike,
Set Europe's dearest killing, thrusting alike
At life or body's beauty. Too ill for War
Was I, whose life was organist, and more
Writing. But health came, the return home, dress
Changed. A little longer the tenderness
So dear, of friends, after drill, that love which had given
Help to work; shared Bach's thought going to Heaven,
Or Beethoven's music loved in company —
Half-light playings of music, of poetry
Readings. . . .   Training took all strength, none was left
For shaping or word or sound. Forgotten the gift.
Rattle-tattle, bugle-call, button-cleaning, leather shining.
Midland, East England, South England; digging, hard-training. . . .
Songs a few; verses few. But overseas better
Chance came. Signallers might, more than the letter
Of Linesmen, Infantry, night-watchers accomplish.
Candles were lit, more time was, and the great wish
Of reading, writing, making was more possible
Than to others of greater danger more honourable.
Nevertheless, Songs and verses. Laventie, by Arras,
Crucifix Corner, Caulaincourt, Rouen, by Ypres.
Something was fashioned out; Work in all odd-sort corners.
Yet time there was for dreams, which so often discerners
Are of the future paths, gatherers of old
Thought-wrack; treasurers, hoarders of time's gold.
Chance of work? Yes, but one hoped so in the coming
Peace, the hoped for universal true homing
Of Line and all Force.

Wound brought on Hospital, then
Was more chance of writing. Some true work. Eastward again
To war-chance.
Gas brought England, and some hope-fulfilling.
The leave, walking, and friendship; but Joy too willing
For hope would not bend down to so short a day
Of labour. Better taste joy, and go quick away
To the hard task. Country seen, friends loved, work's hope
   renewed. . . .
Depot again was not of right labour's hope,
Little comforted there; but the kindest fine scope
Of Hospitality made bright dun closed-in dull lives.
Dreadful the tale to follow.
And the spirit forgives
Best in freedom, horror on horror best put in the black
Oblivion of Time, not ever to be told, or called back.
There was no shadow of happiness, and small chance of
That work my spirit had right of, had learnt to love.
Gloucestershire restored again, though evil forces made
Difficult. The spirit strove for its earlier unafraid
Trust in life. Work at munitions purified, strengthened
Body and spirit. Beauty shone nobly on the well lengthened
Days; but working late was not allowed to me
Or was difficult. Freedom not yet was my legacy
Of right — Nor had I learnt yet the worth of an hour,
Or the all-watching night come into my power.
Cornwall, Gloucester again. London to work —
London that held such hopes, but perils lurk
And are dread there. Hopes broke, work was destroyed,
For all my hopings. Evil flowed black like a tide
Of darkness over me.
Goodness freed, at the last.
But out of London — West Country; Songs, other work passed
From my hand. Walking, making, living on small
Riches, but friendship helped me. Without any call —
Friendship reached out a hand, or where had I been?
Music shared, book-talk shared, and a serene
Hope gained. Many songs, other things, then a good farm
Took me, and body labour took away harm
With fine muscle-using, wood hewing, labouring with spade.
Hedging, plough-helping, stone shifting, Labour was good.
Gone out was danger, ill longing of unspiritual food.
May-Time was more, with poems, or music to sketch;

In the great Roman-trod hill-sides, with water to fetch,
Wood to carry, Tasks — then to return
At evening high up where last sunset light did burn
Looking high over to the British borders
Of old, these camps-slopes sentries and true warders,
Guardians of Rome's power. Yet it is difficult
In a house not one's own to work, and the fire felt
Not into much work grew or was forced. Some poems
Captured the sense of Rome; but one's own home's
Shelter, not to disturb sleep — this not yet
Was granted. Chances I remember to have read late —
Sketched often in the open — Quartetts, songs
Where-to the real sense of earth still clings, belongs.
Much loved all this; but something most evil drove
Me from that place, where desperate work with love
Was mixed. An evil took me; the farm I left —
Beautiful West England of every gift
Dowered, it would seem. London once more, where never
Had stronger been my struggle or hard endeavour.
Success a hundred times deserved, and all
Evil, as best might be, shunned. Work came, but small
Return for so much trying. A War-mourning
Had nobleness, many songs, a Violin thing
Pleased my ambitiousness. A good room that was.
Many streets helped me with their width, a place
Of Labour London never was more to me.
Little more than tea, coffee; coffee and tea
My fare. To Gloucester again for holidays. Still
Sketching, hoping, poems and lyrics making.
Late staying up perhaps; but always shaking
A little with fear to disturb the sleepers over.
It was not one's own house. Better in streets to be rover,
Sketching at notes easily to be completed
In short time, while the quick mind no-ways waited.
Many times walking in the grimy dark, or
Moonlit streets till the time came: the true working-hour.
No fault was mine save drink, and that kept often
The brain clear — Tea preserved me to making then.
But in tea-houses one may not work, there is business,
One may not loiter; and resting places are less
In City ways than anywhere almost.
But a Morley's extract of old time plays; at last
Here were Elizabethans, Greene, Dekker, and Marston —

Shirley, Massinger, Ford, and greater Jonson —
Something of each; Carefully in honour reading,
Learning slowly the new mastery, needing
Such swift mastership after the slower
Foreign scholarship of the more modern hour
Of music. . . . This was revelation, this new
Guidance to what I hoped for — the saying true
And clear out what truly was to be shown of life.
Then an organist's post gave me once more subsistence.
Walking the flint ways, daylight or darkness dense,
Sketching or trying to think — but again I left that;
Went to the dear loved farm, but illness out
Cast me — and so my life to the finest year
Of all comes; the working, hoping, pain-without-fear.
My Aunt with kindest hospitality
To her house and garden made me wholly free —
In her kindness trusting reward which never came —
But honouring work, honouring old poet's name,
And work performed. Hope filled me; Papers I read
For that hard work should bring me daily bread,
And finding none, on my few shillings was
(Of pension) content to work and know my place
Of waiting — worker. Tea, fire, my chief desires.
To dawn often I laboured, and with keen cares
Kept sleep away with wary avoidance till
Sun's fire topped the steep of the Eastern Hill.
Employment came, but not long kept — the expected
Body-labour, the cleansing work, directed
Controlled, till work-end came, once more I was free
For thought, and writing, and free artistry
Denied. Denied must be content; on twelve
Shillings and odd earnings I must serve.
So through the Winter, the Spring, wherein I was reader
Of Midsummer Night's Dream, on that sweet thought the feeder.
On, on to summer; my nights to working so given,
Days to sketching, walking, watching, water, earth, heaven —
Labouring as might be — seventeen miles, home again,
Fair payment of body's usage for using pen,
Back at dusk; talking (scribbling the while) not to lose
Much of the precious work-time. Her habit, use,
Was — bed-at-eleven, when I might settle hard to
Quartetts, or verse, or reading. Summer drew so
To height. Digging, wood chopping, leaping, and such

To increase body's joy, never, never too much.
Night-long often, till others full waking time
Working in strict discipline, music or strict rhyme.
Chaucer, Carlyle, Borrow, Jonson to my aid
Calling. A life of pain, a spirit unafraid
Of duties' costs.
                 Then my misfortunes began.
Influences wrought on me after evil plan.
My body pained, work spoiled, and not my fault —
Since such activity rarely did halt
Rarely falter . . . O little I deserved this thing —
Was I wasting time? Was I playing? Was it slacking?
This life carried onward to one good end,
Yet ready to be abandoned should orders send
Me to some body-using, or money earning.
An office-post for twelve weeks to me turning
By other men's kindness I had; no real fault mine
I lost it — influences drove me, there was much pain.
Still I laved body, still worked when courteousness
Let me so; But worse and worse still my distress
Became. I wished Life's end, because of much pain.
Demanded that — many times, many. But why again
Should I, the striver, be punished? So few men led
Life that so little loved easiness of bed
Or slumber. Fruit pulp, milk, tea, salt, water I took,
Hanging despairingly on many an old book.
Strange things happened, many times death denied
To a spirit that loved working, and had such pride
In achievement, and making's pain. I must leave that
House, where my hopings, strivings had been so great.
I would have gone on tramp. Many hindrances let
Me from this course. Pain. obstacles, hurt head, the wet
Ending of water I feared, but longed much for another.
A Promise failed, a pension that would have saved, rather
Led to destruction perhaps. Friends took me, they thought
Out of danger, but much pain, wrong, was there on me wrought.
Friends helped again; but here I am walking a ward —
A twelve hour day — small comfort for him whose true word,
True though was labour. Why punish so one who so paid
For success, such worthy strong efforts, why ever denied
To me Chance of Work, Bread-earning, who loved sun and stars
More than most others. And saw the bronzed cloud-bars
Between work-spells at cold dawn? . . .

                                        O if such pain is
Not of account — a whole life's whole penalties
To cancel . . . Grant pity, grant chance of Work, Grant that
Freedom of effort in other days held to be great.
Prices I paid, small rest took. Others slept, still
Warding sleep, I watched meadow and tree and hill —
Farm workers still at slumber . . .
                                        Who earned more a good
Fate; how many followed the thing he should
In all England; with such chance?
                                        Honour, I pray
And rescue one who worked, knew every aspect of night and day.
Would pray for death, beneath which Chance, Change; this life
Is horror, and bad horror. For here now no strife
With self or evil is possible, nor yet is brief
The minute. Pain or Wearing without relief.
                        Stone House
                        Dartford
                             Kent.
                        I. B. Gurney.[5]

AFTERMATH: 1937-1959

Memory, let all slip save what is sweet
Of Ypres plains.
Keep only autumn sunlight and the fleet
Clouds after rains.

Blue sky and mellow distance softly blue;
These only hold
Let I my panged grave share with you.
Else dead. Else cold.[1]

XVII

The funeral was a simple affair. Alfred Cheesman took the service, and Herbert Howells played the organ. Family and friends were there, and, rather to everyone's surprise, a sprinkling of civic dignitaries. When it was all over, Gerald Finzi described the scene to Howard Ferguson:

You'll have seen about Gurney — in fact, the press has given him in his death more attention in a week than they gave his life in 47 years. I thought the enclosed headlines from the Gloucester *Citizen* would amuse you, knowing what precious little attention his native city paid to him before. I went to his funeral, a sad little affair at Twigworth, and H.H. played 'Sleep' and 'Severn Meadows' on a wheezy little organ, whilst his brother Ronald stood by, looking exactly as though he had won a medal, so pleased, so complacent and high-collared! Poor Marion Scott, in tears at the end, but remarkably brave and calm considering how much it must have meant to her. And now for 'The Late Christopher Bean' all over again, for there's no doubt that the *Music and Letters* articles have really set the ball rolling and people are discovering that they had MSS. of his; that they knew him quite well 'and were always amazed at his genius'; that they visited him regularly when he was in the asylum; that they were his best friends, etc., etc. . . . .

But, Lord, I'm glad these articles came out before he died, even though he was practically beyond understanding what and whom they were about. It's been worth all the trouble and irritation and obstruction, (which reminds me, have you got the two Violin pieces yet?!) and something, however much in the background, I'm honestly proud to have done, since his own 'friends' hadn't the spirit to do it. . . .[2]

On the same day he wrote to Marion Scott, sending her the newspaper obituary that had so grated on his sense of fitness (the headline ran: 'One of Gloucester's Greatest Sons'!):

We were so very glad to be at Twigworth. Though I never knew Gurney, you know how much his work has always moved me, and I don't think that anything more beautiful exists than the best of it. I was glad to hear from Herbert that Ronald Gurney seemed to wish that he and Ivor could have started all over again. However, I'm afraid that it never has been, nor ever will be, possible to avoid such misunderstandings, when a radiant mind is born amongst sterile, unimaginative minds.

Finzi was by nature the soul of gentle kindness and understanding, a sensitive and imaginative composer whose response to literature was as deep as Gurney's own. He was not a man to rage against his fellows, but he had been sorely tried, and the events leading up to the publication of the *Music and Letters* symposium and the twenty O.U.P. songs had left a tincture of cynicism.

He had first come across Gurney through his music in 1920, when he himself was nineteen and a student. 'Sleep' seemed to him then, and ever after, 'one of the greatest songs of the world' and he lost no time in finding out what he could about its composer.

Distressed that so little of Gurney's work had reached publication, Finzi began to prod Marion Scott about the desirability of remedying the situation. On 25 February 1925, she wrote to him: 'So far I have not been able to see either Dr. Vaughan Williams or Mr. Plunket Greene about the idea we talked of for an edition of Gurney's songs . . .'. And a few months later (5 May): 'I am going to beg a great kindness. If I am asking too much please feel *no* hesitation in refusing, for the thing is a big job — nothing less than a request from me to you for help over making the string parts of Ivor Gurney's *Western Playland* . . .'. He agreed to help, gladly committing himself to the service of Gurney's music, though perhaps not guessing how long the task would take, or to what extent Marion Scott's ill-health and advancing years would oblige him to take charge. Nor could he have guessed that his youthful enthusiasm would eventually lead him into conflict with her instinctively more cautious approach.

Nothing was done in 1925, save the completion of the Carnegie project and the preparation of the six Edward Thomas songs, *Lights Out*, published by subscription in 1926. Thereafter interest lapsed. Marion Scott collected together such manuscripts as she could, but made no very sustained attempt to garner everything, and did nothing to catalogue or otherwise assess what she had.

Finzi returned to the attack in 1935, using as his excuse the publication of a biography of Sir Charles Stanford by Harry Plunket Greene and its friendly references to Gurney.[3] He suggested that *Music and Letters* might be willing to carry a symposium of articles on Gurney and his work, and that Vaughan Williams and Walter de la Mare ought to be among the first to be approached for a contribution. Marion Scott liked the idea and began to make tentative arrangements. She moved slowly, however, as muted enquiries from Finzi and his wife show:

14 June, 1935.
I wonder if anything has happened yet about the Gurney plan? Forgive me for worrying you, but I have just thought that we might get a 'benediction' similar to the one promised by Vaughan Williams from Masefield. If you approve I could tackle him through some friends, unless you would care to . . .

And again, in early August 1935: 'I wonder if you ever received my husband's letter asking you if you approved . . .'

Marion Scott replied on 21 August:

I feel infinitely sorry and apologetic that I have not written before. Yes: your letter did reach me, and I committed the error of waiting to reply hoping that I might have something more definite to say about the various plans for I.B.G's things. I simply don't know how to apologise sufficiently. The worst of it is too that I have not been able to do anything in the matter of approaching Mr. de la Mare . . . To be quite frank I had such a *desperately* rushed time all last spring and in the summer that I had only a certain amount of time which I could devote to I.B.G's affairs, and all that went on going to see him and interviewing doctors, etc., for he fell so sharply ill early in May that the Hospital people didn't know for a few days how things would go. Then after they got him better he had a relapse and was laid up again. I know it doesn't sound very heroic of me either to have to admit that I was so absolutely done up with the incessant work by day and loss of sleep at night due to the motor traffic in our road that I couldn't then tackle all that the projects for this campaign involve. So things drifted on, and eventually I just *had* to let them wait until I had had a holiday. No one regrets this more than myself. . . .

It never seems to have occurred to her that in Finzi she had a willing donkey to hand, ready to do all the work.

And so matters rested until 1937, when Finzi again brought the subject up, adding to it the pressing need to sort out, catalogue, and generally assess Gurney's manuscripts in the hope that some at least might prove to be worthy of publication. Despite her plea of illness and overwork, he persisted and was soon able to make a preliminary report:

30 January, 1937.
The sorting has been even more difficult than I expected, chiefly because there is comparatively little that one can really be sure is bad. Even the late 1925 asylum songs, though they get more and more involved (and at the same time more disintegrated, if you know what I mean) have a curious coherence about them somewhere, which makes it difficult to know if they are really over the border. I think the eventual difficulty in 'editing' the later Gurney may be great: a neat mind could smooth away the queernesses — like Rimsky-Korsakov with Mussorgsky — yet time and familiarity will probably show something not so mistaken, after all, about the queer and odd things. However, there are some obviously incoherent things and a good many others of which one can say that it would be better for them not to be published.

For the remainder, my crude and arbitrary method of grouping into √√ for good; √ good or adequate; (√× when I don't quite know my own mind); × bad; must seem ridiculous — like a Baedeker guide! Then again, a day and a half to go through more than a hundred songs, etc., is hardly the way to keep one's perspective, though I appreciate your insistence on having the MSS. back. So the groupings mustn't be taken too seriously, nor my trite little remarks, which are just quick first impressions. But at any rate here is the first rough sorting which may eventually be of some use to you. Perhaps you could keep this list with the ones already sorted, i.e. 3 portfolios and red binder. I should be grateful if the black binder could be left as it is, and then a little later on I should like to take it away again, together with the remaining MSS. (including the song with Stainer & Bell that you mentioned, if they are not going to do it) and so finish the work. As to what happens then, I've lots of suggestions, but had better leave them until we meet. Howard Ferguson's help has been invaluable. He reads so well — and Gurney's accompaniments *are* very awkward sometimes — and his sympathy and understanding of the work are half the battle. As a rule we entirely agree over the markings. . . .

There were a great many misprints. Dynamics are badly needed, but Ferguson thinks an 'urtext' is what is needed, with editorial markings in

brackets. You may be able to fill in missing dates and poets, as you collate
with other MSS.

Little by little, progress was made, and on 14 March Finzi was
able to tell Marion Scott:

We spent Friday with the V[aughan] W[illiams]'s, going through the
Gurney songs and, as a beginning, about 25 were chosen with a view to
making two books of 10 songs each. They would be sets, not cycles, but
even so, a certain amount of contrast would still have to be considered,
and the margin over the 20 would allow for any to be put in or taken
out, according to the needs of the sets. V.W. would like just to have
another look at the songs when we have got the 20 into a satisfactory
order. The ones left over — and there are plenty of good ones to form
other sets later on — I will return to you when I am next in London. . . .

It was these songs that went into the two volumes that were
with the printers when Gurney died; and it was Finzi's unremit-
ting efforts that formed the basis of the symposium that *Music
and Letters* produced to herald their publication. But by the time
that everything had been settled, Finzi permitted himself a singularly uncharacteristic outburst to Howard Ferguson:

15 August, 1937.
You'll be glad to hear that O.U.P. have agreed to publish the 20 Gurney
songs. Foss hopes to have them out at the same time as the *Music and
Letters* articles in Jan. It's terrible to think that all this might have been
done years ago, if his work had not been left in the hands of that possessive, incompetent, mulish old maid Marion Scott. You know the inside
of it all and how impossible she has been, but that was nothing to the
3 days Joy and I spent in London doing the final cataloguing. This had
been agreed on about a month before. The first thing we found was that
she had mislaid part of the *List 1* music. This turned up next day. Then
she had not even managed to get copies of the published work to put
with the complete works. She put every obstacle in the way of our
phoning the publishers, but we managed to get our way and the copies
arrived on the last day. Then, in the afternoon of the last day, I suggested
looking into that large wooden packing case in her room, which she
always assured me had nothing of importance in it. I bundled everything out on to the floor and found about 30 complete songs of G's best
period, dozens of notebooks, some with complete songs in, and a few
thousand papers of various MSS., including 'lost' Violin sonata movements and so on. Joy and I worked till about 9.30 that night — the

temperature of Maid Marion's room was 90° — and begged that we should be treated like the piano tuner and left alone, whilst the Scott family dined in state. It is incredible when you realise that everything was supposed to be ready for the cataloguing, sorted out and in order two months ago. But what can you expect from someone who hasn't 'had time' to copy out those two little Violin and Piano pieces you asked for nine months ago! I'm so polite to this fragile fool that I've not got the heart to remind her that I *made* time to copy out 24 of his songs in a month. However, the cataloguing seems to be done. 17 portfolios of coherent work and a chestful of asylum stuff, and its taken me about four years of incessant prodding to make the woman move. Now, she says, all the music must go back into the bank! I'm reminded of the little beetle in *The Insect Play*, guarding his pile. I think Howells and V.W. are quite right in feeling that she has an unconscious resentment against anything being done for Gurney unless it is done by herself, but beyond 'guarding the pile' she is incapable of doing anything. Now there'll be all the bother over again if the poems are ever to see the light. I forget whether I told you that Maid Marion, having promised to make a selection from the poems for de la Mare and his article (in *Music and Letters*) (she would not hear of Joy and me doing it — said it would be a nice quiet job for her when on holiday) sent him the whole collection, sane, incoherent, unsorted. Poor de la Mare. . . .

When finally the symposium appeared, backed up by two appreciative articles by Richard Capell in the *Telegraph* and, ironically, by the news of Gurney's death, the effect was decidedly encouraging. 'Press notices,' wrote Marion Scott, 'continue to pour in from all parts of England, Scotland, Wales and Ireland.' It would, she thought, 'have fairly staggered Ivor. I can almost hear him exclaim "Christopher!!" — which was his favourite ejaculation when astounded.'[4] The impression made by O.U.P.'s two volumes of songs was also encouraging and was followed by two broadcast programmes of his works, on 21 and 23 July, with Isobel Baillie and Sinclair Logan among the soloists. Thereafter sales were slow but steady, and little by little Gurney's reputation as one of England's finest song writers became an acknowledged fact of musical history.

Nevertheless, even though he had proved Gurney's genius, Finzi did not relax his efforts. He wanted to see more volumes of the songs and at least a selection of the poems in print. He began active work on the third volume of ten songs in 1941, but publication during wartime was out of the question and it was not until

August 1949 that any firm agreement was reached with O.U.P., and not until 1952 that the volume finally emerged from the press.

In the meantime steps were taken towards assembling and publishing a selection of the poems. Towards the end of 1945 Edmund Blunden was approached as a likely editor, but, despite his interest and enthusiasm, it proved impossible to get the project off the ground until 1951. And in that year the quest for a publisher began in earnest. Sidgwick and Jackson seemed the obvious choice, and for a time they made encouraging noises. Then Rupert Hart-Davis was approached; then Collins; then Hamish Hamilton. But while Hamish Hamilton were dallying, the firm of Hutchinson agreed to take a selection of Gurney's best unpublished poems, to be gathered together in a volume with a substantial biographical and critical introduction by Blunden. By June 1953 the matter was fixed.

Even so, there were problems. Would Marion Scott be fit enough to supply Blunden with biographical material? Would she, even, be willing to part with her memories? Gerald Finzi, writing to Blunden in Hong Kong on 23 August 1953, was far from certain:

I'll do my best to keep Marion Scott up to the mark. Prodding people is not a pleasant job, but I have had to do it to her for 20 years or so. Yet G. had no more devoted friend and would-be comforter. I still fail to understand why G's contemporaries, Howells, Arthur Benjamin and a few others, who truly recognized his worth, left his work in limbo and made no effort on its behalf, though they pay tributes enough now that it is in print. And in the case of the verse I think we all owe you a tremendous debt for doing what no one else seemed able or willing to undertake.

What you might do, sometime or other, is to let Richard Church know, if you haven't done so, the position about Marion Scott. It may be necessary for him to chivvy her, to bang on her door, so to speak, if things are held up. And to bang hard! There will always be an accident, or influenza by way of an answer, but one must be ruthless. And if he needs support, then he can write to me.

Yet she has befriended many generations of R.C.M. students in the past. Oddly enough I got the B.B.C. to do a work by my first teacher, a young man called Ernest Farrar, one of 'our rising young composers' who was slaughtered in your bloody war. Then I was about 14 and he just over 30. Now I am over 50 and he is still just over 30. Anyhow, it was from him that I first heard of M.S. and in those days she was young, delightful and even said to have love affairs!

But this time Marion Scott confounded everybody, for on Christmas Eve she died.

Ominous rumbles began to emerge from Gloucester almost immediately. Until this point Marion Scott had acted as Gurney's legal representative and had administered his estate. Tiresome and possessive as she was, she at least knew the value of what she was guarding. Now that possession had passed back to the family, there could no longer be any certainty that the manuscripts would be preserved or that permission for future publications would be granted.

The difficulties seem to have arisen quite simply and naturally out of the family's feeling that it had been cold-shouldered by those who were trying to bring Gurney's work to publication. Who were all these 'London people', with their posh accents, their education and money, who always knew what was best to be done and who obviously thought that ordinary Gloucester folk were scarcely one step removed from peasantry? It was not pleasant when strangers published articles about Gurney that implied that the family was 'poor' and 'uneducated' and 'unappreciative' of his genius.[5] It was not pleasant when bouncy American undergraduates lit upon his life and work as a suitable case for a thesis, complete with all the latest psychological theories and redolent with every kind of remote aesthetic jargon. It was not pleasant to reflect that Marion Scott had obtained her control over the manuscripts in exchange for the cancellation of the debt owed to her for her contribution towards his asylum expenses. Nor was it pleasant to think that she had tried to pass on that control by leaving her 'debt' to Gerald Finzi in her will. It was, in short, high time that all these intellectual fandangoes were called to a halt.

Finzi was worried. On 22 March 1954, he wrote anxiously to Edmund Blunden in Hong Kong:

I don't think the law has any hold over the next of kin who have letters of administration. The question of ownership of the MSS. may have to be gone into, but what I am doing at present is trying to undo what the lawyers have done (or rather the way they have done it) by making personal contact with Ronald Gurney and visiting him in Gloucester. He responded to my letter better than I had hoped and I shall visit him early in April. Meanwhile his sister (Winifred) is giving interviews to the local press and saying that someone ought to write her brother's life, etc., etc.

Evidently the talk succeeded, for the poems were published in the autumn of 1954 and Ronald astonished everybody by sending Blunden a copy for Christmas![6]

But the uncertainty continued, and when during the following year Finzi began to stir O.U.P.'s enthusiasm for a fourth volume of ten songs they met with Ronald Gurney's blank refusal to allow any further publications. On 2 August 1955, Finzi wrote to explain the situation to Edmund Blunden:

I then got old V.W. to write to him (Ronald) and point out his responsibility, even though, as a brother, he had a poor opinion of I.G. V.W. also offered to buy the MSS. R.G. made no reply. V.W. wrote again, and then again. After which R.G. replied that he did not consider his brother's work to be of any importance and that his reputation was based on the efforts of a few friends. He had asked an expert, who told him that his brother's work was not popular! (V.W. thought that the expert was probably a dance band musician or something of that sort.) But R.G. added that he *might* possibly give the MSS. to the Gloucester Public Library and V.W. replied taking this for granted, and telling him how good of him it was, and that he was writing to the public library to let them know. . . .

But for the time being nothing came of this ploy, and the manuscripts remained with the family and permission to publish was withheld.

And there the situation might have remained had not Gerald Finzi himself died, in September 1956. In the spring of the following year Joyce Finzi renewed the attack and early in May was able to tell O.U.P. that she had been to Gloucester and

. . . managed to bring back all the MSS. of the Ivor Gurney songs which my husband and Howard Ferguson marked very good and good when they went through and catalogued his work twenty years ago.

Ronald Gurney allowed me to do this to complete the work my husband started and which he was so keen to see completed. Though

Mr. Gurney seemed quite willing for the estate to bear the possible cost of copying (I assured him that Howard Ferguson would do his editing for love) he naturally didn't want to be involved in much expense. It is important at this stage to express every enthusiasm for the project without any qualifications!

The fourth volume was published in the summer of 1959. On 4 December Joyce Finzi telephoned Howard Ferguson in great elation. She had received a letter from Ronald Gurney and it read:

You will rejoice and your husband rest easier, to hear that today I handed over the Box complete, together with 4 published volumes of the O.U.P. and the 2 Carnegie Trust volumes, therein, to the Gloucester Reference Library on Permanent Loan. I have also handed over, separately, on likewise Permanent Loan, most of the Poems.

It was a noble gesture, and though Ronald Gurney was to live for many more years, and be troubled by many more people seeking information, he did nothing to disturb the manuscripts or make it impossible for other men to consider them and the strange, sad history they contain.

What did they expect of our toil and extreme
Hunger — the perfect drawing of a heart's dream?
Did they look for a book of wrought art's perfection,
Who promised no reading, nor praise, nor publication?
Out of the heart's sickness the spirit wrote
For delight, or to escape hunger, or of war's worst anger,
When the guns died to silence and men would gather sense
Somehow together, and find this was life indeed,
And praise another's nobleness, or to Cotswold get hence.
There we wrote — Corbie Ridge — or in Gonnehem at rest.
Or Fauquissart or world's death songs, ever the best.
One made sorrows' praise passing the Church where silence
Opened for the long quivering strokes of the bell —
Another wrote all soldiers' praise, and of France and night's stars,
Served his guns, got immortality, and died well.
But Ypres played another trick with its danger on me,
Yet still the needing and loving of action body;
Gave no candles, and nearly killed me twice as well,
And no souvenirs though I risked my life in the stuck tanks,
Yet there was praise of Ypres; love came sweet in hospital
And old Flanders went under to long ages of plays thought in my
    pages.[7]

CONCLUSION: 1977

Had I a song
I would sing it here
Four lined square shaped
Utterance dear.

But since I have none,
Well, regret in verse
Before the power's gone
Might be worse, might be worse.[1]

XVIII

Three questions remain. Two, concerning his achievements as a composer and poet, present few problems and might almost be dismissed with a simple and enthusiastic verdict. The third — the nature of his mental collapse, and its causes — can only be approached with circumspection, and answered, if at all, with the utmost diffidence. All three, however, must be tackled if any kind of assessment is to be made of Ivor Gurney's life and its significance.

Gurney's Mental State

A natural revulsion against all forms of military carnage has led most commentators on Gurney's asylum years to cast him in the role of 'war victim', laying the blame squarely on his experience in the trenches and citing gas and shell-shock as the final blows that crushed him. Such documentary evidence as we have, including his own autobiographical writings, does not support this diagnosis, but shows it rather to be simplistic and sentimental. The truth of the matter would seem to be far more complex, and buried deeper and more fundamentally in Gurney's own nature.

While it would be wrong to pretend that his war experiences were anything less than horrible, or that, like every soldier on those bloody fields, he was not deeply scarred by them, Gurney's letters from the front and his poetic re-enactment of the scene in later years have a buoyancy and an elation that transfigure even their bitterest and most disgusted moments. They do not read like the cry of a man at the end of his tether, but suggest that he had reached a considerable degree of detachment in accepting and absorbing the horrors. It is, of course, possible that once out of the front line, in hospital and free to recollect those horrors in tranquillity, Gurney suffered the kind of hysterical revulsion that the army liked to describe as 'shell-shock'; but again his letters and poems do not really bear this out. Their hallmark is a kind of stoic irony — not blank terror and despair.

What does recur throughout his writings is a sense of outrage that his sufferings have not brought the reward of fame and achievement that he always believed went hand in hand with 'pain'. This feeling of baffled anger — almost that of a child denied — dominates his asylum poetry and must surely represent a crucial element in those factors that led to his breakdown.

Yet, as we have seen, his actual achievement was considerable, and the degree to which it was acknowledged by performance and publication might have satisfied a lesser ego. But Gurney nursed the highest expectations of his talent and showed few signs of any realistic appreciation of its exact nature — its strengths, or its weaknesses. Moreover, the friends he made in his formative years were more noted for their warmth and affection than for any critical edge. It was all too easy to bask in the love and admiration of Cheesman and the Hunts and imagine yourself a great man. Significantly, when he came face to face with a truly critical artistic intelligence, in the shape of Sir Charles Stanford (and, one suspects, Dr. Herbert Brewer), he made very heavy weather of the situation.

Somewhere in between the critical and the admiring was Marion Scott, and her influence may ultimately have been the greatest and most helpful. Something to the good must also have come from F. W. Harvey and Herbert Howells.

In Gurney, of course, there were other influences of even longer standing. He was an exceptional and gifted child in an otherwise ordinary family. It was not a happy home and he took the earliest opportunity to transfer his affections — 'adopting', as it were, other people's families as his own. His mother, in particular, seems to have lacked a natural ability to show warmth and affection, and in consequence he sought this in close friendships with a series of maiden ladies old enough to have taken her place.

Sex, as such, does not appear to have entered his life in any serious way. His relationships with Margaret Hunt and Marion Scott were played out in terms of spiritual affinity, and even his 'passion' for Annie Nelson Drummond has a marked air of unreality (though the memory lasted long enough for him to dedi-

cate later poems and music, cryptically, to 'Hawthornden').[2]
Arthur Benjamin, a close acquaintance and himself a well-
integrated homosexual, believed that Gurney bore the same
inflexion but never recognized the fact.[3] Herbert Howells, an
even closer friend, found the notion 'unthinkable', and declared
that Gurney 'would have died first'.[4] Their opinions are not,
however, mutually contradictory, and one is led to the conclusion that sex simply did not enter Gurney's calculations in any
shape or form.

Immature, or at least negative, in sexual matters, he was also
singularly ill at ease with his own body in general terms. From
quite early years he was plagued by digestive troubles, aggravated
by erratic eating habits, and these grew worse as he grew older.
Enemas are mentioned frequently in his writings and seem to
have been a regular feature of his daily routine — a 'timetable'
scribbled in the back of a notebook belonging to about 1921
reads: '7–8.30 Preparation, 9–5 Office, 5.30–9.30 Walking,
9.30–11 Aunt, 11 Enemas.' It is also just possible that he was in
some way punished for indulging in them during one of his army
hospitalization periods.

Asylum writings make frequent reference to the need to 'wash
my body' (the more sensual word 'lave' occurs also), and, with
other references, suggest a very considerable degree of self-
disgust. The need to obtain physical fitness is also a recurring
motif, coupled with an admiration for that type of animal well-
being he found in many of his army comrades: an admiration not
without its homo-erotic overtones, but probably best thought of
as the natural envy of a mental man for the purely physical and
uncomplicated.

All this suggests a type of mind and body that found it difficult
to reach a state of equilibrium and self-acceptance, and which
was in no way aided by a satisfactory emotional life. In such circumstances the advent of schizophrenic psychosis is scarcely
surprising.

The condition of paranoid schizophrenia is thought to be
largely determined by genetic factors. It may lie dormant, or only
mildly in evidence, for many years and then manifest itself for no
other reason than the passage of time.[5] In Gurney's case, pro-
longed bouts of depression were a feature of his adult life. Often,
as in 1913, they followed a period of intense creativity — a

vacuum, as it were, following the sudden release of pressure. They seem to have been held at bay during his years in the trenches — largely, one suspects, by the distraction of external events — but to have become more frequent as soon as he returned to England and began to pick up the creative threads in earnest, and in some desperation to cash the accumulated balance of his suffering. It is arguable that these episodes were not separate, but periodic relapses which finally led to a more constant abnormal state of mind. The delusions which he then suffered are typical of paranoid schizophrenia.[6]

It is for reasons such as these, evident in a wealth of tiny biographical detail amply documented in his letters and poems, that Gurney's mental troubles may reasonably be attributed to some basic defect in the brain chemistry — aggravated, or even caused by his erratic and singularly unhealthy eating habits. Illness would have declared itself, war or no war.[7]

Nor is it possible to ignore evidence that suggests that his mother may have suffered from a similar disposition, though to a much lesser degree. Her apparent inability to show affection accords very well with the known symptoms of latent schizophrenia.[8] Bearing in mind her capacity for creating family tension, her extremely vivid and imaginative style of letter-writing, and her lack of maternal warmth, Florence Gurney may have passed on to her son all the essential ingredients of his genius and his undoing.

Gurney, it would seem, was marked out from birth for mental problems. But it is no comfort to reflect that modern drug therapy might have controlled his behaviour sufficiently to have made asylum unnecessary, and that, as a relatively free man, his creative powers might have remained intact for at least a few more years.

Gurney, the Poet

Surviving manuscripts indicate that between about 1913 and 1926 Ivor Gurney wrote nearly 900 poems. The two volumes published during his lifetime contain 46 and 58 poems respectively, and a handful of individual poems appeared in various magazines, mostly during his years in the asylum. Edmund Blunden's 1954 volume contained 78 new poems taken from manuscripts of all periods. A selection of 140 poems from all these sources (including

73 from unpublished manuscripts, and 10 that had appeared only in magazines) was published in 1973 under the editorship of Leonard Clark. Of the 600 or so unpublished poems, a further selection could be made with confidence — though it is fair to say that the bulk is not publishable, except perhaps as evidence of a disintegrating mind.

At a conservative estimate, then, Gurney was the author of at least 300 viable poems, and a great many of these are of the highest quality. He wore the title 'War Poet' with enormous pride, and certainly came in the end to understand that his literary gifts were out of the ordinary. Yet he never doubted (or had reason to doubt) that his true vocation was music, or that it was the supreme form of all self-expression. In an unpublished essay entitled 'The Springs of Music', written some time in the twenties, he made his attitude quite clear: for in talking about Wordsworth's *The Prelude* he says:

(it) is but the shadow and faint far-off indication of what Music might do — the chief use of Poetry seeming to be, to one perhaps mistaken musician, to stir the spirit to the height of music, the maker to create, the listener worthily receive or remember. . . .

and later, commenting on his own creativity, he wrote that 'the brighter visions brought music; the fainter, verse or mere pleasurable emotion.'

Though first prompted into writing poetry seriously by expediency, publication and a degree of success nourished his ambition and, whether he ever quite acknowledged the fact, it soon became a form of expression parallel to and almost as important as the composition of music. Gurney thus joins that select band of artists whose creative outlet found more than one effective channel.

That it was a genuine gift, and not merely a stop-gap alternative, is perhaps best demonstrated by the clear progression of style from the poems in *Severn and Somme* — some awkward and technically immature, some fluent but commonplace, a few undeniably fine, but nearly all derivative — to the poetry he wrote after the war. Development on this scale would not have been possible to anyone who merely dabbled in the art.

Quite what influenced this growth, other than the maturing

fires of the front line, is difficult to say, for Gurney's enthusiasm for poetry (and music, for that matter) seldom seems to have led to speculation about technical matters. When commenting on the work of other men it is their feeling for 'beauty' that impressed him, and not their grasp of technique. Nevertheless, he certainly absorbed influences, and two of the most obvious in helping to bring about his mature style were those of Walt Whitman and Gerard Manley Hopkins.

He came across both in the trenches: Whitman through a pocket edition, sent out by Marion Scott, and Hopkins through the samples included in Bridges' *The Spirit of Man* (1916). He is also known to have been introduced to the first collected edition of Hopkins (1918) by his friend John Haines. But such effect as they had on his writing was rather to confirm the validity of a naturally 'loose' manner of expression than to stimulate an active concern for technical experiment. Thoughts about the nature of 'sprung rhythm' or the problems of 'free verse' do not seem to have interested him in any real sense. He was a poet and composer of instinct rather than calculation; and this is one reason why he is so difficult to categorize.

Two features stand out most obviously in contributing to what Blunden aptly described as Gurney's 'gnarled' poetic style.[9] One is his cavalier way with punctuation, which, as it stands, is often crucially misleading to the unprepared reader. This, presumably, would have been tidied up in due course — as it was, at Marion Scott's insistence, in the case of the volumes published during his lifetime. The other concerns his tendency to omit minor but important connecting words and generally to telescope his thought so that the meaning becomes ambiguous and even totally obscure. Both indicate a certain impatience under pressure of utterance, as well as an unwillingness to revise, polish and bring to perfection through painstaking self-criticism. Both, to some extent, can be remedied by reading the poem aloud — clear indication that he tended to write by sound rather than by sense. But both, exasperatingly, give to his work at least part of its individuality, and thus cannot easily be 'corrected' without destroying more than is gained.

To what extent either is to be attributed to a genuine 'style', or merely to a mind innately inclined to make sudden, inconsequential leaps — a kind of stutter in the thought process, due perhaps to incipient mental disturbance — is, however, another matter and is as difficult to disentangle as any of the properties of genius.

The range of matters that came under Gurney's poetic observation is very considerable. High on the list of priorities was his acute awareness of nature. What interested him were the ordinary, everyday things, made extraordinary by the very fact that they passed, for the most part, unnoticed:

> One comes across the strangest things in walks:
> Fragments of Abbey tithe-barns fixed in modern,
> And Dutch-sort houses where the water baulks
> Weired up, and brick kilns broken among fern,
> Old troughs, great stone cisterns bishops might have blessed
> Ceremonially, and worthy mounting-stones;
> Black timber in red brick, queerly placed
> Where Hill stone was looked for — and a manor's bones
> Spied in the frame of some wisteria's house,
> And mill-falls and sedge pools and Saxon faces
> Stream-sources happened upon in unlikely places,
> And Roman-looking hills of small degree
> And the surprise of dignity of poplars
> At a road end, or the white Cotswold scars,
> Or sheets spread white against the hazel tree.
> Strange the large difference of Up Cotswold ways;
> Birdlip climbs bold and treeless to a bend,
> Portway to dim wood-lengths without an end,
> And Crickley goes to cliffs are the crown of days.[10]

The omission of the word 'that' in the final line is very typical — but whether it reflects the influence of Hopkins, or merely indicates a lapse in Gurney's attention is open to argument!

In none of these country poems does he romanticize his subject. Though he can go into ecstasies over the beauties of his beloved Cotswolds and Severn Plain, he does so with a countryman's true clarity of vision. Like John Clare, he knows too much about the countryside to be tempted into sentimentality. Often his observation has a child-like quality:

> The ordered curly and plain cabbages
> Are all set out like school-children in rows;
> In six short weeks shall these no longer please,
> For with that ink-proud lady the rose, pleasure goes.

I cannot think what moved the poet men
So to write panegyrics of that foolish
Simpleton — while wild-rose as fresh again
Lives, and the drowsed cabbages keep soil coolish.[11]

Again, one is left wondering at such words as 'coolish'. A stroke
of genius, or merely a reach-me-down rhyme for 'foolish'? But a
further examination of the veiled alliteration in the last line, the
admirable choice of 'drowsed', the cunning interior rhymes in
lines 3, 4, and 6, suggest that Gurney's ear was remarkably in
tune with his vision. The entire poem, however, stands as an
example of the way in which his meaning can sometimes elude
final definition, even though at a casual reading it may seem to be
quite clear.

Nature, too, can be read as a lesson — as in 'Generations'. It
is one of his finest and most concentrated poems, extraordinarily
in advance of its time (the use of the word 'prudent', for example, uncannily anticipates W. H. Auden):

The ploughed field and the fallow field
They sang a prudent song to me;
We bide all year and take our yield
Or barrenness as case may be.

What time or tide may bring to pass
Is nothing of our reckoning,
Power was before our making was
That had in brooding thought its spring.

We bide our fate as best betides
What ends the tale may prove the first.
Stars know as truly of their guides
As we the truth of best or worst.[12]

This quality of modernity, a laconic, unsentimental statement of
observed facts, transmuted into poetry by force and concentration of expression and a very exact choice of words, comes very
much to the fore in those poems in which Gurney re-enacted his
war experiences. In, for example, 'The Silent One', he encap-
sulates the patient suffering of all conscripted fighters — black
ironic humour their only protection against a stupidity and horror

that goes almost too deep for the devices of literature. Measured against this most truthful report from the battlefield, even Wilfred Owen's work can seem a shade contrived and literary. Gurney, obsessed with poets past and present, could write as if poetry had never existed before and he were inventing it from scratch out of the raw materials of his experience:

The Silent One

Who died on the wires, and hung there, one of two —
Who for his hours of life had chattered through
Infinitely lovely chatter of Bucks accent:
Yet faced unbroken wires; stepped over, and went
A noble fool, faithful to his stripes — and ended.
But I, weak, hungry, and willing only for the chance
Of line — to fight in the line, lay down under unbroken
Wires, and saw the flashes and kept unshaken,
Till the politest voice — a finicking accent, said:
'Do you think you might crawl through, there: there's a hole.'
Darkness, shot at: I smiled, as politely replied —
'I'm afraid not, Sir.' There was no hole no way to be seen
Nothing but chance of death, after tearing of clothes.
Kept flat, and watched the darkness, hearing bullets whizzing —
And thought of music — and swore deep heart's deep oaths
(Polite to God) and retreated and came on again,
Again retreated — and a second time faced the screen.[13]

Comparison of such poems as this and, for example, 'Bohemians' (pp. 90-1) with those he published in *Severn and Somme* and *War's Embers* — like, for example, the Rupert Brookeish sonnet 'Now, Youth' (p. 56) and the much more deeply felt 'To his Love' (p. 117), still heavily indebted to the pastoral literary tradition, however — is instructive. It is as if the reality of war had burned away all artifice and exposed the naked poetry of daily experience. Even the sonnet form emerges clearer and more meaningful from such refining fires:

Butchers and Tombs

After so much battering of fire and steel
It had seemed well to cover them with Cotswold Stone —
And shortly praising their courage and quick skill
Leave them buried, hidden till the slow, inevitable

Change should make them service of France alone.
But the time's hurry, the commonness of the tale,
Made it a thing not fitting ceremonial,
And so the disregarders of blister on heel,
Pack on shoulder, barrage and work at the wires,
One wooden cross had for ensign of honour and life gone —
Save when the Gloucesters turning sudden to tell to one
Some joke, would remember and say — 'That joke is done',
Since he who would understand was so cold he could not feel,
And clay binds hard, and sandbags get rotten and crumble.[14]

The part of Gurney's poetry that is concerned with his sufferings at Barnwood and Dartford varies very considerably in quality.
Sometimes the pain is so acute that the outcry can scarcely be
held in poetic form. Examples such as 'Why have You made life so
intolerable' are given in this book (pp. 162-3). In others the form
collapses altogether, and the outcome is interesting only as naked
autobiography and not as poetry in any absolute sense. But certain earlier pieces, written when he was aware that collapse was
imminent, harness the same laconic, everyday turn of speech that
makes his war poems so memorable. Who else, in the twenties,
was making poetry (genuine poetry, not merely squibs to frighten
the middle classes in Sitwellian fashion) out of such uncompromis-
ingly ordinary ingredients?

Old Tale
If one's heart is broken twenty times a day,
What easier thing to fling the bits away
But still one gathers fragments, and looks for wire,
Or patches it up like some old bicycle tire.

Bicycle tires fare hardly on roads, but the heart
Has a longer time than rubber. They sheath a cart
With iron; so lumbering and slow my mind must be made —
To bother the heart and to teach things and learn it its trade.[15]

In comparison, the 'realism' of Brooke and the early Georgians is
contrived and self-conscious: born of the study and not of
experience.

While it would be wrong to claim for Ivor Gurney the status
of a neglected *major* poet, it would seem reasonable to suggest

that he is a minor master of very considerable accomplishment whose work does not deserve to be overlooked. The chief obstacle in the way of an appreciation of his finest coherent works lies less in their occasional oddities of manner and syntax than in their autobiographical reference. To understand the poetry it is essential to know something of the life — and it is for this reason that the present book has been given its slightly unorthodox shape. Possibly the most damning criticism that can be levelled against Gurney's poetry is that it seldom becomes so completely externalized as to stand on its own feet. Yet having made the charge, it is impossible not to recognize that this weakness is also a source of strength and individuality. In a very real sense, poetry was for Ivor Gurney a form of therapy — but it is also true poetry.

Gurney, the Composer

Taken item for item, Gurney certainly wrote rather more poems than individual pieces of music. But comparison on such a basis is misleading, for the complexity of even a short piece of music is much greater than that of the average poem, and it can be fairly argued that his achievement as a composer is even greater than his achievement as a poet. It is no accident that his finest songs won an almost immediate acceptance as classics of their kind.

In all, the manuscripts of some 265 songs have survived.[16] Of these, eighty-two have been published — including the four major cycles: the 'Elizas', *Lights Out*, *Ludlow and Teme*, and *The Western Playland*. The present writer considers that four more songs, requiring a minimum of editorial interference, are immediately publishable; and that perhaps another dozen or so might be salvaged, assuming that considerable editorial licence were thought permissible. Thus, approximately one-third of his song output has artistic validity: the remainder being of curiosity value only. It seems an unimpressive total — until one remembers that the list contains some of the finest songs written by any English composer, and that the total song output of Peter Warlock (justly famed as a 'great' song writer, with a rather longer creative life than Gurney's) amounts to little more than a hundred songs.

The situation with regard to his instrumental music is less cheering. The quantity is there, but quality is largely absent. Manuscripts exist of 2 piano sonatas, and some three dozen piano pieces or separate sonata movements; there are 7 complete (or nearly complete) sonatas for violin and piano, 9 separate movements and a dozen short violin and piano pieces. There is a string trio, most of a piano trio, 4 complete string quartets and half a dozen separate quartet movements; five choral works; and two pieces for orchestra, the 'Coronation' March, and the 'Gloucestershire Rhapsody'. Of these, two sets of piano pieces (*Five Western Watercolours* and *Five Preludes*) and two short pieces for violin and piano have been published. The remainder, as we shall see, is unpublishable. Even the published pieces are of little account.

Gurney's reputation as a composer must, therefore, stand or fall by his songs, and we may fairly ask what it is that distinguishes them from those of his contemporaries and immediate successors.

The earliest of his mature songs, the group known as the 'Elizas', dates from 1912. The last which can be called completely coherent were composed in 1922 — for his ability to control musical thought slipped from his grasp rather sooner than his control over language. The bulk of his finest songs belong to the years between 1918 and 1922, his output rising to a peak in 1919 and 1920 of about 50 songs a year. A sudden outburst of 50 or more songs occurred in 1925, but by that time he had lost the power to express his ideas in any sustained, coherent way.

One of the most immediately striking features of Gurney's work as a song composer is his choice of words. A handful of 'obvious' poets are represented: Shakespeare, Herrick, Ben Jonson, John Fletcher, Walt Whitman — men whose lyrics it is almost impossible for an Englishman to avoid setting to music. So too, for the period, is the considerable presence of A. E. Housman (nineteen settings in all). But unlike most of his fellow composers, Gurney was drawn to his contemporaries, many of whom could be classed as 'Georgians'. The list is formidable, and taken in order of numerical prevalence includes: Edward Thomas, Robert Bridges, W. B. Yeats, Wilfrid Gibson, Walter de la Mare, F. W. Harvey, Bliss Carman, W. H. Davies, Edward Shanks, Hilaire Belloc, Robert Graves, Rupert Brooke, John Masefield, Thomas Hardy, J. C. Squire, John Freeman, John Haines, James Elroy Flecker, William Kerr, Edmund Blunden,

John Davidson, Ralph Hodgson, John Drinkwater, and Francis Ledwidge.

The subject matter which stirred his imagination is also very varied. It ranges from the powerfully dramatic ('Edward' and 'The Twa Corbies') to the philosophical contemplation of life and death ('Even such is Time' and 'By a Bierside'); from the muted love song ('Thou didst delight mine eyes') to the passionate nostalgia of 'Severn Meadows'; from pastoral elegy ('The Latmian Shepherd') to the rumbustious and rather commonplace heartiness of 'Captain Stratton's Fancy'. Provided only that the poem suggested melody, Gurney, it seems, could respond with equal felicity over a very wide range of emotions.

As with his poetry, the question of influences is not easy to pin down. Very early unpublished songs reflect the kind of music he heard in Gloucester — everything from drawing-room ballads to the prettier morsels of Grieg and Brahms. And Brahms's hefty piano textures crop up as an influence even in some of his later efforts — as in 'Edward' or the setting of Robin Flower's 'A Sword', both worked for their drama and grim power.

For the most part, however, the influence that might have been anticipated — Schubert — is conspicuous only by its absence, even though his admiration for the composer was immense. Gurney's whole approach to song was more French than German. Neither in his vocal lines nor his piano parts was he interested in finding out melodic shapes to illustrate individual words or dramatic situations. His songs are not miniature symphonic poems, even though they always catch the necessary atmosphere. It is the overall response that takes precedence, not the response to detail. Indeed, his preferred method of composition might lead one to expect just such an approach, for he was accustomed to absorb each poem and then set it to music entirely from memory. In the process he often contrived to 'rewrite' a word here and there!

The typical Gurney song projects long, flexible vocal lines against a warm harmonic background, which is animated by unobtrusive piano figuration. Controlling this wash of delicate sound calls for subtle playing and a degree of sympathetic interpretation not always catered for in the composer's markings.

A very few of his songs depend on self-contained vocal melody — 'Down by the Salley Gardens' is one. By far the greater number allow for a subtle give and take between voice and piano. The vocal line is 'melodic', in the sense that it flows naturally and is very singable: but its melody is wayward and only kept under control by its relationship to the piano accompaniment. 'Accompaniment', in fact, is not the most apt word for Gurney's piano parts: voice and piano are part of a unified texture.

Though certain songs employ very simple harmonies in keeping with simple thoughts — as, for example, 'Nine of the Clock' — the generality make use of a wide range of soft discords — sevenths, ninths, and so forth — which provide the kind of rich, warm, romantic palette that is in tune with his whole approach to piano writing. Enharmonic changes abound, and his harmonic schemes often involve extreme modulation — from which he extricates himself sometimes with great dexterity, and sometimes only by means of a desperate jerk. The harmonic style is, in essence, rhapsodic — with all the virtues and shortcomings implied by that very 1920ish predilection!

It would be wrong to pretend that Gurney's songs are without blemish — though the faults often seem such an integral part of his style that any editorial attempt to smooth out the difficulties only detracts from the overall effect. His songs are like his poems — 'gnarled' and full of quirks. But once the style has been understood, it seems inevitable and right.

The problems mainly concern over-elaborate piano textures in which far too many notes chase around the keyboard without any very obvious sense of direction. Allied to this is a tendency to allow a rhapsodic manner to degenerate into general aimlessness. There is also a factor that pulls in the opposite direction — a tendency, paralleled in the syntax of his poetry, to telescope events so that modulation, in particular, is achieved under pressure and is guaranteed, sometimes, by only the most tenuous link.

Significantly, when Gurney was required to think in terms of instrumental textures — as for example in the five 'Elizas', which were originally designed for a small chamber ensemble — these faults almost totally disappear. And when circumstances forced him to take a less self-indulgent approach — as in those songs he wrote actually in the trenches — the textures are instantly braced and made purposeful. The piano, it would seem, could betray him into inspired improvization at the expense of positive musical thought.

These, however, are problems that can be surmounted by imaginative interpretation and do not invalidate the very powerful and individual quality of his music.

Of the major cycles, the 'Elizas' is almost perfect, and one song ('Sleep') has entered the repertoire of nearly all singers. 'Lights Out' is a less satisfactory venture, displaying too many of Gurney's weaknesses for comfort. The two Housman cycles are scored for piano and string quartet. One, *Ludlow and Teme*, manages this notoriously tricky combination with great tact and is an extremely effective cycle. The other, *The Western Playland*, is less well managed: the textures are far too busy and self-defeating, and the cycle is finished off, disastrously, by a singularly vague instrumental coda. It is possible that had Gurney maintained his mental stability some of the problems would have been ironed out, at the insistence of his publisher or on the advice of his friends; but, as it is, they remain to weaken what in other respects is a very fine cycle.

It is interesting, however, to compare both with Vaughan Williams's *On Wenlock Edge* — written for a similar combination and using several of the same poems. Though it lacks something of Gurney's spring-like lyrical freshness, Vaughan Williams's work triumphs because it is a true cycle, linked emotionally and dramatically in one great and purposeful arc — music spun from a genuinely symphonic cast of mind.

This, as his instrumental music makes all too clear, is a quality of mind that Gurney lacked. While the song writer could depend on another man's verse to provide a formal framework for his musical thoughts, the instrumental writer was at the mercy of his rhapsodic inclinations. Despite excellent initial ideas, his sonatas and quartets, without exception, degenerate into note-spinning. The shorter pieces necessarily fare better, but most of them are early and do not represent his mature voice. Examples of these weaknesses can be seen in the handful of published pieces, of which the *Five Preludes* are probably the most effective, even though they echo Chopin and to some extent Scriabin, and show little of the true Gurney individuality. The *Five Western Watercolours* are featureless and frankly dull, and neither of the two short violin and piano pieces ('Apple Orchard' and 'Scherzo') should have been published at all (Marion Scott's piety here did Gurney a disservice).

We are left, then, with a song composer: somewhat flawed, but undeniably individual and certainly touched with genius. His finest songs have a rightness that cannot be challenged, and because of this he must be admitted to the galaxy of great British song composers and take his place, where, we may suppose, he would have wished, alongside such names as Dowland, Parry, Warlock, Finzi, and Britten. For a man whose life and work was played out against such appalling difficulties, it is no small achievement.

They will walk there, the sons of our great grandsons and
Will know no reason for the old love of the land.
There will be no tiny bent-browed houses in the
Twilight to watch, nor small shops of multi-miscellany.
The respectable and red-brick will rule all,
With green paint railings outside the front door wall,
And children will not play skip-games in the gutter,
Nor dust fly furious in hot valour of footer;
Queerness and untidiness will be smoothed out
As any steam-roller tactful, and there'll be no doubt
About the dust bins or the colour of curtains,
No talking at the doors, no ten o'clock flirtings,
And Nicholas will look as strange as any
Goddess ungarmented in that staid company,
With lovely attitude of fixéd grace,
But naked and embarrassed in the red brick place.
We see her well, and should have great thanksgiving,
Living in sight and form of more than common living.
She is a City still and the centuries drape her yet;
Something in the air or light cannot or will not forget
The past ages of her, and the toil which made her,
The courage of her, the army that made not afraid her,
And a shapely fulness of being drawn maybe from the air
Crystal or mellow about her or above her ever:
Record of desire apparent of dreamer or striver,
And still the house between the Cotswolds bare
And the Welsh wars; Mistress of the widening river.[17]

— I hAVE RECORDING

Appendix

Gurney's Published Works

MUSIC

Oxford University Press

SONGS

Volume 1 (1938)

'The Singer'	Edward Shanks	1919
'The Latmian Shepherd'	Edward Shanks	1920
'Black Stitchel'	Wilfrid Gibson	1920
'Down by the Salley Gardens'	W. B. Yeats	1920
'All night under the moon'	Wilfrid Gibson	1918
'Nine of the Clock'	John Doyle*	1920
'You are my sky'	J. C. Squire	1920
'Ha'nacker Mill'	Hilaire Belloc	1920
'When death to either shall come'	Robert Bridges	1920
'Cathleen ni Houlihan'	W. B. Yeats	1919

Volume 2 (1938)

'The Scribe'	Walter de la Mare	1918
'The boat is chafing'	John Davidson	1920
'Bread and cherries'	Walter de la Mare	1921
'An Epitaph'	Walter de la Mare	1920
'Blaweary'	Wilfrid Gibson	1921
'A Sword'	Robin Flower	1922
'The folly of being comforted'	W. B. Yeats	1917
'Hawk and Buckle'	John Doyle*	1920
'Last Hours'	John Freeman	1919
'Epitaph in an old mode'	J. C. Squire	1920

*Robert Graves's pseudonym

Volume 3 (1952)

'Shepherd's song'	Ben Jonson	1919
'The happy tree'	Gerald Gould	1920
'The cherry trees'	Edward Thomas	1920
'I shall ever be maiden'	Bliss Carman	1919
'Ploughman singing'	John Clare	1920
'I praise the tender flower'	Robert Bridges	1912
'Snow'	Edward Thomas	1921
'Thou didst delight mine eyes'	Robert Bridges	1921
'The Ship'	J. C. Squire	1920
'Goodnight to the meadows'	Robert Graves	1920

Volume 4 (1957)

'Even such is Time'	Walter Raleigh	1917
'Brown is my love'	Anon 16th century	1920
'Love shakes my soul'	Bliss Carman	1920
'Most holy night'	Hilaire Belloc	1920
'To Violets'	Robert Herrick	1920
'Up on the Downs'	John Masefield	1919
'A Piper'	Seumas O'Sullivan	1920
'A cradle song'	W. B. Yeats	1920
'The Fiddler of Dooney'	W. B. Yeats	1917
'In Flanders'	F. W. Harvey	1917

Volume 5 (forthcoming 1979)

'Walking song'*	F. W. Harvey	1919
'Desire in Spring'*	Francis Ledwidge	1918
'The fields are full'*	Edward Shanks	1919
'Severn Meadows'*	Ivor Gurney	1917
'The Twa Corbies'*	Ballad	1914
'The night of Trafalgar'	Thomas Hardy	1913
'The cloths of heaven'	W. B. Yeats	1919
'By a Bierside'	John Masefield	1917
'The isle of peace'	Ethna Carbery	1911
'The apple orchard'	Bliss Carman	1919

INSTRUMENTAL MUSIC

Two pieces for violin and piano (1940)

1. 'The Apple Orchard'	1919
2. 'Scherzo'	1919

*Published separately, 1927-8

Stainer and Bell

SONG CYCLES

Ludlow and Teme	A. E. Housman	1920

(Baritone, string quartet, and piano
Carnegie Collection of British Music 1923)
    'When smoke stood up from Ludlow'
    'Far in a Western brookland'
    ' 'Tis time, I think'
    'Ludlow Fair'
    'On the idle hill of summer'
    'When I was one and twenty'
    'The Lent Lily'

The Western Playland	A. E. Housman	1921

(Tenor, string quartet, and piano
Carnegie Collection of British Music 1926)
    'Reveille'
    'Loveliest of trees'
    'Golden friends'
    'Twice a week'
    'The Aspens'
    'Is my team ploughing?'
    'The Far Country'
    'March'

Lights Out (1926)	Edward Thomas	1918–25

    'The Penny Whistle'
    'Scents'
    'Bright clouds'
    'Lights out'
    'Will you come?'
    'The Trumpet'

INDIVIDUAL SONGS

'Edward' (1922)	Ballad	1914
'Star-talk' (1927)	Robert Graves	1920
'Sowing' (1925)	Edward Thomas	1918
'Captain Stratton's Fancy' (1920)	John Masefield	1914

INSTRUMENTAL MUSIC (piano)

Five Western Watercolours (1923)		1920

Winthrop Rogers (now Boosey and Hawkes)

INDIVIDUAL SONGS

'Under the greenwood tree'*	Shakespeare	1912
'Orpheus'*	Shakespeare	1912
'Spring'*	Thomas Nashe	1912
'Tears'*	John Fletcher	1912
'Sleep'*	John Fletcher	1912
'The County Mayo' (1921)	James Stephens	1918
'The Bonnie Earl of Murray' (1921)	Ballad	1918

INSTRUMENTAL MUSIC (piano)

Five Preludes (1921)	1919–20

Boosey and Hawkes

INDIVIDUAL SONGS

'Carol of the Skiddaw Yowes' (1920)	Ernest Casson	1919
'I will go with my father a-ploughing' (1921)	Seosman Mac Cathmhaoil	1921
'Come, O come my life's delight' (1922)	Thomas Campion	1922?
'Since thou, O fondest and truest' (1921)	Robert Bridges	1921

Chappell

INDIVIDUAL SONG

'West Sussex Drinking Song' (1921)	Hilaire Belloc	1921

POEMS

Severn and Somme (Sidgwick & Jackson, 1917, reprinted 1919).

War's Embers (Sidgwick & Jackson, 1919).

Poems by Ivor Gurney, with a memoir by Edmund Blunden (Hutchinson, 1954).

Poems of Ivor Gurney, 1890–1937, with an Introduction by Edmund Blunden and a Bibliographical Note by Leonard Clark (Chatto & Windus, 1973).

*All published in 1920 as separate songs but regarded by Gurney as a cycle, the 'Elizas'.

Bibliography

PRIMARY PUBLISHED SOURCES

Edmund Blunden, 'memoir' in *Poems by Ivor Gurney* (Hutchinson, 1954), pp. 9–16. Reprinted in *Poems of Ivor Gurney* (Hutchinson, 1973).

Leonard Clark, bibliographical note in *Poems of Ivor Gurney* (Hutchinson, 1973), pp. 27–32.

Howard Ferguson, preface to *Gurney Songs*, Vol. 4 (Oxford University Press, 1957).

Ivor Gurney 'symposium', *Music and Letters*, Vol. XIX, No. 1, January 1938, pp. 1–17. Containing articles by Harry Plunket Greene, Marion Scott, Sir John Squire, Walter de la Mare, Edmund Blunden, Ralph Vaughan Williams, and Herbert Howells.

Marion M. Scott, prefaces to *Gurney Songs*, Vols 1–3 (Oxford University Press, 1938 and 1952). 'Ivor Gurney: Musician and Poet', the *Monthly Musical Record*, January 1938, pp. 41–46.

William H. Trethowan, *The Brain and Music*, Ch. 23 (pp. 416–18 especially) (Heinemann, 1977).

Helen Thomas, 'Memoir of Ivor Gurney', the *R.C.M. Magazine*, Vol. LVI, No. 1, Easter Term 1960, pp. 10–11. Reprinted in the *Musical Times*, No. 1414, December 1960, p. 754, and in *Time and Again* (Carcanet Press, 1978).

SECONDARY PUBLISHED SOURCES

Mervyn Burtch, 'Ivor Gurney: a revaluation', the *Musical Times*, October 1953, pp. 528–30.

Charles W. Moore, 'Ivor Gurney, English Poet in Song', the *Nats Bulletin*, Vol. XX, No. 3, February 1964, pp. 12–14. *Ivor Gurney, poet and songwriter* (Triad Press, 1976).

Notes

The chief source of material for any study of the life and work of Ivor Gurney is contained in the Ivor Gurney Archive in the City of Gloucester Public Library. This consists of his music manuscripts; the manuscripts of his poems, together with copies made by Marion Scott (and others), and typed copies by Mr. and Mrs. Gerald Finzi; an extensive collection of his letters; letters and documents relating to his medical history and to the publication of his work; and a general miscellany of smaller items, including a number of photographs. At the time of writing, this collection had not been catalogued, and it will therefore not be possible to identify the present references in anything but a very general way.

The second source of material consists of personal interviews conducted by the author over a period between 1963 and 1977. These were frequently backed up by letters and written autobiographical statements. This material will eventually be placed in the Ivor Gurney Archive.

A detailed analysis of Gurney's medical history has been undertaken by William H. Trethowan, Professor of Psychiatry at the University of Birmingham, in a paper entitled 'Ivor Gurney's Illness', which, it is hoped, will soon be published.

Though it was possible to trace a fairly detailed account of Gurney's war experiences through his letters, the chronological and geographical sequence of events was confirmed and clarified by *The Story of the 2nd/5th Gloucestershire Regiment*, edited by A. F. Barnes, M.C., and published by The Crypt House Press, Gloucester (1930).

Printed source materials can be found listed under Gurney's Published Works, and Bibliography.

In the following notes, the Gurney Archive is identified by the abbreviation G.A.; the author's interviews, etc., by the word 'reminiscences'; Gurney's published poems by the date of publication (see Gurney's Published Works); and *The Story of the 2nd/5th Gloucestershire Regiment* by the editor's name, 'Barnes'. Volume XIX, No. 1 of *Music and Letters* (January 1938), containing the Gurney symposium, is abbreviated to *M & L*.

All material quoted in the biography is to be found in the Gurney Archive, whether it is identified in the text by date, writer, and recipient, or by explanation in the notes that follow.

Notes

I

1. 'The Songs I had', *Poems*, 1954, p. 21.
2. G.A. Asylum letter, undated.

Gloucester: 1890–1911

II

1. 'Generations', *Poems*, 1954, p. 100.
2. G.A. Letter, undated: Florence Gurney to Marion Scott.
3. Reminiscences: Mrs. E. Ford (letter, 1975), Mrs. M. Rouse (letter, 1963), Mrs. E. Sterry (letters, 1975), and many others.
4. ibid.
5. Winifred Gurney reminiscences
6. ibid.
7. G.A. Unpublished poems.
8. G.A. Letter, undated: Florence Gurney to Marion Scott.
9. Dorothy Hayward reminiscences.
10. William Bubb reminiscences (letter, 1963).
11. Herbert Howells reminiscences.
12. William Bubb reminiscences (letter, 1963).
13. Winifred Gurney reminiscences.
14. 'Down Commercial Road (Gloucester)', *Poems*, 1919, p. 77.
15. G.A. Letter, undated: Florence Gurney to Marion Scott.
16. Winifred Gurney reminiscences.
17. G.A. Letter, 19 April 1937: Alfred Hunter Cheesman to Marion Scott.
18. G.A. Unpublished poems.
19. Ethel Gurney reminiscences.

III

1. *Gloucester Citizen*, 6 August 1906.
2. ibid., 27 April 1907.
3. Winifred Gurney reminiscences.
4. 'The Fire Kindles', *Poems*, 1917, p. 15.
5. Herbert Howells reminiscences.
6. Herbert Brewer autobiography, *Memories of Choirs and Cloisters*, p. 174. (The Bodley Head, 1931.)
7. ibid., p. 84.
8. Although Marion Scott, and others, believed that Gurney signed himself 'Dotted Crotchet', I have been unable to locate any articles or correspondence under this pseudonym. The incident as retold here does, however, accord with the reminiscences of Mrs. Margaret Rouse (1963).
9. G.A. Alfred Cheesman reminiscences, 1937.
10. 'The Farm', *Poems*, 1919, p. 15.
11. Herbert Howells reminiscences.
12. Winifred Gurney reminiscences.
13. Herbert Howells reminiscences.

14. *Housman* 1897–1936 by Grant Richards, p. 81. (Oxford University Press, 1941.)
15. G.A. Alfred Hunter Cheesman reminiscences, 1937.
16. G.A. Emily Hunt reminiscences, undated.
17. This version of 'The Old City (Gloucester)' differs from that published in *Poems*, 1973, p. 40. Lines 15–17 are quite new. Source: G. A. Letter to Marion Scott, June 1927.

London: 1911–1915

IV

1. 'Longford dawns', G.A. Unpublished poems.
2. *M & L*, pp. 2–3.
3. G.A. Marion Scott lecture notes, 1938.
4. Herbert Howells reminiscences.
5. ibid.
6. *M & L*, p. 14.
7. *My System*, by Lieut. Muller — an energetic and self-disciplining guide to health.
8. *M & L*, p. 13.
9. Saint-Saëns's new work was the oratorio 'The Promised Land', Gloucester, 1913.
10. Sir Arthur Bliss autobiography, *As I remember*, p. 28. (Faber & Faber, 1970.)

V

1. G.A. Unpublished poems.
2. G.A. Emily Hunt, letter to Marion Scott, 8 May 1917.
3. The reference is to the militant suffragettes.
4. F. W. Harvey 'A Gloucestershire Lad', p. 9. (Sidgwick & Jackson, 1916.)
5. This version differs very considerably from that printed in *Poems*, 1954, p. 25. A comparison shows the immense difficulties an editor may encounter in arriving at a definitive version of Gurney's poems. Source: G.A. Unpublished poems.

France: 1915-1917

VI

1. 'Song', *Poems*, 1917, p. 42.
2. *M & L*, p. 4.
3. G.A. Asylum letter of appeal, undated: 'To His Lordship the Bishop of Liverpool, from perhaps the first war poet'.
4. I can find no evidence to support Marion Scott's statement (*M & L*, p. 5) that Gurney was first 'in the Yeomanry, where the other men gave him a very rough time'.
5. G.A. Letter to Marion Scott, undated.
6. G.A. Letter to Mrs. Ethel Voynich (novelist), undated.

7. G.A. Letter to Herbert Howells, undated.
8. 'To the poet before battle', *Poems*, 1917, p. 17.
9. G.A. Letter to Marion Scott, September 1915.
10. G.A. Letter to Marion Scott, undated.
11. Letter from 'Mr. Bathe of Tewkesbury' to Peter Bayley, July 1975.
12. G.A. Letter to Marion Scott, September 1915.
13. G.A. Letter to Mrs. Ethel Voynich, September 1915.
14. G.A. Letter to Marion Scott, 6 October 1915.
15. G.A. Letter to Marion Scott, 9 November 1915.
16. G.A. Letter to Marion Scott, March 1916.
17. Barnes, p. 23.
18. G.A. Letter to Marion Scott, 22 February 1916.
19. Barnes, p. 24.
20. ibid., p. 25.
21. ibid., pp. 29–30.
22. G.A. Letter to Marion Scott, 25 May 1916.

VII

1. Barnes, p. 36.
2. ibid., p. 37.
3. ibid., p. 38.
4. ibid., pp. 56–7.
5. Haig's consultations with Higher Authority are mentioned in most accounts of the war (e.g. *In Flanders Fields*, Leon Wolff, pp. 27, 28. Longmans, 1958).
6. Barnes, p. 42.
7. ibid., p. 50.

VIII

1. Gurney, in so far as his calligraphy permits accurate reading, seems to have been uncertain about the gender of 'la guerre', but since he later opted for the feminine it seems better to correct these early errors.
2. G.A. Letter to Marion Scott, 16 August 1916.

IX

1. 'Song', *Poems*, 1917, p. 42.
2. A reference to the poem 'To certain comrades': *Poems*, 1917, p. 13.
3. G.A. Letter to Marion Scott, undated (September 1916?).
4. G.A. Letter to Marion Scott, 29 September 1916.
5. G.A. Letter to Herbert Howells, 30 October 1916.
6. G.A. Letter to Marion Scott, 25 October 1916.
7. G.A. Letter to Marion Scott, 15 February 1917.
8. G.A. Letter to Marion Scott, 27 July 1916.

9. G.A. Unpublished poems.
10. 'Dicky', *Poems*, 1919, p. 70. A memorial to Richard Rhodes (p. 88).
11. 'The Bohemians', *Poems*, 1954, p. 67.

X

1. Barnes, p. 53.
2. ibid., pp. 54–5.
3. G.A. Unpublished poems. Lines 4–14 of a 21-line poem.
4. Barnes, p. 58.
5. ibid., pp. 58–9.
6. *Poems*, 1973, p. 69.
7. G.A. Letter to Marion Scott, undated — probably early August 1917.
8. G.A. Letter to Marion Scott, 28 July 1917.
9. Barnes, p. 67.
10. *Poems*, 1919, p. 13.
11. G.A. Unpublished poems.

England: 1917–1922

XI

1. G.A. Unpublished poems.
2. G.A. Unpublished asylum poem.
3. G.A. Gurney's calligraphy is very obscure at this point. The missing phrase seems to read 'leaking in through the string covering of post and use', but 'string' might equally well be 'strong', and 'post' might be 'frost' (though 'use' does not appear to be 'ice'!).
4. G.A. Letter to Marion Scott, 26 September 1917.
5. G.A. Letter to Marion Scott, 12 October 1917.
6. G.A. Letter to Marion Scott, 1 October 1917.
7. 'Ballad of the Three Spectres', *Poems*, 1917, p. 43.
8. 'Afterglow', ibid., p. 47.
9. 'To his love', *Poems*, 1919, p. 45.
10. 'Photographs', ibid., p. 87.
11. G.A. Letter to Herbert Howells, undated and partly destroyed.
12. G.A. Letter to Herbert Howells, 16 October 1916?
13. Miss Drummond eventually went to America, where she married a Mr. McKay.

XII

1. G.A. Letter to Herbert Howells, undated.
2. G.A. Letter to Marion Scott, 21 November 1917.
3. G.A. ibid.
4. G.A. Letter to Marion Scott from Dorothy Gurney, 20 June 1918.
5. G.A. Letter to Marion Scott, 4 March 1917.
6. G.A. Unpublished asylum poems.

XIII

1. Ronald Gurney reminiscences.
2. Winifred Gurney reminiscences.
3. Reminiscences: Winifred Gurney, Ethel Gurney, Ronald Gurney. Similar statements made by friends of the Gurney family.
4. In Edinburgh Gurney was befriended by the Revd. T. Ratcliffe Barnett, author of such books as *Reminiscences of Old Scots Folk* (T. N. Foulis, 1916). Nothing is known of this association, apart from the Revd. Barnett's rather gushing invitation: 'My House an Ever Open Door to You.'
5. *M & L*, p. 6. Original letter from Geoffrey Taylor to Marion Scott, 23 October 1937, in the Gurney Archive.
6. G.A. Letter from John Haines to Marion Scott.
7. Winifred Gurney reminiscences.

XIV

1. G.A. Letter to Marion Scott.
2. G.A. Unpublished poems.
3. *M & L*, p. 6.
4. The MSS. were discovered by Christopher Hassall and given to the Oxford University Press in 1959, who, not wishing to publish them, presented them to the Gurney Archive.
5. Ethel Gurney reminiscences.
6. ibid.
7. G. A. Unpublished asylum poems.

Asylum: 1922–1937

XV

1. 'Drachms and Scruples', *Poems*, 1973, p. 125.
2. Gurney Medical Records.
3. G.A. Letter from Walter de la Mare to Marion Scott, 9 May 1923.
4. 'What evil coil', *Poems*, 1954, p. 33.
5. 'To God', *Poems*, 1973, p. 49.
6. G.A. Letter, undated, Florence Gurney to Marion Scott.

XVI

1. Reminiscences of Mr. Fletcher, head nurse at Dartford.
2. Gurney Medical Records.
3. G.A. Marion Scott lecture notes, 1938.
4. G.A. Letter from Mrs. Ethel Voynich to Marion Scott, 4 March 1938.
5. G.A. Unpublished asylum poems.

Aftermath: 1937-1959

XVII

The letters quoted in this chapter are to be found in two volumes of typed extracts, compiled by Howard Ferguson (G.A. 'Letters to and from Gerald Finzi concerning Ivor Gurney').

1. 'Memory, let slip', *Poems*, 1973, p. 41.
2. G.A. Letter from Gerald Finzi to Howard Ferguson, 1 January 1938.
3. *Charles Villiers Stanford*, by H. Plunket Greene (Edwin Arnold, 1935).
4. G.A. Letter from Marion Scott to Gerald Finzi, 4 January 1938. In an undated letter to Winifred Chapman Gurney himself spells the expression 'Kerhistopher'.
5. Ronald Gurney reminiscences.
6. G.A. Letter from Edmund Blunden to Gerald Finzi, 24 December 1954.
7. 'War Books', *Poems*, 1954, p. 71.

Conclusion: 1977

XVIII

1. 'Had I a song', *Poems*, 1973, p. 94.
2. A literary pun on 'Drummond' (i.e. 'Drummond of Hawthornden', the poet William Drummond, 1585–1649).
3. Arthur Benjamin reminiscences, made in casual conversation with the author in about 1955. His letter to Marion Scott of 15 September 1922 (G.A.) contains the following sentence which seems to point to the same thing: 'I used to know a great deal about Ivor; and on that knowledge — the details of which it is impossible for me to discuss with you — I think that psycho-analysis is the only chance.'
4. Herbert Howells reminiscences.
5. William H. Trethowan, *Ivor Gurney's Illness*, and conversation with the author.
6. ibid.
7. ibid.
8. ibid.
9. *Poems*, 1954, Blunden's introduction.
10. 'Cotswold Ways', *Poems*, 1954, p. 23.
11. G.A. Unpublished poems.
12. 'Generations', *Poems*, 1954, p. 100.
13. 'The Silent One', ibid., p. 65. The punctuation at the end of line 13 has been added to clarify the meaning.
14. G.A. Unpublished poems.
15. 'Old Tale', *Poems*, 1973, p. 62.
16. The current total in the Gurney Archive — others may yet turn up.
17. G.A. Unpublished poem.

General Index

Index of Works

GURNEY'S MUSIC

GURNEY'S POETRY

INDEX OF FIRST LINES